Adjustment

A longitudinal study

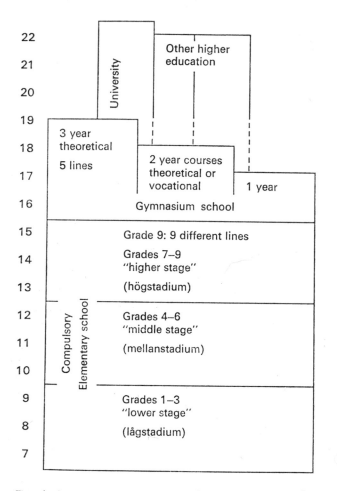

The school system for the main group of the Örebro project.

1) after 1969 there is no differentiation in grade 9.
2) after 1969 all 1-, 2-, and 3 year courses are integrated in the gymnasium
   school.

Adjustment
A longitudinal study

Magnusson, David
Dunér, Anders
Zetterblom, Göran

Department of Psychology
University of Stockholm

A Halsted Press Book
John Wiley & Sons
New York–London–Sydney–Toronto

Almqvist & Wiksell
Stockholm

© David Magnusson, Anders Dunér and Göran Zetterblom
Almqvist & Wiksell Förlag AB, Stockholm 1975

Published in U.S.A., Canada, United Kingdom
and Latin America by Halsted Press, a Division of
John Wiley & Sons, Inc., New York.

Library of Congress Catalog Card Number 75-11593
Halsted Press ISBN 0-470-56347-8
Almqvist & Wiksell ISBN 91-20-97032-3

Design Kerstin Bring

Printed in Sweden by Almqvist & Wiksell Uppsala 1975

Acknowledgements

Many people have contributed to the project. It involves real team work. We would like to express our appreciation to many groups who have participated in the study and made it possible.

During different stages of the project various people at The Swedish Board of Education have assisted us. The interest and support of Dr Eskil Björklund, Dr Sven-Erik Henricson, Dr Esse Löfgren, Professor Sixten Marklund and Dr Nils-Erik Svensson have been very valuable.

We owe a special debt to our co-workers in Örebro. The local school authorities, represented by Eric Samuelsson, Arvid Åberg, and Gunnar Wångrell, as well as the heads of the Örebro schools, during the project Axel Assarsson, Olle Persson, and Jerker Robertsson, have assisted us from the beginning. The headmasters assisted us with scheduling, and the cooperation of all the teachers has been stimulating. They have generously given of their time in terms of observing and rating pupils.

We also owe a special debt to the members of the community advisory group in Örebro, who has worked with us, discussed our problems from both practical and ethical points of view and who have provided many constructive ideas: Majvor Blohm, Bengt Brodin, Arne Dimberg, Sven Frænki, Harry Jonsson, Hans Lindroth, Lars-Gunnar Olsson, Inga-Greta Rundberg, and Sven Öbrink.

We should also thank all those pupils and parents who participated in the study and who have answered our questions with interest and patience.

The project is of a cross-discipline character. In the planning and execution of the project we have very valuable cooperation from Professor Marianne Frankenhaeuser (the endocrinological study), Dr Anders Persson (the EEG study), and Professor Per Olof Åstrand (the physical strength study).

Much of the work in the project has been conducted in conjunction with the research training of students in the graduate program. The first group of students, Rolf Beckne, Dorothy Been, Ingrid Josephson, Birger Lejdare, and Karin Nordenstam, started the work in 1964 with the development of the instruments for the first data collection. Chapter 4 reports partly what they found in their first analyses of the data. The next generation of students worked with special problems dealt with in Chapters 6–13. Marta Henricson, Birgitta Olofsson, Carin Crafoord, Anna Nygren, Gunn

Johansson, and Berit Adebäck will find their research included in the book. We should like to express our appreciation to all these contributors and to all other students who have been involved in other aspects of the project.

We gratefully acknowledge the administrative work that is usually not apparent in research reports. Rolf Beckne, Börje Nyman, Göran Zetterblom and Fredrik Hjortsberg-Nordlund have been our administrative assistents. Without their daily labours the results might have been chaotic. Anyone who has experience from longitudinal projects would know of the cumulative effects of continuous data collections.

We are also deeply indebted to Erik Leander and Lars R. Bergman for their contributions during the planning of many studies, data organization and statistical analyses.

The translation was made by Dr Albert Read.

The project is financed by The Swedish Board of Education.

Stockholm
September 1974

David Magnusson
Anders Dunér

Contents

Introduction

The present report concerns a longitudinal, inter-disciplinary project dealing with the adjustment of individuals.

The project began in 1964 after preliminary analyses of problems, definitions of objectives and planning. The first collection of data, covering all the students in three grades of the schools of Örebro (born in 1950, 1952 and 1955, a total of ca. 3 300), was made in 1965. Data have been collected continuously since then, primarily in 1968 and 1971. In the intervening years the data collected have been concerned chiefly with studies of specific problems of the project, including intensive studies of small samples.

A project of this kind requires a variety of resources. A clear, precise priority of the tasks within the framework of a total research strategy is necessary if the complicated scientific and organizational problems are to be solved satisfactorily. Hitherto, the resources have been devoted to two main areas: (a) discussions of theories, models and methods as a basis for defining problems, choosing variables, constructing instruments and general planning, and (b) the collection of data and analyses of reliability and structure of data. In conjunction with this, certain cross-sectional studies have been performed. There have been many administrative and organizational problems to solve for planning, collection of data, processing and reporting.

The results now available are concerned mainly with cross-sectional studies. The basis of the studies that utilize the longitudinal character of the project has improved continuously and such studies will naturally be given very high priority when planning future work.

A primary condition for achieving the goal of the project is that the population investigated can be followed for many years. As a first step it is planned to follow the subjects until they all have reached the labour market, and it will probably be considered desirable to prolong the follow-up to cover their working life.

In the work planned for the immediate future, the collection of data will be concentrated to some smaller, well-defined groups, according to relevant criteria. Examples of these groups are delinquents, highly gifted individuals, overachievers and underachievers.

Part I of this report discusses the concept of adjustment and considers some research strategies that have guided us in the planning and realization of the project.

Part II reports on the collection of data and describes the investigation groups, instruments, variables, etc.

Part III deals with the problems, instruments, variables and collection of data for the various sub-projects. The results presented in this connection are intended primarily as examples of what can be gained by studies within these domains.

The project cannot be described in a single volume. The purpose of this book is to report (*a*) a general frame of reference for the project, (*b*) the basic information about subjects, variables, and instruments, and (*c*) some cross-sectional studies performed to date on central problems. The book will also serve as a basic reference when results are reported from the longitudinal studies.

Part I
Adjustment as a concept and object of research

The concept of adjustment is discussed and the goals of school are then considered in terms of adjustment. The charactcristics of different measures of adjustment are described.

From this discussion follows the purpose of the project. The strategy for attaining this purpose is outlined. Fundamental methods are discussed as well as methodological problems.

Chapter 1
Adjustment to the social system Frame of reference and purpose of the investigation

A. The concept of adjustment

1. *The functioning of living systems*

The concept of adjustment is associated with what may be called living systems: systems of organs, psychological systems or personality systems, groups of individuals, i.e. social systems, closely structured social systems such as social organizations. Such systems as are engaged in exchange with the surrounding world are regarded as open systems. They are influenced by many factors, and there are various expectations on their functions, for instance claims for activities or products. The exchange includes information about the environment and about the way the system works in relation to its surroundings. The living system transforms this information into modifications of its own structure, its own way of working, or into attempts to change the environment. Such a process may involve changes in the system to compensate for changes in the environment, so that certain internal conditions for the system are preserved. Examples of this type of process are the homeostatic processes for regulating body temperature during variations in the ambient temperature (Katz & Kahn, 1966). Equally important in the process of adjustment of living organisms are their active efforts to influence conditions in the environment.

In the process of adjustment, forces are balanced mutually within the systems with forces originating from the environment. The immediate goals of this process may be characterized generally as a type of equilibrium within the system and in the interaction of the system with the environment. The continuous interactions of the system with the environment assume that this equilibrium is not static but dynamic.

The process of individual adjustment to society, which is the subject of the project presented here, fits into this general frame of reference.

2. *The adjustment of individuals*

The development of an individual from childhood to adulthood occurs in a process, which is characterized by continuous interaction between the individual and his environment. This process can be conceived and studied as a process of adjustment.

a) *The individual.* The individual may be described as an open system involving two closely connected subsystems, one psychological and the other biological.

The main subject of the present project is the adjustment of the individual's *psychological* system. Psychological systems include systems of cognitive, conative and emotional processes. The total system of all such variables is designated the personality of the individual (see e.g. Parson, 1959).

The psychological adjustment process of an individual is closely bound up with states and changes in the *biological* system. Examples of this intimate interaction are readily found in development during adolescence, when physical growth leads to changes in the strength of drives, which results in psychological adjustment reactions.

b) *The environment to which adjustment is made.* The outcome of the process of adjustment for an individual is dependent on the character of the environment with which he interacts. Three main aspects of the environment need to be taken into account in a study of individual adjustment: the physical environment, the micro-social environment and the macro-social environment.

The *physical* environment is defined by the physical characteristics of the environment in which an individual lives, the city plan, the way to school, the character of the schoolbuildings, facilities for leisure time activities, etc. In some respects the physical environment is the same for different individuals. In other respects different individuals may face quite different physical environments, as is the case for such an important aspect as facilities for leisure time activities. The physical characteristics of an environment determine to a great extent the kind and range of possible activities. Many city areas offer few possibilities for healthy activities as compared with other physical environments.

The *micro-social* environment may be defined as the social system with which the individual interacts directly, in the family, at school, in peer groups at leisure times, etc. and which is at least partly specific for each individual. Micro-social systems differ typically with respect to economic resources, language, ways of thinking, habits, attitudes, and norms. At school many children meet other children with conspicuously different micro-social systems for the first time.

The *macro-social* environmental system is defined here as the society to which an individual belongs, with its social, economic, political and cultural structure, its laws and regulations, its usages and customs. This system is common in a national group.

One important aspect of the macro-social system is the dominant value structure; we are often unconscious of this or find it too obvious to discuss, yet these values guide our behaviour and help us make decisions. In an overstimulated situation the values have an economic function as we can concentrate our efforts on current choice problems. The value system is sometimes compared to a map, which we use to find our way in life. This cultural map is different in different cultures.

The psychological system is dependent on the other systems and on the physical environment for its development, but it should be emphasized that *we regard the person as the active, intentional subject in the interaction process*. The person influences the social systems and he/she has possibilities to change the physical environment. The continuous adjustment process also results in changes in the psychological system: learning of facts, habit formation, attitude and value changes etc.

The concept of adjustment assumes certain goal-directed forces or guiding mechanisms within the system. The guiding mechanisms in the biological system may be regarded primarily as products of natural selection, preserving such mechanisms as guarantee the continued existence of the species. The guiding mechanisms in the psychological system may be regarded largely as acquired during an individual's interaction with his social environment. The structures of secondary needs, evaluations, attitudes and norms are developed during the process of socialization (Bandura & Walters, 1965). These structures start from a relatively narrow base of biologically conditioned primary needs and guide the individual's future adjustment reactions. This is accompanied by the development of perceptual functions, methods of solving problems and patterns of reaction used in the process of adjustment.

3. *The role of an individual in a social system*

As a member of a social system, the individual is the object of expectations of other members of the system. These role expectations, taken together, constitute the individual's role in the system. Agreement between the role expectations and the rewards associated with the role on the one hand and, on the other, the individual's needs, values and capacity can be regarded as a state of equilibrium, an aspect of his adjustment to the system in question.

The expectations that define the role, as well as the rewards, may also be subject to change. This type of change may be a modification of the role demands or rewards as an effect of the individual's behaviour in the role. If so, there has been an adjustment of the social system to the individual. Social systems are characterized by varying degrees of inertia, depending on their size, aims, earlier development and so on, and consequently the individual has varying possibilities of becoming adjusted by influencing the system. In the case of a supreme social organization such as the state, the process of adjustment is usually one-sided, and the individual must modify his behaviour according to prevailing rules, which can be altered only via social organizations. A similar situation is often present in respect of role demands in a large firm, in school, and so on. In small, more informal systems, the individual has better chances of achieving adjustment by influencing role demands and rewards.

It is important to observe that one individual may belong to several social systems, i.e. he may have several roles. One way to achieve adjustment in the total situation lies in the choice of roles or social systems. The individual may leave a system to which he is poorly adjusted. He may also seek a social system which gives him rewards that compensate the frustrations he is exposed to in other systems which he cannot leave. Such behaviour is an example of activity in the adjustment process.

4. Intrinsic and extrinsic adjustment

The relation between the individual and a social system may be viewed from two main aspects. One of these is the agreement between the individual's behaviour and the demands that define his role in the system as judged from the viewpoint of the system. The other is the agreement between the individual's needs, motives and evaluations on the one hand, and on the other the rewards he gains as experienced by himself. The first of these aspects may be called the individual's *extrinsic* adjustment and the second his *intrinsic* or subjective adjustment. From the definitions given follow (*a*) that the measures of extrinsic adjustment are to be found in reports and judgments by others, and (*b*) that the main direct measures of intrinsic adjustment are to be obtained in reports from the individual himself. Derived measures as indicators of intrinsic adjustment may be obtained from behaviour data and as reports and judgments by others.

The demand for a certain role behaviour may emanate from a production process in which the individual is involved—it is then a question of what we usually call achievements—or from the social needs of members of a system—then it is a question of a certain social behaviour or interaction.

It should be observed that the individual's subjective adjustment in relation to a certain social system is dependent not only on his needs and the rewards he receives. Adjustment also concerns his expectations of need satisfaction in the relevant relationship.

5. *Indicators of maladjustment*

Discrepancies between the demands made on an individual in a social system and the individual's behaviour elicit measures within the system, aimed at influencing the individual so that the discrepancies are reduced, and possibly at a modification of the demands. When the discrepancies exceed a certain level, the system expels the individual. At a place of work this means that the individual is dismissed. Transferring an individual to a less responsible position, which implies a change of role, or removing him to another subsystem, has similar implications. In some societies a drastic measure is to take the individual into custody or isolate him in an institution. Viewed from another angle, such a measure may be regarded as an attempt to influence the individual so that he can later satisfy the demands of society.

Every step taken by a society which implies sanctions against an individual may be used as a criterion of extrinsic maladjustment to that society. It may be more difficult to find equivalent criteria within social systems at lower levels, at places of work, for example, since the sanctions there do not often have the same formal character.

When the discrepancy between the individual's intrinsic needs and the situational conditions exceeds a certain level, the individual may leave the system if that is possible. This deliberate act is an element in an active process of adjustment, adjustment by choice of system or role. It may be an indicator of a disturbed state of adjustment, but to ascertain this it is necessary to know the underlying circumstances.

If, for one reason or another, the individual considers it impossible to leave the system, and cannot affect his adjustment by influencing the external situation or by modifying his own intrinsic structure, we may expect this to affect his personality system or one or more of its subsystems. This can take the form of various symptoms which may be manifest or extrinsic behaviour, or certain states or processes in the biological system. It may be added that phenomena which are symptoms according to some criteria, may also be regarded as adjustment reactions. Change of work may be an indication of maladjustment but also an active step in a natural adjustment process.

B. The goal of the school in terms of adjustment

The aims of the school system may be transformed into and expressed in terms of adjustment. One task of the school is to give social training. This means that the school, in the social environment it offers, must transfer to its students certain standards which are intended to guide their future adjustment in their relations with other people. This refers to everyday norms for human coexistence and cooperation as well as to the norms society has institutionalized by legislation and bodies set up in the interests of justice. At school, too, the students have opportunities to develop, in interaction with teachers and schoolfellows, various functions and patterns of behaviour which may be used in later adjustment.

Further, the school must prepare its students for work, which involves the creation of attitudes to work and habits of work as well as the training of skills. One purpose of this is to prepare the students for adjustment to their vocational life.

An important part of the aims of the school is to encourage the personal development of the individual, taking into account each student's special talents. This includes the task of helping students to obtain better insight into their own possibilities in respect of both capacity and motivation. Various aspects of insight are important variables in the process of intrinsic adjustment. Such insight is also of fundamental significance for the individual's prospects of achieving adjustment by choice of education and occupation.

It must be re-emphasized that the concept of adjustment also includes the individual's influence on his environment, which may alter the environment in keeping with his needs and values. The school tries to transfer to the individuals techniques which will make them capable to cope with problems in the social system.

The objectives of the school are part of a steering programme emanating from the supreme social system; society transfers the programme to the social system of the school by curricula, the organization of the educational system, etc., and by the training of teachers and other school staff.

As an illustration of how the objectives are expressed in the organization of education may be mentioned the efforts made to postpone the grouping of pupils in classes with different goals. By keeping the classes undifferentiated, an endeavour is made to create a social environment in which students are faced with the necessity of adjusting themselves to schoolfellows at different levels of intelligence and from different social backgrounds. School democracy may be taken as an example of attempts to instil democratic methods of work, alien to many authoritarian job situations outside the school context. This will subsequently influence conditions in society, as the students may take these opinions to workshops, offices, etc., and demand more democracy there.

In the educational system, there are many individually designed measures for leading the students to the desired adjustment levels. Most of these belong to the teachers' daily tasks and are usually designated "individualization of instruction". Special measures aimed at the individual, e.g. in the form of instructive discussions with the student, are applied when the student is to choose alternative courses and at the end of the compulsory school when the student is about to decide about further education. The purpose of these measures is to help the student understand his interests and abilities.

C. Adjustment to the school situation

Besides functioning as an environment which influences its students in various ways, the school provides a situation in which the adjustment of individuals can be observed. When the students first come to school they have, by inheritance and environment, already been provided with fundamental guiding mechanisms and patterns of behaviour for their adjustment reactions. It goes without saying that the influence of situations outside the school environment continues during school attendance.

The student's role in the school situation is defined by demands for certain behaviours emanating from the teacher, classmates, and parents. The demands may be classified as demands on achievement and social behaviour respectively, or interaction. The pupil is also faced with a definition of the demands on achievement via teaching material.

Achievement demands in the school situation are at two levels. In the first place, there are certain absolute minimum demands, fixed so that almost every student is assumed to be able to satisfy them. The students in the compulsory school who cannot satisfy these demands receive some kind of special training. In other types of schools, an inability to satisfy the minimum demands means that the student is not promoted to a higher class, and repeated failure leads to expulsion.

The demands on achievement at the other level are determined individually. These demands imply that the teacher, having judged a student's capacity, expects achievements at a corresponding level. If the student's results are far below the expected achievements, the teacher may take action even though the student has exceeded the minimum demands. The parents' views of the student's adjustment from the aspect of achievement may differ from that of the teacher. Ambitious parents may, for example, overestimate their children's ability and therefore make unrealistic demands on their scholastic achievements.

A teacher's demands on students' social behaviour in the classroom have two main aspects. In the first place, school work requires the student to obey the teacher's instructions and to observe certain rules of behaviour.

That restrictions are placed on the members' behaviour is a necessary condition for the goal-directed process of social organizations. Training adjustment in group situations in this sense is, as mentioned earlier, one important task of the school. The other principal aspect is the requirement that the students' social behaviour shall be characterized by activity. The student has not only to show a certain amount of restraint in his behaviour, he or she must also develop the ability to make a positive contribution to the work of the group, to be active in group contexts, and so on.

When, formerly, the restrictive type of demand on students' behaviour predominated, a system of disciplinary measures was used to maintain these demands. Development in society towards a less authoritarian and more individualized view of education has led to endeavours to individualize the measures and give them a more therapeutic character. Psychological investigations, transferring students to special classes, social measures, etc., are steps taken to remedy adjustment disturbances.

Even behaviour that does not deviate greatly from the demands for achievement or social interaction may lead to intervention. Such behaviour may, for example, be manifested in exaggerated strain or nervousness when confronted with tests, possibly in the form of psychosomatic symptoms. Part of a teacher's duty is to observe such signs of disturbance as may call for measures to help the pupil achieve better adjustment. It is also the duty of the school to initiate steps by other bodies in society, the child welfare board, or clinics of child psychiatry.

D. Mapping the character of measures of adjustment

It is possible at a certain point of time to obtain numerous different measures of various aspects of adjustment, and each of the measures may have high reliability in the traditional meaning of the term. Estimates of reliability are often accepted for determining the utility of the measures as a basis for diagnosis and prediction, and decisions to take certain steps. More knowledge of the character of the measures is necessary, however, in order to judge their fitness for use for different purposes.

1. Grouping the measures of various aspects of adjustment into syndromes

Some examples have been given above of conceivable relations between different aspects of extrinsic and intrinsic adjustment in the school situation. The first thing to be done when studying problems of adjustment is to attempt to empirically uncover patterns of relationships between different measures of adjustment. Such studies may make it possible to establish certain recurrent constellations of adjustment disturbances that may be designated syndromes. Measures of syndromes may be assumed to be more useful than measures of single aspects of adjustment.

2. *Studies of the stability of individual measures of adjustment*

Similar kinds of maladjustment may be due to different causes. There are, on the one hand, students with permanent maladjustment, due to certain stable characteristics in the individual or in the environmental situations. On the other hand there are students with acute disturbances, acute symptoms of maladjustment, due to their being in situations which make too great demands on their ability, or in which their prospects of satisfying their needs are too poor, but in which adjustment is improved when the situation changes or when an act of adjustment occurs.

By studying the stability of single measures of adjustment—or syndromes of such measures—over time we can improve our possibilities of identifying at an early stage such disturbances in adjustment as are liable to become worse or permanent.

The analysis of stability of adjustment measures over a period of time must also refer to individuals. Even if, for groups of individuals, we find weak relations between measures of adjustment disturbances obtained on two occasions, it is possible that adjustment disturbances persist in the individuals who were disturbed on the first occasion but that the symptoms of disturbance have changed. If the individuals were in different phases of a development on the first occasion, a relationship between measures of adjustment may not appear in studies at group level. It is important, however, to find such systematic shifts as may exist in the symptom pattern, sequences that may make predictions possible even though symptoms are unstable.

3. *Study of the predictive value of measures of adjustment with reference to later adjustment to education and work*

This problem implies an extension of the study of stability of adjustment measures to a longer period of time. The question we are concerned with is, "What behaviour in the school situation is an indicator of such deep, chronic disturbance that it is of long-term predictive value in respect of adjustment?" Among patterns of behaviour usually regarded as manifestations and indications of maladjustment there are probably some which, alone or in combination with others, are merely normal reactions of an individual in an unsuitable environment. On the other hand, there are

27

probably behaviours or symptoms that frequently pass unobserved, or to which little importance is attributed, but which in certain combinations may be indicators of a fundamental maladjustment.

E. The purpose of the project

One side of the ultimate purpose of the project is to identify characteristics, types of behaviour or reactions which, alone or in combination with each other, or with certain environmental factors, indicate that an individual runs the risk of ending up in a state of prolonged and serious maladjustment. Another side of the purpose is to investigate the role of environmental factors, especially factors in the school, in the development process of the individual person. An attempt is made to acquire knowledge of the causes of extrinsic and intrinsic maladjustment, thereby providing a basis for therapeutic and prophylactic measures from the school or other organs of society and for more general changes of these institutions.

Within the framework of this total aim, the project will treat, among other things, the following sub-problems:

a) The mapping of patterns of adjustment, behaviour, norms, and attitudes in students of different ages.

b) A study of the stability of single adjustment symptoms or patterns of symptoms, and of sequences of changes that occur.

c) A study of the predictive value of certain items and patterns of behaviour over a long period in relation to various criteria, such as adjustment to work, and criminality.

d) Mapping the current situation and the long-term development for special groups of children, e.g. over-achieving and under-achieving children, creatively gifted children, and children socially isolated in school.

e) A study of the importance of certain school factors for adjustment to the school.

f) Mapping the background of various types of adjustment and behaviour and changes occurring in them, e.g. the background of development towards criminality or the background of various types of behaviour in the choice of a career.

Chapter 2
Investigation strategy and
methodological problems

A. The individual and the environment in the present project

Our primary aim is the study of psychological adjustment. It is then natural that the main emphasis in the collection of data is on variables covering the *psychological system* of the individual in its behavioural, cognitive, conative, and emotional aspects.

The character and outcome of the psychological adjustment process within an individual depend on the specific characteristics of the biological system and the physical, micro-social and macro-social environment with which the psychological system interacts. A fully effective study of psychological adjustment should then include all these factor domains.

With few exceptions, *biological* variables have not been included in earlier studies of psychological adjustment. Since psychological adjustment and the functioning of the biological system are so interdependent, neither intrinsic nor extrinsic adjustment can be studied effectively by taking only psychological variables into account. The necessity of allowing for biological conditions in studies of motivation can serve as a good example. Therefore factors representing important aspects of the biological system of an individual have been studied in the present project. Since very little research has been done on biological variables and psychological adjustment, this part of the project has an exploratory character.

Preparations have also been made for the study of the *physical environment* of the individuals. The living area, the way to school, the facilities for leisure time activities, the school building and its equipment have been mapped for each individual. These data have not yet been used in the project but are stored for future treatment.

The *micro-social* system of an individual is an important and active part in his adjustment process. It has been included in most studies on psychological adjustment. As the main emphasis in this project concerns the micro-social system, it has been covered as thoroughly as possible.

In its main aspects, the *macro-social* system is common to all individuals studied. Most results in the project must be interpreted in the light of the prevailing macro-social system and the changes in this during the course of the project. Some aspects of the process of career in education and profession cannot be meaningfully understood without referring to, for instance, the situation at the labour market.

B. Fundamental methods of approach

1. *Research in open and closed systems*

Observations may be made in an open or a closed system. This is one of the main aspects of the evaluation of the dependability of psychological research data and of the possibilities of drawing general conclusions from them.

In a *closed system* all the variables are assumed to be known and measurable, and therefore possible to check. This affords good possibilities of arriving at definite conclusions concerning their causal structure. Most laboratory experiments are planned in a closed system.

Laboratory experiments are usually made under conditions that differ greatly in some respects from those prevailing in "real" situations. This is valid, e.g., for motivational conditions in the persons studied, which impairs the possibilities of applying the results obtained in laboratory situations to other situations.

In an *open system* there are many different variables operating. Some of them are directly measurable, while others are known, but measurable only indirectly. In an open system there is a great risk that unknown variables affect the results, and the certainty of the conclusions is therefore less than in a closed system. An investigation made in people's ordinary life situation is carried on in an open system.

An investigation made in an open system is, therefore, subject to many methodological difficulties. However, the problems studied in the present project cannot be attacked—at least not in the initial phases—except by studying the students' adjustment under the influence of all the factors present in the actual school situation.

2. *Field studies or field experiments*

Experimental techniques are usually applied in the laboratory situation. Some variables are manipulated, others are kept constant, and the effects on the dependent variables are studied.

Experimental techniques may be used within the framework of actual life situations, too. Then certain interventions are made in the situation, which means that the conditions are altered systematically. *Field experiments* in studies of adjustment may imply, for example, that an attempt is made by certain measures to improve the conditions required for good adjustment, while conditions for a control group are kept constant. If the subjects of the experiment have been assigned to experimental and control groups randomly, certain conclusions may be drawn concerning the steps taken.

To plan and carry out such an experiment so that meaningful conclusions can be drawn from the results requires a certain amount of knowledge of the variables for the individuals and for the social system in the prevailing situation. Such knowledge can be obtained by analyses of situational and individual factors accompanied by observations and measurements of the variables which, according to the analysis, may be assumed to be active in the context, i.e. in a *field study*. As now planned and partly realized, this project is such a field study. In the long run the project may yield a basis for a study of certain restricted problems by experimental techniques and under conditions which approach those of a closed system.

3. *Variables and investigation methods*

To study adjustment in the frame of reference given in Chapter 1 it is necessary to collect information about many variables within the relevant systems. Important aspects of the psychological and biological systems should be measured. The micro-social system for each child has to be described. Variables must be specified to measure intrinsic and extrinsic adjustment on different occasions and in different situations.

A survey of relevant variables is given in the following, with examples of investigation methods.

a) *Psychological characteristics of the individual.* For some characteristics, which are clearly of importance for different aspects of adjustment to school, there are well tested paper and pen instruments that can be used in studies of large groups of individuals. This is true in the first place of intellectual capacity. There are also tests to measure other types of cognitive functions, e.g. creative ability.

The above examples of characteristics refer to aspects of an individual's capacity. The state of the individual as regards the guiding mechanisms of importance to his adjustment—attitudes, values, standards, interests, etc.—may likewise be studied with the help of standardized instruments. But here we are often concerned with variables that ought to be studied in greater detail with individually administered techniques, e.g. interview, if efficient knowledge is to be obtained.

b) *Biological characteristics of the individual.* Some data describing aspects of an individual's neurophysiological and hormonic reaction pattern require time-consuming and costly investigations. Other interesting measures of biological variables, such as the physical development of a growing individual, may be obtained by means of simple methods suitable for large-scale studies.

c) *Variables describing social systems.* One of the principal aspects of a description of a social system is the contact pattern or general pattern of relations between the individuals in the system. Sociometric techniques can be used to map this aspect of the system.

Certain basic data, facts referring to families, which may be expected to serve as indicators of a student's environment in the home, may be collected by means of written questionnaires. However, important aspects of the microsocial system for an individual can only be studied by individual techniques.

d) *Extrinsic adjustment variables.* The extrinsic adjustment of students to school with respect to achievement can be studied in marks and the results of achievement tests. Teachers may also make other evaluations to complement ordinary marks. Marks and standardized tests of achievement provide measures of actual achievement. A teacher's evaluations may attempt to measure an individual's achievement in relation to his capacity. An estimate of achievement relative to the individual's potential capacity of a more objective nature can be obtained by relating actual achievement to the student's intellectual capacity as measured by intelligence tests. Both under-achievement and over-achievement in school work in relation to capacity may be regarded as signs of disturbed intrinsic adjustment. Over-achievement may be regarded as evidence of a compensatory effort in school work that may impair allround development of personality, while under-achievement may be an indication of discomfort and disharmony in the school situation.

Measures of the aspect of a student's extrinsic adjustment concerned with social behaviour and interaction in the school situation are judgements by teachers and peers, the sociometric choices of peers, etc. Some information on a student's adjustment to his or her home may be obtained by questionnaires, but here more important data will probably have to be collected by personal interviews.

Adjustment to the macro-social system may be studied in general from data collected by social authorities and the police, or by questioning the student himself.

e) *Intrinsic adjustment variables.* Information about a student's intrinsic adjustment to school, home and society can best be obtained from the individual in interviews and conversations. In studies of large groups it is often necessary to work with statements by the students in written questionnaires, about experienced comfort and satisfaction, anxiousness, etc., in the total school situation or in certain aspects of it, such as contacts with schoolfellows. Judging from theories about the formation of symptoms in cases of lack of intrinsic adjustment, the question of somatic disturbances may also be relevant.

Another type of data relevant in this context is other people's observations of symptoms of intrinsic maladjustment in the individual. The line of demarcation between such data and data concerning extrinsic disturbances may be diffuse. Extrinsic adjustment disturbance is often regarded as a symptom of intrinsic maladjustment. Certain kinds of behaviour and reactions to which no great importance is ordinarily attached by other people may, perhaps, be classified as symptoms of intrinsic maladjustment to the prevailing situation.

4. *The longitudinal approach*

Investigations aiming at mapping how adjustment disturbances arise are usually of the *ex post facto* type. They are concerned with groups of individuals who, according to certain criteria, are maladjusted—criminals, for example. The investigation groups are then studied in the current situation by psychological, psychiatric, medical and other investigation methods, as well as retrospectively, by interviews with the individual himself, interviews with people who know him, data from the registers of various institutions, and so on. Comparisons are made with corresponding data for a control group of normally adjusted persons matched in certain ways. Some of the weaknesses of this investigation design are:

1. Data describing the individual's state at the time he is chosen a member of an investigation group, that is just when he has shown distinct symptoms of maladjustment, will contain items that are effects of the adjustment disturbance we wish to study. These secondary phenomena may be consequences of the fact that the individual, on account of his primary adjustment disturbance, has been led into changed habits of life or affected by the reactions of his surroundings and the steps taken by society to remedy his disturbed adjustment. We must make serious attempts to obtain data which describe the person at the time when the extrinsic maladjustment began to appear, and earlier.

2. Registered data describing the individual and his situation before his maladjustment became manifest do not give, as a rule, a sufficient basis for mapping the background of the maladjustment.

3. Retrospective data suffer from lapses of memory and the like.

4. There is a risk of criterion contamination when retrospective data are collected. If, for example, we apply to a teacher or an employer for information on a person who has become a criminal, there is a risk that

the person giving the information interprets the individual's earlier behaviour in the light of his knowledge about later behaviour.

The alternative to an *ex post facto* investigation is a longitudinal study. By collecting information at different points in time about a group of growing individuals, we can obtain data which cover the aspects we consider relevant to the causes of adjustment disturbances, and which are not contaminated by components that are secondary in relation to such disturbances. Since it may be assumed that the earlier development of an individual is of prime importance for the rise of adjustment disturbances later in life, such follow-up studies should be started as early as possible. Early studies may be concerned with a child's family situation, the parents' upbringing methods, and so on. Later there will be opportunities of studying the child's own behaviour. The demand for the collection of data early in a person's life must be balanced against the costs and administrative problems connected with such a study, especially since the investigation group must be sizeable.

5. *Successive age groups*

Only one age group is usually followed in longitudinal studies. Some problems are connected with such a design.

Of decisive importance for the outcome of a longitudinal study are, among other things, the choice of problems, the formulation of hypotheses, the choice of techniques and instruments for data collection. Early mistakes in these respects cannot usually be repaired later on and may have strong effects, sometimes disastrous, on the results. Since great costs in money and personnel are invested and tied for a long period in a longitudinal project, it is important that the study of an age group is carefully prepared. One of the most effective ways of preparation is the study of a pilot group. In this (*a*) preliminary results can be obtained and used as basis for the choice of problems for further investigations and for the formulation of hypotheses, and (*b*) methods and instruments for data collection and data treatment can be tried out.

Changes in the macrosocial system may have specific effects on the research group. With only one age group it is not possible to estimate the degree and extent of such influences, which are confounded by age effects.

In the successive collection of data on a group of subjects, later results may be affected by the subject's earlier participation in answering the instruments, the so called panel effect (see e.g. Berglund, 1965). With only one age group at hand it is not possible to estimate this effect.

In view of these and other problems connected with the use of only one age group in a longitudinal approach, the technique of *successive age groups* has been used in the current project. Two age groups have been followed, of which one has served as pilot group and the other one as main group. The details in the use of successive age groups are given later on (p. 51).

6. Size of investigation group

The definitions of adjustment disturbance used most commonly imply that a line of demarcation is drawn round low frequency phenomena. If we wish to make a longitudinal study of an unselected population, therefore, the group must be rather large if we are to obtain sufficient data to elucidate the various aspects of the problem of maladjustment. Further, the use of moderator technique may be required in many cases. With this technique the main group is divided into more or less homogeneous sub-groups with, in some respects, similar features in what are deemed possibly relevant causal variables or intervening variables. Such analyses also require a relatively large initial investigation group. Bearing this in mind it was considered that an investigation group should comprise at least 1 000 persons.

7. The school as a stimulus and observation situation

The school situation contains a large number of variables that may be assumed to be relevant for a study of problems of adjustment. At the same time, the school situation provides conditions on which the investigation strategy of the project can be based. In the first place, the school creates, by its curriculum and organization, a stimulus situation that is the same in its main aspects for all the individuals of certain ages in the population during a period that must be regarded as being very important for the development of the adjustment patterns of these individuals. In the second place, this situation provides good possibilities of collecting a large number of data, especially when the children have advanced so far that they can read and write without difficulty.

If the resources available for the investigations are to be used efficiently in a longitudinal study of the type discussed earlier, the investigation group should consist of a total year group in a community. If, in the introductory phase, the studies were concerned with only certain classes, the number of classes involved in the investigations would increase during the longitudinal study, since the composition of the classes changes at the transfer to higher stages of the school.

Further, to make it possible to follow the students after they have left the compulsory school, an investigation community should be chosen where the migration of young people is small. Thus, a town with possibilities for further education and employment, and with a differentiated economic life, should be chosen.

8. *Summary. Main features in the design of the project*

Among other things the school functions as an instrument of society for measures concerned with the intrinsic and extrinsic adjustment of the individual. One ultimate purpose of the project is to produce knowledge that may be used as a basis for the future design of the school—in accordance with this function.

The relation of the project to the activities of the school may be viewed from other angles, too. The school offers an investigation situation in which it is relatively easy to satisfy certain demands which may be formulated for a research project concerned with problems of adjustment.

Such demands may be summarized in the following main items:

a) In the first place, the individuals should be studied under real life conditions.

b) In view of the limited knowledge available on problems of adjustment, the research work can begin with field studies. Any experiments made later can be based on the knowledge acquired during the field studies.

c) A large number of variables representing different aspects of the individual–environment system should be studied.

d) The project should be carried out as a longitudinal study of successive groups, to be started at a time when individuals are still in the developmental process during which the patterns of their adjustment reactions are formed.

e) The investigation group must be of a considerable size so that it may be expected to contain a sufficient number of individuals who later find themselves in different types of adjustment situations, including serious states of maladjustment.

The project is a longitudinal study of a population of students followed from the first opportunity when written investigation methods administered in large groups can be used, which was considered to be in grade 3. The pupils were then ten years old. Another age group has been studied simultaneously as a pilot group from grade 6, when the pupils were thirteen years of age. The pupils have been studied relatively intensively up to the age of sixteen years, while they were attending the compulsory school. (A third group was studied only in grade 8.)

Investigations of the total population have been complemented with intensive studies. Starting from the data collected for the total population, small groups of students were chosen who are of particular interest from the aspect of adjustment. These groups have been studied with methods which, on account of costs and for other reasons, cannot be applied to the total population.

The students have now left the compulsory nine-year school. Their development in further education and work is being followed.

C. Methodological problems

The design of the investigation, according to the strategy outlined in section B, leads to numerous methodological problems. Relevant problems are discussed in Nesselroade & Reese (1973). A few methodological issues will be mentioned in the following.

1. *Reducing the number of variables*

For each individual, data are collected for a large number of variables. In describing complex systems it is necessary to work with models with a limited number of variables which represent different central constructs.

The frequently numerous items in questionnaires are usually concerned with a limited number of factors, which may be described empirically by factor analysis. The scales obtained have higher reliability than single questions. In addition they may often be more complex and more valuable from the aspect of prediction. In a later step, these factor scales may be included in further factor analyses. They may be grouped together with variables that are measured with other instruments into new, more general factors. The factor structure obtained also elucidates the meaning of the factor scales.

Some of the variables studied have the character of symptoms. Groups of symptoms obtained by factor analysis may be designated syndromes. In many cases, syndromes may be meaningful as components in a model used as an aid in the study of a system. Factor analysis may also be used as a method to obtain maximally meaningful variables or factors for use in the formation of a model or theory.

2. *Dependence and causality*

After the information has been organized for a limited number of central variables, the next step in the study is concerned with the dependency structure of those variables. It is necessary in a system to study several variables at the same time; the correlation between two isolated variables is often uninteresting. Multidimensional methods are available for such an analysis of the dependence between variables in a system. Multiple regression analysis and stepwise regression analysis give information on how a dependent variable can be predicted or estimated from the independent variables included in the system. Here a dependent variable may be, for example, an adjustment variable.

Correlational analyses give information on interdependence, but not necessarily on causal relations; the correlation is symmetrical. A correlation may be caused by a third variable which it has not been possible to measure but which has influenced both the original variables. A dependent variable may also function as an indicator of an essential but immeasurable factor in the chain of causes. The possibility of making causal interpretations increases if a start is made by constructing models, i.e. systems of hypotheses (see e.g. Blalock, 1964). Hypotheses may, for example, be formulated in terms of regression coefficients and be tested by multiple regression analysis. Some models have been tested within the project by Gagnerud (1969). Measurements of the same student groups on several occasions pave the way to more plausible causal interpretations than cross-sectional investigations, since the time shift can be utilized in the analyses.

3. Changes in single variables

Changes in the values of individuals in measurements of the same variable or groups of variables form what is perhaps the most important type of information if one wishes to study factors in the context of their importance for the development of the individual. The possibilities of deriving measures of change also constitute one of the greatest advantages of the follow-up design. There exist, however, methodological difficulties which make the more immediate ways of calculating individual change values unsatisfactory (e.g. Harris, 1963). Therefore the problems of measuring change have been the focus of research within the project (see Bergman, 1972). Regression effects lead, for instance, to a tendency for individuals with very high initial values in a variable to have a negative change, if this is expressed as a difference between raw values.

One method of avoiding this difficulty is to calculate residual measures, which are used as individual values. The residuals are the differences between the values obtained for individuals and the values predicted for them from an earlier measurement. Such derived measures have certain weaknesses, too (see Cronbach & Furby, 1970; Werts & Linn, 1970; Bergman, 1971). Correlations between them and external variables tend, for instance, to be underestimated in the case of positive correlations. Nevertheless, this method is probably useful in certain situations when a convenient screening of variables is wanted.

When the dependency of change on a variable Z is of interest, a regression analytical approach may be useful which uses the pre-test measurement of the change variable together with Z as regressors. The regression or correlation coefficient between the post-test measurement and Z, when the pre-test measurement is partialed out, may under certain assumptions be viewed as an indicator of how change in the dependent variable depends on Z. Problems connected with such a study are treated by Werts & Linn (1970). The above approach is easily extended to incorporate additional variables like Z. Such variables are entered into the regression equation as additional regressors.

The model of the type outlined here may also be applied in studies of relations between changes over time in two or more different variables (Bergman, 1971). If such relations can be shown to exist, they may increase the probability of a causal interpretation.

4. *Changes in groups of variables*

Correlation analyses of data from one occasion may give some information about the character of the groups of variables obtained and their importance in the total picture of adjustment. Knowledge is greatly increased, however, if the syndrome can be studied with data from different points in time.

a) Comparisons between correlation matrices from different occasions may show how far the behaviour in which a syndrome is manifested is the same on both occasions—the stability of the syndrome or factor structure.

b) The correlation, for one variable at a time, between the data obtained on different occasions gives information about the extent to which the values of individual children are the same on different occasions—the stability of individuals in this behaviour.

c) Correlation analyses of data from different occasions may also show if disturbances, which on one occasion are manifested in one type of behaviour, correspond at other ages to other types of behaviour. Seemingly unstable syndromes may thus be of interest for prediction if a behavioural transformation has occurred with age.

5. *Age-, time-, and generation effects*

In a longitudinal study with only one age group it is not possible to separate the effects of individual development (age effects) from other effects as those of changes in the macro-social system (in the labour market, in customs, attitudes etc.) during the studied period (time effects). With a cross-sectional design it is not possible to separate age effects from effects of changes in the macro-social system occuring before the investigation which have caused systematic differences between the age groups (generation effects). A longitudinal design with several groups in different ages (generations) makes it possible to single out the age effects. Such a design is described by Baltes and Nesselroade (1970). In their bifactorial development model several generations are studied, each generation in several ages. Measurements are made at certain intervals. On each occasion one sample is taken for each age. These same samples are studied on the subsequent occasions in successively higher ages. In the complete design an age group can be compared with other groups of the same age on all the other occasions. In their terminology the present study can be regarded as an example of a longitudinal sequence. (See Chapter 3, Figure 3: 1.)

6. *Classification of individuals*

The total structure of the material is studied by means of dimension analytical methods. This, however, is only one step towards the study of individuals. Since the purpose of the investigation is to throw light on generally valid features of the problem of adjustment, it is not enough to describe one individual at a time. It should be possible in the analyses to form groups of individuals that are, as far as possible, similar to each other in certain respects fundamental to the problem—homogeneous groups. Groupings according to values in a single variable are often difficult to interpret and may easily become misleading. This is because it is the interaction between different variables and the way this is manifested in symptoms that decides how far behaviour can be classed as adjusted or not.

In grouping, therefore, it should be possible to use information from different kinds of data, as well as from the interaction between different variables. A definition of meaningful latent variables is required. Then the profiles of single individuals must be taken into consideration. Traditional methods based on regression analysis satisfy these conditions only rarely and to a limited extent. An individual-directed method for continuous scales, latent profile analysis (LPA), or, if the classes are known, discriminant analysis, is more suitable for this purpose. Latent profile analysis is a development of latent structure analysis (Lazarsfeld, 1959), and is described by Gibson (1959) and Mårdberg (1973).

LPA gives point ratings of classes of individuals—agglomerations of points—in a latent space, on which the model is based. The variables of the basic material need not satisfy any demands on form of the distributions. Classification of individuals may be used with advantage for the study of changes between different occasions. Changes in class affinity may be related to other measures, which may refer to personality, socio-economic background or physiological variables, or to events which occurred between the measurement occasions.

Since class affinity is based on a complex information material, such analyses may be more meaningful than studies of changes in single variables.

7. *Moderator variables in system studies*

One objection that may be raised against psychological research based on data from large groups is that the causal patterns one wishes to study are really unique for individuals. If this is so, the only possible method is the study of single cases.

As discussed in paragraph 6 above, it need not be assumed, however, that the relations between the concepts in a system model are completely general. Group investigations may be performed by dividing the sample into certain homogeneous classes. A structure in data may be found for each such class even in situations where corresponding analyses made on the total material give unclear results.

The division of the total group into groups or classes is performed according to certain moderator variables. Subdivision may be performed between the sexes and between students from different social backgrounds. For some problems it is possible to use the division into classes obtained by latent profile analysis for such moderator analyses.

Using, for instance, regression analytical methods, the structure within a problem domain will be described for each of a number of moderator groups. The differences between the moderator groups can be tested for significance by means of variance analysis of regression coefficients.

D. Earlier longitudinal studies

Most studies of development or adjustment problems have applied cross-sectional methods. In some projects endeavours have been made to elucidate the process of development by a longitudinal approach. In most cases a limited problem has been dealt with; in a few cases a broader field of problems has been the focus of large projects. A few examples will be given of longitudinal studies from the domains which are the focus of the current project.

1. *Stability of traits*

The use of the concept of trait in the prediction of behaviour has made it necessary to estimate stability. Thorndike (1933) discussed a number of investigations on the stability of intelligence and Bloom (1964) reanalysed results from longitudinal studies with reference to cognitive factors. He used data from developmental studies where other personality traits were measured repeatedly, too. There are e.g. the Berkeley Growth Study (Bayley, 1949), the Fels Institute's Study of Human Development (Kagan & Moss, 1962), the California Guidance Study (Macfarlane et al., 1962; Bronson, 1967), the California Adolescent Growth Study, the Oakland Study (Stewart, 1962; Macfarlane, 1963), and the Menninger Foundation study (Murphy, 1960). Kagan (1964) discussed ten such longitudinal studies of development and possibilities to predict behaviour from measurement of personality traits early in life.

2. Stability of maladaptive behaviour

Few studies have been devoted to the important problem of what maladjusted behaviour is normal for a particular age and what is a symptom of a disorder that should be treated. The problem has been discussed for centuries for the adolescent period. Is adolescence a period of inevitable "Sturm und Drang", a phase when disturbances in behaviour and adjustment are normal? This question is also the question of the relative importance of environment and heredity for individual development.

Rousseau (1762), Hall (1904), Anna Freud (1958), Shapiro (1963), and others regard the period as one of inevitable stress. Locke (1690), Mead (1928), and Douvan and Adelson (1966) are some of those who oppose this opinion. Masterson (1968, 1972) argues that the "Sturm und Drang" opinion is dangerous, because many adolescents with serious adjustment disturbances never get the treatment they need. Weiner (1970) has given an account of this controversy through the ages.

It seems, however, necessary to study even earlier signs of disorder. What should be alarming, which child needs treatment? What behaviour is normal for the age, which child should we not be worried about? Kraus (1973) found that most adjustment problems in school were evident before the end of the third grade. These children were identified as problems in the primary grades and did not "grow out of it". The problems were of different kinds according to teachers' judgments. Other studies of this kind of problems are those of Glavin (1972), Stennett (1966) and Rubin and Balow (1971). Roff, Sells and Golden (1972) found that peer rejection is not an isolated characteristic but a factor tied to social forces of considerable generality and of great significance for development.

The National Survey of Health and Development has been following a large group of young people in England since their birth in 1946. A report by Douglas (1964) covers the period up to the end of the primary school. Douglas, Ross & Simpson (1968) have reported the study to the end of the secondary school, when the subjects were sixteen years of age. Much information was collected from schools, parents, doctors and school nurses. Among other things, occupational plans, educational aspirations, interests and hobbies during the students' thirteenth and fifteenth years were studied. This investigation, like so many other survey investigations, has thrown light on the importance of the socio-economic background in the utilization of the education offered by society. In England, this influence was found to increase from the primary to the secondary school level. Results reported hitherto deal with development of achievement and school attendance up to the secondary school level. Persistent conditions of uncertainty in the home, for example, have been shown to be related to development of achievement and tendency to choose further education. A behavioural syndrome—nervousness, agressiveness and anxiousness are included in the description—has emerged, with a distinct correlation with impairment of achievement during the school period studied. Such factors behind different developmental trends are interesting for problems of careers, and should be studied in other investigations in other environments.

3. *Different aspects of adjustment as criteria*

It is also of interest to study the impact of certain kinds of early adjustment disturbances on later development with different aspects of adjustment as criteria. In a–d below studies are reviewed using four criteria.

a. Achievement in theoretical studies. Predictions are of great importance to make a streaming system just and effective and to help the individual choose a suitable education (Vernon, 1957).

b. Choice of educational line and occupation and adult economic status. Lately the importance of social background factors in this process has been thouroughly studied (see Coleman, 1966; Mosteller & Moynihan, 1972; Husén, 1972).

The analyses of social mobility made by sociologists are of great importance. Carlsson (1958) processed data from several investigations, including a follow-up study by Boalt (1954). Thorndike & Hagen (1959) followed a group of men who, fourteen years earlier, had applied for military air training and been tested in many ways. A questionnaire was used to study the current situation. Comparisons between and within 124 occupational groups in respect of test results gave a description of the predictive value of the tests in these 10 000 careers. Another example of a study in which data collected originally for another purpose have become the starting point of a follow-up investigation is Terman's (1925) study of the development of highly intelligent children. During the 1940's and 50's the group was studied in respect of vocational career (Terman & Oden, 1947, 1959). A longitudinal study now being made is the so-called Project Talent (Flanagan, 1962). Extensive testing of young Americans at high school level has been performed. The follow-up will be continued for a long time.

Youth from the capitals of Scandinavia are studied continuously in Project Metropolitan (Janson, 1965).

In one investigation, a year group of students in a Swedish county has been followed through the upper secondary school (gymnasium prediction study). The choices of subjects and streams were analysed, as well as further education after the nine-year comprehensive school, by Jansson & Ljung (1970). By their choice of subjects for grade 7, made in grade 6, more than half of the students from the lowest socio-economic group had lost the chance of going to the higher secondary school. For the highest socio-economic group the corresponding proportion was 2 per cent. In grades 7, 8 and 9 of the comprehensive school the percentage of students from the lowest socio-economic group with a suitable combination of subjects for higher secondary school studies dropped to 36 per cent. At the transfer to the higher secondary school, too, a smaller proportion of students in the lowest socio-economic group than in other groups made use of the possibilities of applying for a higher education.

A survey investigation elucidating the corresponding situation in Scotland is a follow-up study made by the Scottish Council for Research in Education, reported by Macpherson (1958) and Maxwell (1969).

In Sweden, the collection of data on a sample representative of the whole country has been started in the individual statistics project (Härnqvist, 1966). A data bank of information about 10 per cent of all the children born in 1948 is being built up for longitudinal studies. The first data were collected in grade 6, referring to school, results of achievement tests as well as a test of intelligence, and parents' occupations and education. A questionnaire concerned with plans for work and education, interests and attitudes to the school was also used. An analysis of changes in intelligence during a five-year period has been made by Härnqvist (1968), while Svensson (1971) has used the data for a study on the problems of under-achievers, including differences in achievement between sexes and socio-economic groups.

The longitudinal design has also been applied in a few studies of the mechanisms behind the process of educational and vocational choice.

Super (1957), on the basis of Ginzberg (1951), has developed a vocational choice theory on which a longitudinal project, the Career Pattern

Study at the Teachers' College, Columbia, is founded (Locascio, 1966; Super et al., 1967). The problem studied is how the individual changes his occupation during the choice process and passes through a certain sequence before he becomes stabilized in a certain category. Gotkin (1966) has reported the result of a ten year follow-up of a group of boys within the project.

Changes during the vocational choice process have also been the main problem for Tiedeman & O'Hara (1963) and others at Harvard, who have built up a data bank in order to be able to utilize longitudinal data on the developmental process.

c. Clinical or personality adjustment. The clinical aspect of adjustment as a criterion in a longitudinal study has been used in some of the stability studies mentioned. Of special interest are also such studies as the follow-up by Robins (1966). She used information about children and contacted both groups as adults and rated their personal and social status. She analysed especially data for those children with antisocial behaviour and related them to the diagnosis sociopathy in the adult group. Robins claims to be able to predict adult sociopathic personality from child characteristics.

d. Delinquency. Most studies of criminal behaviour have had a retrospective character. It is difficult to apply the longitudinal design, as it is necessary to study a very large group to get a sufficient number of delinquents to form an investigation group. West (1969) reports a study from a dense, urban working-class neighbourhood where the delinquency rate is so high that it is possible to start from only 400 boys. In the project, boys were studied from eight to 16 years in an attempt to observe the onset of delinquent behaviour and explore factors which distinguish the delinquent minority from their fellows. An important study with a longitudinal approach is also the follow-up of the boys in the investigation groups of the Cambridge-Somerville Youth Project for treatment of risk groups with respect to delinquency (McCord & McCord, 1959).

For many reasons the investigation group that is the object of a longitudinal study should be a representative sample of a normal population. Information about such a group may be useful for the study of various problems with different criteria of adjustment.

In a Swedish study many problems are studied within the same investigation group. All the children in the third grade in the schools of Malmö in 1938 were the subjects of a study of the relation between social background and intelligence (Hallgren, 1939, 1946). In addition to tests of intelligence, teachers' ratings of scholastic aptitude were used. Also marks and information on socio-economic background were collected. The male part of this group has been followed up by Husén, first in order to study the effect of formal education on the results of intelligence tests (Husén, 1950) and then in order to ascertain how information on the children's intellectual and social background in their tenth year can predict development and adjustment in life up to the age of thirty-seven (Husén, 1969).

Education, attitudes, own children's education, vocational career, attitude to vocational career, feeling of success, criminological status, social welfare data, married/unmarried and number of children were studied as criteria of adjustment. Data were collected from official registers and by questionnaires sent by post to the subjects. In this the Swedish census statistics were found to be of great value in the tracing of individuals.

Results of intelligence tests and teachers' ratings of aptitude for study were found to predict line of education and achievement to some extent. This prediction was partly counteracted by the relation between social background and education. Of the group classed as highest in intelligence, one-fourth never continued their education after the compulsory school; these children were mainly from the lowest socio-economic group. Of these only 10–15 per cent continued their education after the compulsory school.

In the vocational career, too, relationships with social background could be observed. The higher the father's level of occupation, the quicker the individual climbed in social status from the aspect of occupation. The group which had to pass the white-collar line found it most difficult to climb in social status. Adult education may have some prospects of changing this pattern. A third of those judged as weakest in respect of study ability had attended adult schools and shown interest in further education. The group that had participated in voluntary education also differed from the other groups in social mobility.

Husén also took an interest in the slightly mentally handicapped in the investigation group, who, as expected, were at a lower vocational level. The members of this group revealed less mobility upwards during the period studied. They also found it more difficult to achieve good social and occupational adjustment, but in this case other factors besides intelligence were at work.

Part II
The current project

A survey of the project is given, with information about the investigation groups, variables and methods, the location for the project, the planning, data collection, information etc.

The total group investigations are presented, with reference to individual, environmental and adjustment variables in the basic data. The groups are described during the first five years together with the drop-out in this longitudinal investigation.

Part II

The current input

Chapter 3
Survey of the project

A. Choice of investigation town

Örebro, a town with about 100 000 inhabitants, was chosen for the investigation. Örebro is an old Swedish town that has expanded at a normal rate in recent decades. It satisfied the demands that could be made on an investigation town in several respects. The year groups of students in the nine-year compulsory comprehensive school were of a suitable size— c. 1 000 in each. Örebro has a well-developed educational system. After the comprehensive school the young people can move on to the various branches of the gymnasium school (higher secondary school, continuation school or the very diverse vocational school). At the post-gymnasium level are a university annex, a college of social work and administration, a college of gymnastics and athletics, and a college of education. Further, there are training schools for pre-school teachers, occupational therapists, laboratory assistants and nurses.

Formerly, the economic life of Örebro was dominated by the footwear industry. During recent years it has become more diversified and now there are engineering works, printing shops, food and paper industries. Örebro also has a great deal of commerce and is the service centre of a large region. It has a large hospital with many special clinics, among them a child-psychiatric clinic, which was considered to be valuable to the project, since some special studies could be made there.

Örebro counts as a large town in Sweden, where the national population is only about 8.2 millions, but it cannot, of course, be said to represent a big city environment. It is, moreover, an inland town. Consequently it does not provide a basis for studying some of the severe problems of youth that tend to be associated with major ports and other big cities, e.g. extensive prostitution, illicit liquor and drug markets. The conditions prevailing in Örebro must naturally be born in mind when assessing some of the results of the project. (Cf. page 57 on generalization.)

B. Investigation groups

The project concerns the pupils who were attending grades 3, 6 and 8 of the Örebro comprehensive school in the school year 1964–65.

The pupils attending grade 3 form the *main group* and the most comprehensive data have been collected on them. Those attending the other two grades form *pilot groups.*

In the following, the letter M denotes the main group and the letter P denotes the pilot group that was in grade 6 in 1965. No designation has been used for the pilot group that was in grade 8 in 1965. The occasion when particular measures occurred is indicated by a suffix, representing the average age of the group at that time:

M_{10} is the main group in grade 3, i.e. in 1965, aged 10
M_{13} is the main group in grade 6, i.e. in 1968, aged 13
M_{15} is the main group in grade 8, i.e. in 1970, aged 15
P_{13} is the pilot group in grade 6, i.e. in 1965, aged 13
P_{16} is the pilot group in grade 9, i.e. in 1968, aged 16

When the first investigation was undertaken, in the spring of 1965, the numbers of pupils in the three grades were as follows:

Grade 3 (M_{10}): N = 1 025
Grade 6 (P_{13}): N = 960
Grade 8: N = 1 330

Most of the children, about 88 per cent, had been born in 1955, 1952 and 1950 respectively; about 10 per cent had been born in the year before these "normal" years of birth for each grade; about 1 per cent had been born in the year after the majority in the grade, i.e. they were under-age. As the principles for judging school readiness were not changed between the years in which these groups started school, each of the grades, with the exceptions given below, comprised an age stratum of the whole population of Örebro.

The following categories were excluded from the groups.

1. Children with serious intellectual shortcomings, i.e. with an intellectual level corresponding to an IQ of 70 or lower. Such children are transferred to a special school during their first school year.

2. Children with grave physical handicaps, e.g. blindness.

3. Children with serious social adjustment disturbances, taken into custody by society and placed in foster homes or school homes outside Örebro. Students who, after a total assessment, have been placed in such homes will nevertheless be included in some follow-up studies.

Custody of the type mentioned in point 3 is extremely unusual with respect to children during their ninth year. Exclusion of this type has not affected the composition of the main group on the first investigation occasion to any great extent.

It must be pointed out that there are very few private schools in Sweden. Children from all social groups attend the comprehensive school. The sizes of the groups during the first five years of the project are reported in Chapter 5.

C. Planning the investigation

The plan of the project includes total group investigations, i.e. investigations concerned with all the pupils in the grades studied, and sample investigations of a small number of pupils taken from the total group.

The total group investigations include the collocation of data collected by the school or other authorities in other connections as well as new collections of data planned and administered wholly within the project.

The sample investigations embody methods which, on account of costs or for other reasons, cannot suitably be used in total group investigations. The samples of students studied may be obtained so as to be as representative as possible in relation to the total group, i.e. by random sampling or some form of stratification procedure, or in such a way that individuals with certain characteristics are chosen by means of data from the total group investigations. The latter approach is usually designated contrast or extreme group investigation.

The general design of the project was laid down during the spring of 1964. In June the same year the National Board of Education granted funds for investigations during the school year 1964–65. Field work started with total group investigations in Örebro in the spring of 1965. A survey of the collection of data up to and including the school year 1967–68 is given in Figure 3: 1.

No data were collected during the school year 1968–69. The investigations made during the years 1969–70 and 1970–71 are surveyed in Figure 3: 2.

D. Variables and investigation methods

Table 3: 1 surveys the variables studied in different sections of the project, and the methods used to measure them.

The variables were derived according to the frame of reference presented earlier from the categories individual–environment–adjustment. It must be pointed out that the frame of reference used implies a functional classification of the variables where some variables should be assigned to several categories. Sociometric measures, i.e., in this case peers' ratings of popularity, may be taken as an example. A student's popularity with his

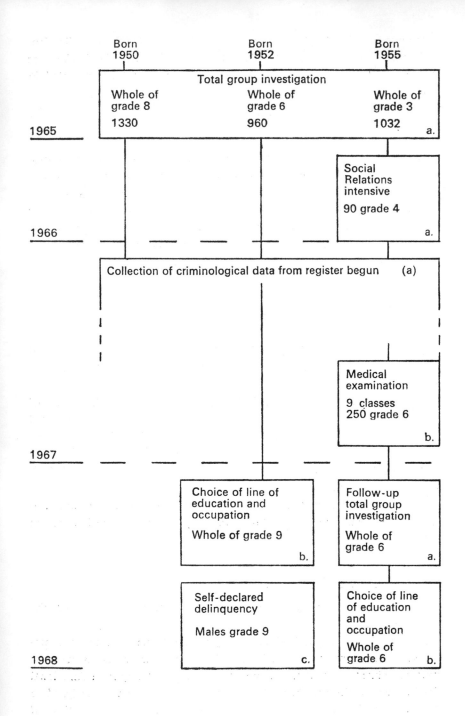

Figure 3:1 Survey of project 1965–1968

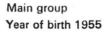

Main group
Year of birth 1955

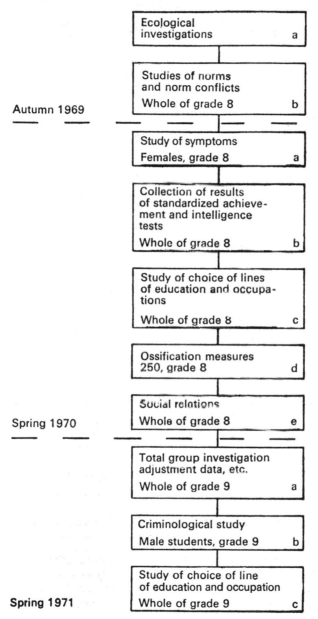

Ecological investigations	a

Studies of norms and norm conflicts	
Whole of grade 8	b

Autumn 1969

Study of symptoms	
Females, grade 8	a

Collection of results of standardized achievement and intelligence tests	
Whole of grade 8	b

Study of choice of lines of education and occupations	
Whole of grade 8	c

Ossification measures	
250, grade 8	d

Social relations	
Whole of grade 8	e

Spring 1970

Total group investigation adjustment data, etc.	
Whole of grade 9	a

Criminological study	
Male students, grade 9	b

Study of choice of line of education and occupation	
Whole of grade 9	c

Spring 1971

Figure 3: 2 Survey of project 1969–1971

Table 3: 1. Survey of variables and methods.

Type of variable	Total group investigation	Sample investigation	Investigation occasion (For symbols see figs. 3: 1–2)
I. Adjustment variables			
A. Extrinsic adjustment			
1. Scholastic achievement	Objective test		
a. Absolute achievement	Objective test		65: a, 68: a, 70: b
b. Achievement relative to the individual's capacity	Objective tests		65: a, 68: a
2. Social behaviour			
a. Behaviour in relation to classmates	Peer ratings Sociometric methods		65: a, 68: a 65: a, 68: a, 70: e
		Teacher interview	66: a
b. Behaviour in classroom	Teacher's ratings		65: a, 68: a, 71: a
		Teacher interview	66: a
c. Behaviour at home	Parent questionnaire		65: a, 68: a
d. Behaviour in society	Register data Student questionnaire		67: a 68: c, 70: a, 71: b
B. Intrinsic adjustment			
1. Experienced satisfaction of needs, etc.			
a. Total experience of school	Student questionnaire Vocational questionnaire		65: a, 68: a, 70: c, 71: a 68: b, 70: c, 71: c
		Student interview	66: a
b. Experience of school work	Student questionnaire		65: a, 68: a, 70: c, 71: a
		Student interview	66: a
c. Experience of teacher contact		Student interview	66: a
d. Experience of peer contact	Student questionnaire Student's ratings of own sociometric status		65: a, 68: a, 71: a
		Student interview	66: a
e. Experience of parent contact	Student questionnaire		69: b, 70: a, 71: a

Type of variable	Total group investigation	Sample investigation	Investigation occasion (For symbols see figs. 3:1–2)
2. General emotional level (anxiety, uneasiness, depression, etc.)	Student questionnaire, symptoms		70: a
		Medical examination	66: a
3. Experienced somatic symptoms	Student questionnaire		65: a, 68: a, 71: a
	Student questionnaire, symptoms		70: a
		Medical examination	66: a
4. Objective somatic situation		Medical examination	66: a
		Measures of adrenalin — noradrenalin	67: b
5. Symptoms in behaviour (disharmony, confidence, well-being, etc.)	Teachers' ratings		65: a, 68: a, 71: a
	Parent questionnaire		65: a, 68: a
	Peer ratings		65: a, 68: a
	Student questionnaire, symptoms		70: c
		Teacher interview	66: a
		Parent interview	66: a

II. Individual variables

1 Psychological characteristics

Type of variable	Total group investigation	Sample investigation	Investigation occasion
a. General intellectual capacity	Objective tests		65: a, 68: a
b. Creative ability	Objective tests		68: a, 71: a
c. Aspiration level	Vocational questionnaires		68: b, 70: c, 71: c
	Vocational differential		68: b, 70: c, 71: c
	Teachers' ratings		65: a, 68: a
d. Norms, attitudes, evaluations	Semantic differential technique		65: a, 68: a, 71: c
	Student questionnaire, situations		69: b
	Voc. quest.		68: b, 70: c, 71: c
	Voc. differential		68: b, 70: c, 71: c
	Student quest., self-rep. delinquency		71: b
	Student quest.		71: a
e. Interests	Student questionnaire		68: b, 71: c

Type of variable	Total group investigation	Sample investigation	Investigation occasion (For symbols see figs. 3: 1–2)
2. Biological characteristics			
a. General physical capacity (working capacity)		Cycle ergometer test	67: b
b. Neurophysiological situation		Electro- encephalogram	67: b
c. Hormonal situation		Adrenalin– noradrenalin measures	67: b
d. Biological age		Measures of ossification	70: d
III. *Environmental variables*			
1. School environment			
a. Teacher relations	Teacher ratings		65: a, 68: a, 71: a
b. Peer personality	See Individual variables		
c. Peer relations	Sociometric measures		65: a, 68: a, 70: e
2. Home environment			
a. Economic situation of home, dwelling standard etc.	Parent questionnaire		65: a, 68: a
b. Parents' educational level	Parent questionnaire		65: a, 68: a
c. Attitudes and norms of parents		Interviews	66: a
3. External dwelling environment	Social ecologi- cal data		69: a
4. Material standard of the school	Social ecologi- cal data		69: a

classmates may be regarded as a measure of how well he satisfies certain demands on social conduct in the school situation, as well as an environmental variable expressing the strength of the social rewards meted out to the student in this situation. Expressed in experimental terminology this means that we can utilize the measure of popularity as dependent or independent variable.

In general, the adjustment variables are regarded as functions of individual and environmental variables. On different assumptions they may be assumed to have influenced the latter types of variables. In some cases, the environmental variables are determined entirely by factors that are independent of the individual but may, in other cases, be viewed as results of the individual's actions. They may then perhaps be used as indicators of individual variables. The individual variables, finally, can never be studied quite independently of the individual's current environment, but are regarded here as being less influenced by environment and as being relatively constant in time.

E. Generalization

The studies are performed in one particular place, which is not entirely representative of Sweden in all respects. But the limitations which this imposes on generalizations should not be exaggerated. It may be that in a few special cases, the proportion of children displaying a particular behaviour or answering a question in a particular way differs from the population of Swedish children of the same age. Surprisingly good agreement with respect to frequencies of answers, for example, has been found, however, between the Örebro results and those from other studies in recent years in other parts of the country, in some cases with the same instruments (see Bergman, 1973). The possibilities of generalizing to a Swedish population are probably quite good. This is no doubt still more true of conclusions concerning explanations of behaviour, causal structures behind functions, and testing of theories and models.

F. General comments on the planning of the project, information and contacts

The presentation given here describes the situation of the project in 1972. The present design has developed from the first general plan drawn up in 1964. The experience gained in the course of the work has been utilized successively in the further development of the investigation plan.

A project of this character is dependent on the possibilities of establishing cooperation with the local education authority, the teachers, parents, and pupils and others affected by the investigation. All these parties have collaborated with great interest in an advisory group with representatives of the above-mentioned groups and of the National Board of Education and the school medical service. This group was formed prior to the first total group investigations and has since met repeatedly; all kinds of problems have been discussed: the planning of the total project and of its goals, the various problems that have been formulated and questions of ethics in the investigations. Preliminary versions of the instruments have been submitted to the group for comments, which have led to modifications of the instruments and of the investigation plans. The work with this group of persons has been of great importance for the favourable outcome of the project.

Teachers and headmasters have been informed at each stage of the investigation about the purpose of the total project and each specific study. This was done in writing from the project staff together with a covering letter from the local education authority. Information meetings have also been convened for teachers.

The parents of the pupils participating in the investigation have been informed about the project directly and by articles in the local press.

It is the business of newspapers to follow and inform about what is going on in society. If they get incomplete or wrong information about a research project they may spread misunderstandings which may generate a feeling of suspicion and discontent in the readers. These feelings may make it impossible to continue the project. The usual strategy seems to have been to try to keep investigations secret from the local press. In the present project the opposite strategy was followed. The newspapers have received written information from the leaders of the project, among other things a complete set of the investigation instruments, and their heads were informed orally by personal contacts. Through their coverage the newspapers have given active support to the investigations; this has undoubtedly contributed to their being performed without disturbance and also to the high frequency of replies to the questionnaires sent to the parents.

Chapter 4
Total group investigations of individual, environmental, and adjustment variables

A. Introduction

In this and the following chapters the variables of the project are presented in greater detail by describing the investigation process and the instruments. The division into chapters is based on the survey of the project given in Figures 3: 1 and 3: 2 (pp. 52 and 53).

The investigations which, in Figures 3: 1 and 3: 2, are called *total group investigation—adjustment data, etc.*, designated 65:a, 68:a and 71:a, comprise what may be called the basic data of the project. The choice of variables and the design of the instruments in these investigations are related to the principal objective of the project as reported earlier. The data collected in the current section of the project are intended to be used in the analysis of certain of the problems studied, but they are also intended to be used in the selection of extreme groups for intensive studies and as background data in studies where the central variables are measured in special investigations. The total group investigations gave the material for a data bank which is the basis of the project.

It proved more suitable to arrange the following account on the basis of groups of variables measured with the same investigation methods than on the basis of the theoretical framework of the variables as presented on pages 51 ff., since some investigation instruments give data that can be assigned to different types of variables according to this frame of reference. In the present chapter, the investigations in which the students themselves are involved are treated first, after that the investigations concerned with the teachers, and finally those in which parents are involved.

B. Intelligence and Creativity

Six written group tests from the battery Differential Intelligence Analysis (DIA), designed by Härnqvist (1961), were chosen to measure the students' *intelligence*.

The first two subtests of the battery, Similarities and Opposites, measure the V-factor according to the conventional division into intelligence factors. The next two, Groups of letters and Number series, contain abstract logical (inductive) tasks. The last two subtests, Cube Counting and Metal folding, consist of spatial tasks. This test battery requires a total of three lessons.

As the name of the test battery implies, it is intended to measure differentially the various factors of intelligence. However, the battery was also used in the project to give a total measure of intelligence, by Härnqvist called General Study Aptitude, comprising the sum of the stanine points for the six subtests. The reliability of this total measure of intelligence, calculated from data on the reliability of the subtests, is about 0.95.

The same test battery was used in the total group investigations in 1965 and in 1968. The distribution of test scores was normalized for each sex-age group tested. In the processing of the results obtained in 1968, consideration was paid to whether the students participated in the tests in 1965 or not. Special norms were made up and applied on those who were retested.

Test WIT III (Westrin, 1967) was used to measure intelligence for group M_{15}. This is a factor type test containing four subtests: Analogies, a test of inductive ability on verbal material, Opposites, a test of verbal comprehension, Number Combinations, to measure deduction ability, and Puzzle, a test of spatial ability.

For the ages we are concerned with here, the test manual reports a reliability of about 0.93 (split-half reliability) for the total scores on the test.

The tests of intelligence were administered by the staffs of the schools. The testing formed part of the ordinary school program.

Creative ability has been measured in M_{13}, M_{16}, M_{18} and P_{19}. The instruments used on M_{13} were Consequences and Divergent figures. A creativity study is reported in Chapter 10 and the instruments are described there (see p. 191). In M_{16} and P_{19} two other instruments were used, Pukort and Titles, which are described on p. 176.

Testing is not the only way of examining children's creativity potential. Davies & Belcher (1971) found that a Biographical Inventory had the best validity in their study. They believe in attitude inventories for problem solving and interest schedules for estimating creativity. Wallach & Wing (1969) studied non-academic achievement as an expression for creative ability. On M_{18} an inventory was used for mapping the non-academic achievement and leisure time activities, which will be used in the longitudinal study of creativity.

C. Scholastic achievement

The results of nationally standardized achievement tests were used to measure scholastic achievement. These standardized tests in grades 3, 6 and 8 are in the subjects Swedish and mathematics; in grade 6 also in English, and in grade 8 in English and German. In analysis of data within the project, a total measure of achievement comprising the sum of the test scores in Swedish and mathematics was used for grades 3 and 6. In this way equivalent measures of scholastic achievement were obtained for these grades.

The standardized tests are concerned with different items of the courses: in Swedish reading comprehension, spelling, knowledge of words, grammar, punctuation, etc.; in mathematics mechanical arithmetic, fractions, mental arithmetic, and denominations.

The reliability (measure of internal consistency) of the total measure of achievement should, according to information on the data available from earlier use of this type of test, be above 0.90.

The results of the standardized tests of achievement as a measure of scholastic achievement have the advantage of not being affected by behavioural variables irrelevant in this context. The teachers' markings, on the other hand, are probably influenced by, among other things, certain features of behaviour in the students which are studied in relation to scholastic achievement (see Svensson, 1971). In addition, a teacher's frame of reference is influenced by the general standard of the class. These are decisive reasons why the results of standardized tests instead of marks have been used as the principal measure of achievement.

One drawback of standardized achievement tests compared with marks is that they do not cover the whole domain of achievement we wish to study. It should also be borne in mind that the achievement tests are in some ways similar to intelligence tests, which may lead to high correlations between these two types of instrument.

In principle, the difference between the students' actual achievement, measured by standardized achievement tests, and the achievement that can be predicted on the basis of his score on the intelligence test DIA is used as a measure of relative scholastic achievement (Thorndike, 1963). The technique of using individual achievement measures as deviations from the regression line for the correlation between intelligence and scholastic achievement has been developed further in more complicated models, reported earlier in the project (see Magnusson & Dunér, 1967).

There are certain difficulties in the use for research purposes of the standardized tests that are administered in grade 8. Only the test in Swedish was the same for all the students. The results from this test are available for the main group, M_{15}.

D. Pupils' experience of the school situation

To measure the pupils' experiences of the school and their satisfaction with their school situation, new instruments were constructed.

Questionnaire for the main group in grade 3—M_{10}
Questionnaire for the main group in grade 6—M_{13}
Questionnaire for the main group in grade 9—M_{16}
Questionnaire for the pilot group in grade 6—P_{13} and for the grade 8 group studied in 1965

The work of constructing the questionnaires in 1965 has been reported by Beckne (1966).

The domains covered by the questions will be clear from the following account.

1. *Construction of instruments, all groups, 1965*

Within each domain a number of questions about the school situation were constructed: "How do you like school?" "Do you experience that your schoolfellows are troublesome during the breaks?" The questions were to be answered by marking one of usually three or four alternatives. The questionnaire may be described as a Likert scale.

Questions were also formulated concerning the students' interests in various school subjects, their home situations and leisure time habits, and more specific situations in higher school studies, e.g. the subject teacher system.

Two versions of the form were constructed for the study in 1965: one for grade 3 and another for grades 6 and 8. The questionnaire was tried out on a small number of classes in other school districts and then modified on the basis of this trial.

2. *Component analysis for the grouping of questions, 1965 data*

The possibilities of grouping into scales the questions intended to measure the adjustment variables were studied by component analysis of data. Separate analyses were made for each grade and sex. The analyses were made on samples of 150–300 students in each group on the basis of tetrachoric coefficients for the correlation between the questions and were performed according to the principal component method. A few questions with extremely skewed distributions of answers were excluded from the analyses. The factor matrix was rotated orthogonally according to the varimax method.

For grade 3 (M_{10}) four factors were extracted and rotated, for grade 6 (P_{13}) six factors, and for grade 8, five factors. Factor scales were con-

Table 4: 1. Coefficients of reliability for scales in the student questionnaire.

Grade	Scale	Retest coefficient	
		Boys	Girls
3	General satisfaction	.79	.75
	Attitude to school meals	.67	.65
	Psychosomatic reaction	.79	.77
	Attitude to way to school	.70	.77
6	General satisfaction	.81	.82
	Psychosomatic reaction (Boys)	.74	—
	Burden of work	.78	.74
	Peer relations	.71	.66
	Anxiousness (Boys)/Anxiousness + psycho-		
	somatic reaction (Girls)	.82	.67
	Anxiousness for peer relations (Girls)	—	.72
8	General satisfaction	.85	.83
	Anxiousness	.85	.88
	Attitude to school meals	.61	.75
	Psychosomatic reaction	.83	.90
	Burden of work	.87	.85

structed on the basis of the results of this factor analysis. The scales obtained are shown in Table 4: 1.

3. *Reliability*

Reliability was studied by re-testing, three weeks after the total group investigation in 1965, a number of classes with a total of ca. 170 students from each of grades 3, 6 and 8. The coefficients of reliability for the different scales are given in Table 4: 1.

4. *Revision of instruments for M_{13}*

On the basis of the results from P_{13}, the questionnaire was revised prior to the 1968 investigation of M_{13}. Some questions with low reliability were reformulated or excluded. All the questions were given five alternative answers. An attempt was also made to cover the scales derived at the component analysis of data from P_{13} by a number of new questions.

5. *Component analysis for the grouping of questions, M_{13}*

The data from M_{13} were also subjected to component analysis. Separate analyses were performed for boys and girls. Data from all questionnaires——494 for boys and 510 for girls—were analysed. The analyses were based on product-moment coefficients for the correlation between questions. The same method was used for component analysis and rotation as earlier. Five factors were extracted and rotated and five factor scales constructed, the same for boys and girls.

Table 4: 2. Intercorrelations for factor scales from the student questionnaire, normal classes, M_{13}.

	2	3	4	5
(a) Boys N = 459				
1. General satisfaction	.37	.44	.68	.29
2. Relations to schoolfellows	—	.31	.32	.24
3. Anxiousness for school work		—	.56	.31
4. Experienced burden of work			—	.29
5. Anxiousness for acting individually in class				—
(b) Girls N = 492				
1. General satisfaction	.50	.39	.57	.41
2. Relations to schoolfellows	—	.33	.45	.33
3. Anxiousness for school work		—	.57	.41
4. Experienced burden of work			—	.39
5. Anxiousness for acting individually in class				—

The questions in scale 1 reflect a general attitude to school, particularly school work, and the scale was given the same title as corresponding scales in earlier analyses, *"General satisfaction with school"*.

The questions in scale 2 are concerned with experience of contacts with schoolfellows and the scale was called *"Peer relations"*.

The questions in scale 3 are concerned with uneasiness and anxiousness in respect of school work, also such anxiousness as is manifested in somatic symptoms. The scale was called *"Anxiousness for school work"*.

The questions that represent scale 4 deal with experience of whether school work is a strain or not. The scale has been called *"Experienced burden of work"*.

In scale 5 the questions are concerned with acting in class, and the scale was therefore called *"Anxiousness for acting individually in class"*.

The intercorrelations for the scales given above were calculated over all pupils participating. These intercorrelations are shown in Table 4: 2.

6. *Student questionnaire for M_{16}*

Before the investigation of the main group in grade 9, the student questionnaire was reconstructed so that the wording of the questions and the presentation of the problems were better adapted to the age of the students. It was also extended in order to obtain information in conjunction with special studies within the project, in the first place the criminological study (see Chapter 7) and the study of adjustment-critical behaviour in girls (see Chapter 8).

Some questions were intended to cover the factors revealed by the component analyses of the answers to earlier questionnaires: *Peer relations, Satisfaction, Burden of work, Anxiousness,* and *Psychosomatic reaction.*

Other questions were concerned with relations to parents and other adults, trust in adults, ambition and other aspects of self-experience. As far as possible, questions were taken unaltered from earlier questionnaires to facilitate a study of the stability of the answers. A report on analyses made on the data and descriptive results is given by Marnell, Dunér & Magnusson (1973).

E. Students' attitudes and values: investigation with semantic differential technique

1. *Background*

Attitudes and values are regarded as very important individual variables. In order to study students' attitudes to themselves and others and their attitudes to phenomena related to the school situation, a form was designed based on Osgood's semantic differential technique. A detailed account of this work and of the data obtained has been given by Nordenstam (1969).

Methodological problems in semantic differential research have been discussed by Heise (1969), Heaps (1972), and McNeil (1970).

The semantic differential technique has been used earlier to measure such attitudes and values as have been considered to be associated with different aspects of adjustment and mental health. These investigations were concerned with, e.g., the concepts *I, My mother, My father* in therapeutic patients and control groups and with changes in the values after therapy (Luria, 1959), the similarity in rating profiles between the concept *I* and other concepts such as *Father, Mother, Husband* and *Wife* for subjects with high and low anxiousness, preparedness, etc. (Lasowich, 1955), and the evaluations of the concepts *I, Mother, Father* and *Asthma* in groups of asthmatic children with varying case histories (Baraff & Cunningham, 1966).

2. *Investigation instrument*

Osgood's semantic differential technique (Osgood, Suci & Tannenbaum, 1957) consists of a series of seven-point scales, the poles of which are defined by two adjectives which are the opposites of each other, e.g.

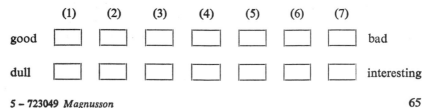

By drawing a cross in one of the squares of each scale, the subjects were to judge a number of concepts, e.g. *School, Child.* The steps of the first scale were defined in the test instructions as follows:

Steps 1 and 7 — *very* good or bad respectively
Steps 2 and 6 — *rather* good or bad respectively
Steps 3 and 5 — *a little* good or bad respectively
Step 4 — *neither* good *nor* bad, or *as* good *as* bad.

For the form used in the total group investigations in 1965, *concepts* were chosen from the following domains:

a) The own person, self-assessment, aspiration level:

I — as I am as a rule; *Ideal self* — as I wish I were; *The future; Solitariness.*

b) Family

Mother; Father; Sister; Brother.

c) Persons of the same or opposite sex:

Girl; Boy; Woman; Man.

d) The school

Teacher; Student; School work.

e) Aggressive impulses and formation of norms

Fights; Disobedience

In the choice of concepts care was taken that they would be easily understood by both young children and older students. The number of concepts was not to be greater than could be assessed during one lesson. The concepts *School work, The future,* and *Solitariness* were used with P_{13} and in grade 8 only.

The *scales* used were chosen from a very large fund of adjectives used earlier, mainly in personality research by Osgood and others. The scales, of course, had to be easy to understand. They also had to be meaningful in the assessment of both abstract and concrete concepts. Further, the adjectives had to be as unambiguous opposites as possible. They should not be confused with adjectives in other scales, or have several meanings so that they might be attributed to the different dimensions.

The form contained the following scales:

1. good   —bad
2. interesting—dull
3. pleasant   —unpleasant
4. clean   —dirty
5. happy   —sad
6. unfair   —fair
7. kind   —unkind
8. strong   —weak

9. brave —cowardly
10. manly—womanly
11. hard —soft
12. fast —slow
13. hot —cold
14. easy —difficult
15. safe —dangerous

Table 4: 3. Pupils' mean deviation (MD) and the percentage of pupils with a deviation of 0–1 steps from test to re-test for concepts in the semantic differential, M_{10} and P_{13}.

	Grade 3				Grade 6			
	Boys		Girls		Boys		Girls	
Concept	MD	0–1	MD	0–1	MD	0–1	MD	0–1
1. Ideal self	0.87	80	0.67	84	0.68	85	0.60	85
2. I	1.10	75	0.97	76	1.09	73	0.95	76
3. Girl	1.49	64	1.02	75	1.15	68	1.02	75
4. Boy	1.21	71	1.42	63	1.13	71	1.21	70
5. Sister	1.38	66	1.04	75	1.20	70	0.98	75
6. Brother	1.11	74	1.23	71	1.23	69	1.18	70
7. Woman	1.45	65	1.00	77	1.13	71	0.99	73
8. Man	1.16	72	1.15	72	1.04	74	1.09	72
9. Teacher	1.14	69	0.98	77	1.38	63	1.11	69
10. Student	1.22	71	1.10	72	1.33	64	1.29	66
11. Fight	1.58	61	1.63	60	1.40	62	1.29	66
12. Disobedience	1.61	61	1.82	54	1.46	62	1.49	60
13. School work	—	—	—	—	1.45	58	1.23	68
14. Solitariness	—	—	—	—	1.69	52	1.40	64
15. Future	—	—	—	—	1.32	65	1.15	68

Scales 1–7 have been given high loadings in the *evaluation* dimension in Osgood's factor analyses. Scales 8–11 are usually assigned to the *potency* dimension and scales 12–13 to the *activity* dimension. Scales 14–15 were considered relevant to the present investigation but have not been found in earlier factor analyses.

To counteract tendencies towards stereotype reply patterns, the 'positive' pole of the scales was to the left and right alternately. Scales belonging to different dimensions were rotated. Different versions of the sheets of the test booklet with the scales rotated in different ways were presented in the same order for only a small number of the students in the same class. The purpose of this was to counteract position effects on concepts and scales in the study of groups.

3. *Reliability*

Ten classes in M_{10}, with a total of 207 pupils, and eight classes in P_{13}, with 169 students, were re-tested after an interval of about ten weeks.

The distributions of the ratings in each concept and scale were often very skewed, with the mean near the positive end of the scale. Thus the conditions for the calculation of product moment correlations were not ideal, and the re-test stability was therefore studied according to the following method, recommended by Osgood et al. (1957) and others.

1. The percentage of the students with an absolute deviation of 0, 1, 2, ... 6 scale steps from the first to the second test occasion was calculated

Table 4: 4. Pupils' mean deviation (MD) and the percentage of pupils with a deviation of 0–1 steps from test to re-test for scales in the semantic differential, M_{10} and P_{13}.

| | Grade 3 | | | | Grade 6 | | | |
| | Boys | | Girls | | Boys | | Girls | |
Scale	MD	0–1	MD	0–1	MD	0–1	MD	0–1
1. Good	1.14	73	0.98	77	1.17	70	1.05	74
2. Weak	1.34	68	1.39	66	1.29	68	1.19	68
3. Dangerous	1.50	64	1.25	71	1.61	58	1.32	65
4. Warm	1.48	62	1.44	60	1.44	60	1.19	67
5. Dull	1.21	72	1.20	71	1.28	67	1.12	73
6. Brave	1.42	67	1.28	68	1.28	66	1.18	68
7. Unpleasant	1.17	74	1.17	76	1.22	69	1.01	76
8. Soft	1.49	62	1.32	67	1.33	63	1.29	66
9. Clean	1.07	75	0.85	80	1.08	73	0.92	77
10. Slow	1.38	68	1.19	72	1.27	68	1.22	66
11. Kind	1.06	76	0.90	78	1.13	72	1.05	74
12. Manly	1.20	71	1.08	74	0.95	75	0.87	77
13. Easy	1.57	60	1.49	62	1.43	60	1.40	60
14. Unfair	1.30	69	1.22	70	1.24	68	1.19	69
15. Happy	1.04	76	0.90	78	1.08	73	0.98	76

for each concept over all scales and for each scale over all concepts. The proportion of pupils who had altered their ratings 0–1 steps is reported for concepts in Table 4: 3 and for scales in Table 4: 4.

2. The pupils' average absolute deviation in scale steps, the mean deviation from test to re-test, was calculated in the same way and is also reported in Tables 4: 3 and 4: 4.

In each group the concepts have about the same relative rank order according to the size of the deviations. *Ideal self* and *I* were, on an average, the most stable concepts.

Of the scales, the evaluation scales and the scale *Manly–Womanly* were most stable in all groups.

Extreme ratings have shown greater stability than ratings on the intermediate scale steps in several of Osgood's investigations. The concepts and scales which tended to be most stable in the investigation reported above, were also usually those that are given extreme ratings.

The data obtained by the semantic differential technique in the investigations within the present project on children and youngsters are somewhat less stable than the data obtained earlier for adults (Osgood et al., 1957; Luria, 1959; Norman, 1959).

4. *Profile analysis*

For each individual tested with the semantic differential technique, a profile can be drawn for each concept, showing how the individual has rated the concept in the fifteen scales. Starting from the structure of the individuals' scale profiles, homogeneous classes of individuals can be formed. Each individual is assigned to the class whose profile is most similar to his own. Such a classification of the profiles for certain concepts was made by latent profile analysis (see p. 40).

The profile analyses led up to a grouping of the individuals into three to five classes for the different concepts studied. The profile classes have a certain generality, so that the same types of profile are repeated for the different concepts. The results of the profile analyses have been used in studies concerned with covariation between attitudes and values and other data of the project (see Nordenstam, 1969).

5. *Revision of the instruments for* M_{13}

When calculating how much time would be required for different investigation methods in the follow-up study it was considered desirable to abbreviate the semantic differential form to about half its original length. On the basis of the analyses of data from the first occasion and considerations of the psychological relevance of the different concepts, seven of the concepts used originally were chosen for a new version of the form, namely

Girl; Boy; I; Woman; Man; Teacher; Future

The series of scales was retained unaltered except for one scale, clean–dirty.

F. Peer relations, motivation and confidence: Peer ratings

1. *Background*

The aspect of extrinsic adjustment concerning interaction with peers can be studied in the pupils' status of popularity among classmates. Such popularity has proved to be a type of variable to which great importance should be attached in the diagnosis and prediction of adjustment (Roff, 1961; Roff & Sells, 1968).

Popularity may, to a certain extent, be assumed to be related to a situation. Some students may, for example, be popular as members of a football team, but less popular in a working group with theoretical tasks, while the opposite may be the case for others. We may also expect, however, to find pupils who are popular with many schoolfellows in most situations, while others are isolated and shut off from every form of community with their classmates.

There is no evidence, however, that extremely popular and extremely impopular students must be found in every class. The social climate in a class may be influenced greatly by other factors than the students—the teacher, for example. A pupil's status among peers is determined by interaction between the individual and the group and may be seen as dependent on factors in the student and on group psychological factors. It is mainly the first-named type of factor that is studied in the project.

Of interest in this context is the pupils' self-assessment (see Magnusson, 1960). It may be assumed that (a) self-esteem formed earlier influences the process of social adjustment in the school, and (b) success or failure in endeavours to create and maintain contacts with classmates affects the current self-assessment.

Judgements by peers at school can also be used in contexts not directly associated with popularity, i.e. in assessments of observed behaviour or personality characteristics. It is feasible that such assessments may, in some cases, be even more important than those made by teachers, or complement teachers' assessments.

2. Self and peer ratings, 1965

For the total group investigations in 1965 three different situations were chosen—the classroom, breaks and leisure time outside the school. A pupil who, in any one of these three situations, has no classmate who will associate with him must have grave difficulties with companions. A pupil who, on the other hand, is chosen first in all three situations by many of his classmates must, with a rather high degree of certainty, be considered to be popular in his class.

In M_{10} only schoolfellows of own sex were rated. In P_{13} and in grade 8, the pupils when rating the variable referring to the classroom, rated also classmates of the opposite sex. This difference in the design of the investigation in the various grades was justified by the fact that earlier investigations have shown that the interaction between boys and girls is much less developed in lower grades.

As a first phase in the investigation the pupils were instructed to imagine that they were to be transferred to another classroom, and that not all of their classmates could go to the new room. They were then given the task of ranking all their classmates in the order they would like them to move. The students ranked classmates of their own sex (all grades), and as a separate task they ranked classmates of the opposite sex (grades 6 and 8).

Afterwards the students were given the task of naming the three classmates of their own sex whom they would like best to be with during breaks, and also the three classmates they would like to be together with during their leisure time outside the school. They should in both cases also rank those three classmates.

In conjunction with the ranking of classmates in the classroom variable, the students assessed their own popularity in the class. This self-rating was performed by the pupils' giving which classmates they thought that most of the others had chosen in preference to themselves, and which classmates had been chosen after themselves. This technique for self-evaluation has been used in earlier studies by Magnusson (1960, 1962).

3. Motivation and Confidence

Finally, the students in grades 6 and 8 had to rate their classmates of their own sex in respect of their *motivation* for school work, and in respect of the *confidence* they revealed in their demeanour in school. The motivation variable was defined in the instructions to the students in terms such as "interest in school subjects", "willingness to do school work" and "think it important to get good marks and endeavour to get on well in lessons and examinations". The confidence variable was defined in terms such as "to be sure of oneself", "to talk calmly and confidently during lessons", "not be afraid of asking questions" and "to seem at home in school". The assessments were made by ranking all classmates of their own sex.

All ratings were made by students' writing rank numbers on lists of names of classmates prepared in advance. The lists were made in two versions with the names of the students in different order, to counteract the risk that the students might automatically follow the ranking they had performed earlier. After they had completed a ranking, the students put their lists into envelopes so that they could not refer to them at the next ranking.

4. The meaning of self and peer ratings

The rankings given to a certain student by classmates in the variables "classroom", "breaks" and "leisure time" may be regarded as an expression of the students' adjustment to demands on certain social behaviour made by peers, and are thus measures of aspects of *extrinsic adjustment*.

Self-rating as an expression of a student's conception of his position in the group is of interest as, among other things, a measure of the satisfaction of social needs which the student enjoys through contacts with classmates. Thus, self-rating belongs to the category *intrinsic adjustment* variables.

The ratings of *confidence* and *motivation* are measures of certain features of behaviour in the student which indicate his intrinsic adjustment.

A detailed account of the collection and analysis of peer ratings and self-ratings has been given by Josephson (1967).

5. Calculation of individual measures

In the variables for which complete ranking was performed, each student received ranking values, one from each classmate. On the assumption that the classmates are normally distributed on the cognitive dimension that each student uses to distinguish between them, the ranking values were transformed to standard scores—z-values (see Magnusson, 1961). Afterwards the mean of the z-values for each individual was calculated. This mean is the individual measure used in the analyses of data. The z-transformation gives extreme positions in the ranking greater weights in the calculation of mean values than positions in the centre zone. The transformation also leads to values for students in classes of different sizes being given the same implications, e.g. the central positions in the rank order receive the same scale value regardless of size of class. A transformation of this type does not, of course, eliminate the fundamental weakness that is characteristic of ordinal data, namely that the true distance between different values may differ greatly in rankings in different classes.

For the variables in which ratings referred to choice and ranking of three classmates, the situations *breaks* and *leisure time,* the total number of choices received by the student was calculated. No attention was paid to the ranking of the choices. The variable comprising the sum of the number of choices received in the situations *breaks* and *leisure time* was designated *leisure.*

Since each student stated how many classmates he thought had been preferred to him, the self-ratings could be expressed as ranking values. On the same assumption and in order to make the self-ratings comparable between classes of different sizes, these ranking values were transformed into z-values in a normal distribution (see Magnusson, 1960).

In all these ratings the class-sex group is the reference group. All between-group variance is thereby excluded after transformations.

6. Agreement in the students' ratings

It is in the nature of sociometric data that we cannot necessarily expect a high degree of agreement between ratings made by different individuals in a group (Bjerstedt, 1956). We expect rather a sociometric pattern with various groupings round several popular individuals. The ratings of motivation and confidence are treated here in conjunction with the sociometric measures.

A crude measure of agreement in the students' ratings on one and the same occasion was obtained by calculating concordance coefficients (Kendall, 1948). Concordance coefficients calculated on ranking matrices, where judges and judged are the same persons and a loss of values occurs

Table 4: 5. Concordance coefficients for agreement between the pupils' rankings within the class for different rating variables.

Variable	Grade 3		Grade 6		Grade 8	
	Boys	Girls	Boys	Girls	Boys	Girls
"Classroom, own sex"	.29	.26	.25	.29	.25	.22
"Classroom, opposite sex"			.57	.52	.44	.48
"Motivation"			.59	.64	.67	.66
"Confidence"			.50	.55	.44	.52

because the judges do not judge themselves, will be somewhat lower than coefficients calculated on complete matrices. For this reason, other things being equal, higher values should be obtained for the variable *Classroom, opposite sex* than for the other variables.

The coefficients of concordance for the variables subjected to ranking are reported in Table 4: 5. It should be observed that these coefficients are not to be interpreted as correlation coefficients for agreement.

It will be observed that agreement is consistently lowest in respect of *Classroom, own sex.* One interpretation of this fact is that more differentiated sociometric patterns function here.

7. *Stability of ratings*

Tables 4: 6 to 4: 8 show some coefficients for the correlations between the variables measured in peer ratings. In the diagonals are given the stability coefficient obtained in a retest study made about ten weeks after the total group investigation in 1965. It should be observed that for peer ratings the correlations refer to the means of the ratings the children received.

The coefficients for stability are relatively high for all peer rating variables. In view of the importance of these variables, the high stability in the ratings of *Motivation* and *Confidence* should be observed particularly. No remarkable changes seem to have occurred in the students' status in class during the period. The stability correlations for the self-ratings, on the other hand, are lower for both grades. This may be explained by the fact that the self-rating value consists of one rating only, while the peer rating values are the means of many ratings. Actually, the self-ratings seem to be more reliable than ratings by single peers.

8. *Correlations between ratings in different variables*

It seems likely that many students prefer the same classmates in the different situations given as frames for the ratings of the popularity variables

Table 4: 6. Measures of stability (diagonal values) for peer and self-ratings and the correlations between these variables (grade 3, M_{10}).

	1	2	3
(a) Boys			
1. Classroom, own sex	.86	.76	.19
2. Leisure		.74	.14
3. Self-rating			.57
(b) Girls			
1. Classroom, own sex	.84	.75	.28
2. Leisure		.79	.19
3. Self-rating			.45

Classroom on the one hand and *Leisure* on the other (see e.g. Bronfenbrenner, 1945).

The correlations between the variables *Classroom, own sex* and *Leisure* are shown in Tables 4: 6 – 4: 7 for M_{10} and P_{13}. There is a tendency towards lower coefficients in higher grades, which can be observed also for other variables.

This suggests that older children differentiate between situations to a greater extent than younger children. Johannesson (1954) and Bjerstedt (1956) have found the same thing. Johannesson stated that there is strong evidence that a general "social acceptability-factor" is typical for children up to about their thirteenth year.

It should be pointed out that the variable *Classroom, opposite sex* was rated by another group of judges (the other sex) than the other peer-rated variables.

Table 4: 7 also shows the correlations between the ratings of the classroom variables of own and opposite sex on the one hand, and on the other the variables *Motivation* and *Confidence*. There is a tendency for the popularity variable to have a stronger correlation with *Confidence* than with *Motivation*.

The correlations between self-rating and ratings performed by peers are also given in these tables. The coefficients are low but all positive. Thus, there is a general association between assessment of own position among classmates and actual ratings by peers. These results are very important for the future work. They justify a further and more thorough analysis of the self-ratings collected.

9. *Revision of the rating methods for M_{13}*

In the investigations made in M_{13}, peers' ratings and the sociometric studies were restricted to the following variables:

Table 4: 7. Measures of stability (diagonal values) for peer and self-ratings and the correlations between these rating variables (grade 6, P_{13}).

	1	2	3	4	5	6
(a) Boys						
1. Classroom, own sex	.83	.66	.74	.34	.44	.39
2. Classroom, opposite sex		.88	.56	.35	.44	.36
3. Leisure			.73	.21	.30	.31
4. Motivation				.95	.84	.09
5. Confidence					.85	.18
6. Self-rating						.62
(b) Girls						
1. Classroom, own sex	.84	.57	.70	.43	.42	.32
2. Classroom, opposite sex		.84	.46	.34	.47	.33
3. Leisure			.53	.26	.33	.24
4. Motivation				.96	.87	.22
5. Confidence					.92	.31
6. Self-rating						.40

1. *Classroom, own sex*
2. *Self-rating*
3. *Motivation*
4. *Confidence*

The methods of collecting the self-ratings were unaltered. The number of variables rated had to be reduced in order to find time for new instruments in the collection of data. The reduction was made in the light of deliberations concerning the importance of the variables in the total investigation programme and the analyses of data reported above.

10. *Rating for M_{15}*

In the investigation in M_{15}, the following variables, which had been used earlier, were rated.

1. *Classroom, own sex* (ranking order)
2. *Self-evaluation*
3. *Classroom, opposite sex* (ranking order)

These variables were complemented with two sociometric questions and three questionnaire items. The new situations considered relevant to teenagers were:

4. *Communication:* The students ranked the five classmates they talked to most during the school day.

5. *Leisure-time friends:* The students were to give an optional number of persons they liked to meet during their spare time. In the case of nonclassmates, approximate age, school, class or work were to be given.

Table 4: 8. Coefficients for the correlations between peer- and self-ratings (grade 8).

	2	3	4	5
(*a*) Boys				
1. Classroom, own sex	.58	.36	.44	.30
2. Classroom, opposite sex		.31	.46	.21
3. Motivation			.78	.11
4. Confidence				.19
5. Self-rating				
(*b*) Girls				
1. Classroom, own sex	.57	.25	.33	.17
2. Classroom, opposite sex		.29	.45	.27
3. Motivation			.71	.03
4. Confidence				.19
5. Self-rating				

The questionnaire items gave:

1. How often the students were with their classmates after school was over for the day.

2. Where the group of friends spent their time in their most common occupations.

3. The size of the group in which the students spent their spare time.

Some groups were somewhat opposed to the investigations with the variable *Classroom, own and opposite sex,* in which the pupils had to rank their classmates in order of popularity. The pupils in these groups declined, for ideological reasons, to differentiate between their classmates and say that they liked any one better than others. Owing to this opposition, four classes had too few judges. The new variables, *Communication* and *Leisure-time friends,* were accepted willingly.

G. Classroom behaviour: Teachers' ratings

1. *Background*

Certain aspects of the students' extrinsic adjustment are concerned with their behaviour in the classroom situation. This refers to, for example, behaviour that directly influences the work of the class. Other types of behaviour are interesting as indicators of intrinsic adjustment. By this is meant behaviour that may be assumed to be symptomatic of internal stress, dissatisfaction, or lack of motivation.

2. *Rating method*

Data referring to the pupils' behaviour in the classroom were obtained from the teachers. The method of collecting data was numerical rating.

This method is labour-saving and easy to learn. Data are obtained directly without any intermediate procedure such as, for example, in graphic ratings. Investigations have shown that methods by which students are judged by comparisons two and two, as in quotient and magnitude ratings, for example, have somewhat higher reliability than conventional graphic and numerical ratings (Dunér, 1965). The gain in reliability is not, however, great enough to justify the much greater amount of work both in the judgment and in the processing of data.

The rating method used in the total group investigations in 1965 may be described briefly as follows:

a) The judgements were made on a seven-point numerical rating scale.

b) The variables were defined by a heading and by descriptions of extreme manifestations of the behaviour in question.

c) To counteract the halo effect, one variable at a time was judged for all students.

d) Boys and girls were rated separately.

e) Reference groups were boys and girls respectively in their own classes.

f) Normal distribution of the ratings was to be obtained as far as possible.

The teachers were given detailed written instructions, and rating forms with the pupils' names entered in advance. The names were in different orders on different forms.

Headings and descriptions of variables are given below. The symbols A and B refer to the two extremes on each scale.

Aggressiveness

A They are aggressive against teachers and classmates. They may, for example, be impertinent and impudent, actively obstructive or incite to rebellion. They like disturbing and quarrelling with classmates.

B They work in harmony with the teacher and have positive contacts with classmates. Their relations to others easily become warm and affectionate.

Most children are between these two extremes.

Motor disturbance

A They find it very difficult to sit still during lessons. They fidget uneasily in their seats or wish to move about in the classroom, even during lessons. They may also be talkative and noisy.

B They have no difficulty at all in satisfying even great demands on silence and quietness.

Most children are between these two extremes.

Timidity

A The behaviour of such children is characterized by bashfulness and shyness. They seem to have poor self-esteem. They are inhibited and afraid to express themselves.

B Characteristic of these students is that they are always open and frank.

Most children are neither particularly inhibited nor markedly and constantly open.

Disharmony

A They seem very disharmonious and unhappy. They are often in restrained or open conflict with their surroundings or themselves.

B They seem to be very harmonious and well balanced, and are seldom involved in serious conflicts with their surroundings or themselves. They seem to be emotionally "at home" in school.

Most children are somewhere between these extremes.

Distraction

A They cannot concentrate on their work, but are occupied with irrelevant things, or sit daydreaming. For a few moments they may work, but are soon lost in other thoughts again. They usually give up quickly, even when the work is suited to their level of intelligence.

B They have a marked ability to concentrate on a task and persevere with it. They never allow themselves to be distracted, and do not give up as long as a task suits their level of intelligence.

Most children are between these extremes.

Lack of school motivation

A They give an impression of feeling averse to learning and to the subject, and they seem to experience a general feeling of discomfort in the school, a feeling of being "fed up with" school. They are uninterested and it is very difficult to get them to take part in ordinary school work.

B Their school motivation is strong and they feel at home in the school environment.

Most students feel neither "fed up with" school nor strongly motivated.

Tension

A These students make, in relation to their ability, too great demands on themselves. They strain themselves to succeed in their tasks. They may be called over-ambitious.

B They utilize in a natural way their intellectual resources and their personality. Their achievements are therefore often attained without strain.

Most students fall between these two extremes.

The rating scale was constructed as follows:

	Most like behaviour B			Mean of class		Most like behaviour A		Degree of certainty
	1	2	3	4	5	6	7	
N.N.								
N N								
N.N.								
N.N.								

The column headed "Degree of certainty" enabled the teachers to use the symbols $+$, 0 and $-$ to indicate the degree of certainty they felt when making their ratings. The purpose of this mode of procedure was to give teachers a chance to express such uncertainty as might otherwise result in failure to make a judgement at all.

3. Processing of raw data

The first processings of the raw data showed that relatively great differences were present between the distributions of the ratings in different classes, in spite of the fact that the judges had been instructed to use the class-sex groups as a reference group and to use the rating scale in such a way that the result would be approximately normal distributions. The intergroup variation found in the raw data may be said to be due mainly to lack of observance of the instructions. This variation was eliminated by transforming the ratings to non-normalized standard scores for each class-sex group. The rating values used in the further processings will thus have the mean 0 and the standard deviation 1 in each such group. After the transformation of scales, each grade and sex in the class-sex groups was treated separately.

4. Correlations between ratings of different variables

The correlations between the rating variables were about the same size in the three grades studied. Table 4:9 gives the correlation coefficients calculated for M_{10}

Table 4:9. Coefficients for the correlations between teachers' rating variables for M_{10}.

	1	2	3	4	5	6	7
(a) Boys							
1. Aggressiveness	—	.67	.01	.66	.54	.54	.03
2. Motor disturbance		—	−.12	.52	.65	.52	.02
3. Timidity			—	.25	.18	.32	.25
4. Disharmony				—	.58	.64	.13
5. Distraction					—	.76	.14
6. Lack of school motivation						—	.14
7. Tension							—
(b) Girls							
1. Aggressiveness	—	.58	.09	.62	.51	.54	.12
2. Motor disturbance		—	−.12	.52	.62	.48	.11
3. Timidity			—	.29	.23	.39	.41
4. Disharmony				—	.64	.65	.35
5. Distraction					—	.75	.26
6. Lack of school motivation						—	.29
7. Tension							—

With the exception of the correlation between the variables *Motor disturbance* and *Timidity,* the correlations are all positive. The general tendency is thus for a student to be judged in a similar way in different aspects of adjustment. A scrutiny of the correlation matrices in Table 4: 9 shows, however, that the mutual correlations between five variables are consistently higher than between these and the two remaining ones. This implies that *Aggressiveness, Motor disturbance, Disharmony, Distraction* and *Lack of school motivation* tend to form together, for the teachers, a syndrome, separate from *Timidity* and *Tension.*

Motor disturbance may be regarded as an expression of extrinsic adjustment, *timidity* as an expression of intrinsic adjustment. The low (negative) correlation between these variables is an indication that they are independent expressions of disturbance.

It was deemed feasible to assume that the correlations between certain of the rating variables might be non-linear. The linearity of the regression lines was tested by calculating eta-coefficients and testing the significance of the deviations of these coefficients from the product moment coefficients. This test was performed in the cases in which inspection of the plots suggested that deviations from linearity were present. The testing of linearity was performed on data for P_{13}. The results of the testings were:

a) Significantly curved forms (angle-shaped) appeared for both sexes in the regressions of *Aggressiveness, Motor disturbance, Distraction,* and *Lack of school motivation* on *Tension.*

b) The regression of *Disharmony* on *Tension* was significantly curved (angle-shaped) for girls only.

c) The regression of *Timidity* on *Aggressiveness* was significantly curved (angle-shaped) for the girls.

The other regressions seemed to be either clearly linear, or they deviated from linearity without distinct form.

It will be observed that it was mainly the regressions of most of the other variables on the variable *Tension* that deviated from linearity. One feasible explanation of this is that, for this variable, both extremes may be conceived positively, for the description of the "tense" behaviour may be associated with strong motivation. Other variables have, from the aspect of adjustment, a favourable and an unfavourable pole. Further, the elaboration of "behaviour B" in the description of the variable *Tension* was rather vague. This may have caused different judges to interpret the variable in different ways.

5. *Profile analysis*

The teachers' ratings have also been studied by the method of latent profile analysis. The method does not assume linear regressions between the variables included in the profiles, and it was thus suitable to apply to the present material (see page 40). Figure 4: 1 gives the latent profiles for boys and girls in M_{10}, P_{13}, and in grade 8.

The same grouping was obtained in five of six grade-sex groups, namely

a) A group of students with values in the positive part of the adjustment scales, except in the variable *Tension*, where they have a central position.

b) A group with values in the negative parts of the scales *Aggressiveness*, *Motor disturbance*, *Disharmony*, *Distraction* and *Lack of school motivation*, but not in the variables *Timidity* and *Tension*, where the students are in a central position.

c) A group with values in the negative part of the scales *Timidity* and *Tension*, in the positive part of *Motor disturbance* and *Aggressiveness*, and otherwise with a central position on the scales.

6. *Rating procedure for M_{13}*

The alteration in the procedure for teachers' ratings made for the investigations in M_{13} referred to the designation of the variable *Tension*, which was altered to *Aspiration*. The latter name was considered to describe more adequately the content of the variable implied. Further, the description of behaviour B was re-worded for the same reason. The new description of the variable runs as follows.

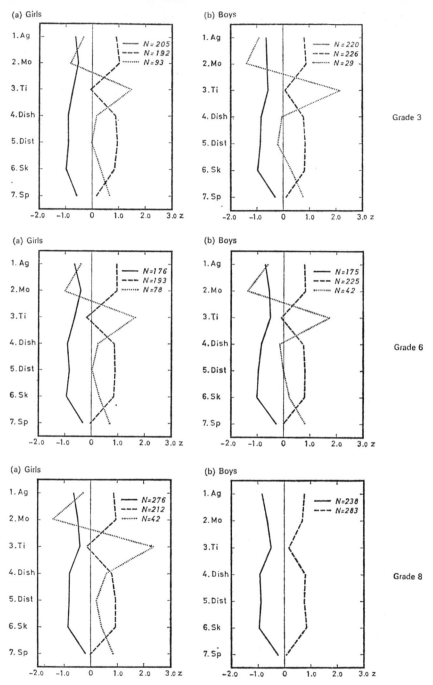

Figure 4: 1 Average latent profiles for three grades according to latent profile analysis of teachers' ratings of classroom behaviour

Table 4: 10. Coefficients for the correlations between teachers' rating variables for M_{13}.

	1	2	3	4	5	6	7
(a) Boys N = 502							
1. Aggressiveness	—	.66	−.09	.61	.55	.59	−.26
2. Motor disturbance		—	−.27	.53	.69	.61	−.33
3. Timidity			—	.17	.09	.15	.05
4. Disharmony				—	.61	.67	−.26
5. Distraction					—	.80	−.44
6. Lack of school motivation						—	−.49
7. Aspiration							—
(b) Girls N = 533							
1. Aggressiveness	—	.56	.03	.63	.51	.59	−.27
2. Motor disturbance		—	−.26	.49	.61	.47	−.32
3. Timidity			—	.26	.14	.30	−.04
4. Disharmony				—	.65	.71	−.24
5. Distraction					—	.78	−.44
6. Lack of school motivation						—	−.45
7. Aspiration							—

Aspiration

A This is characterized by the students making too great demands on themselves in relation to their ability. They stretch their powers to the utmost, when they begin working with their tasks. They may be described as "over-ambitious".

B The students do not seem to make any demands on themselves in respect of achievement, and do not seem to care much what results they get.

Most students fall between these two extremes.

7. Correlations between ratings of different variables, M_{13}

The correlations between the rating variables in data from M_{13} are reported in Table 4: 10.

The alteration of the correlation structure of the teachers' rating data which occurred after the variable *Tension* had been reformulated is that the new definition with the heading *Aspiration* has given a variable with negative correlations with the other variables, except *Timidity*, where the correlation is very low but still positive for boys. Thus it seems as if the teachers tend to evaluate what is called "over-ambition" in the description of the variable positively from the aspect of adjustment.

8. Teachers' ratings for M_{16}

In grades 7–9 of the comprehensive school the students have many different teachers, some of whom have very few lessons in the same class.

This gives rise to great difficulties when the teachers' knowledge of their students is to be used for systematic ratings.

Since it is very important in this period, too, to get some measure of the teachers' opinions of their students, a new assessment procedure, giving a rougher categorization than those used earlier, was developed.

The method is a modified "Guess-who technique". Under the leadership of the class supervisor, the teachers working in a certain class discussed and selected two boys and two girls who fitted best into given descriptions. If there were no students to whom the description could be applied in all details, the teachers were nevertheless to choose students who were most like the descriptions, as far as this was feasible.

The variables of the descriptions were chosen with reference to certain of the long-term problems dealt with in the project, and to the profile classes obtained in earlier teachers' judgments (see Fig. 3: 2). The teachers of a class chose two boys and two girls for each of the following descriptions:

1. *Scholastic ability.* The student has good prospects of pursuing very successfully theoretical studies at university level.

2. *Creative ability.* The student has creative gifts, finds new, adequate solutions of problems and has good prospects of working for innovations and progress in the vocation he/she chooses.

3. *Extrinsic maladjustment, aggressiveness.* The student is motor disturbed, aggressive and disorderly. Unconcentrated in his work, "fed up with" school.

4. *Intrinsic maladjustment, timidity.* The student's current behaviour in school is characterized by shyness, timidity and anxiousness. Afraid of acting in front of others, anxious when confronted with tests and the like. The student lacks self-confidence.

5. *Social maladjustment.* The student shows signs of poor social adjustment: out at nights, plays truant, unable to collaborate with others, abuse of alcohol, etc.

H. Variables in the home environment, etc.: parent questionnaires

1. *The investigation instrument*

A survey of the pupils' home environment can give facts, e.g. parents' education and incomes, number of siblings, dwelling standard, but also information of a more personal character, e.g. parents' attitudes in certain contexts, their systems of norms and child rearing methods. In the total group investigations the collection of data on home environment had to be made by questionnaires. To achieve a satisfactory frequency of replies, the questionnaires had to be rather brief. Further, the contents of the questionnaires had to be restricted mainly to questions of a factual type, easy to answer and not provocative to any parents. For a more detailed survey of the situation in the children's home environments other methods of data collection must be used, personal interviews, for example. Such interviews were carried out in conjunction with an intensive investigation of extreme groups of children with varying adjustment to peers. Then both parents were interviewed. (See Chapter 13.)

The questionnaire used in the total group investigations in 1965 was concerned with the following items:

Complete, incomplete family.

Parents: Age, education, occupation, membership of associations, religious congregations, other activities outside the home, evening work, the mother's gainful occupation, family income.

Siblings: Number, ages, occupations if any.

Family dwelling: Type, size, standard.

Moving, change of dwelling during child's growth.

Parents' contacts with the school.

Help with homework.

The above questions are, as can be seen, intended to elucidate different situations in the children's home environments. The questionnaire also contained some items aiming at ascertaining the parents' observations of the child's intrinsic adjustment. These items were concerned with the child's feelings of well-being at school, signs of anxiousness and uneasiness in respect of school, and observations of certain somatic disturbances in the child in conjunction with school attendance.

In the total group investigation in M_{13}, the questionnaire was augmented with a few questions referring to the child's choice of line of studies: a practical or theoretical education. In M_{16}, a short questionnaire was used. A few items dealt with home and parents, while the main body of questions referred to the choice of educational line or vocation.

2. Classification of families according to parents' education and occupation

One factor of great interest in the study of students' adjustment, above all their achievements, is the socio-economic status of the home. As shown above, the questionnaire answered by the parents gave information that can be used to indicate status in this respect. Since there is reason to assume that the attitudes to school that children acquire in the home, their motivation, their possibilities of getting help with their homework, and other things of great importance in this context are strongly correlated with their *parents' education* (*PE*), this variable was chosen as a measure of the social background.

Starting from the information on parents' education and occupation given in the parent questionnaire, the families were divided into seven groups.

1. University level education.

2. Advanced education above matriculation, but of shorter duration than university studies. Teacher's training college, college of social sciences, institute of social work and administration or an equivalent education.

3. Higher secondary school of engineering, economy or the like.

4. Education at intermediate school level: technological school, commercial institute or equivalent, with lower secondary school certificate or corresponding certificate from the nine-year comprehensive school as qualification for entry.

5. Lower secondary school, girls' school, folk high school ("folkhögskola") or equivalent special education.

6. Vocational training, vocational school or an equivalent training.

7. Unskilled labourer.

The family's status was determined by the parent with the highest education. In about 13 per cent of the families the formal education was at a level distinctly lower than that required for the occupations of these persons. Such families were placed in the educational group corresponding to the knowledge and skills required by the occupation.

I. Socio-ecological investigations

The physical environment is of great importance for children's development and for their possibilities to live a satisfactory life. This environment varies from child to child as the homes are different. But it also varies because the neighbourhoods have different characteristics and because the school buildings and their surroundings are different.

Studies of the social ecology of children from the various schools have been performed. In each study one catchment area was described, including the school, its buildings and equipment, localities and their functions.

An investigation was also made of the social structure of each school, including the teachers' and personnel's satisfaction with the functioning of the social system.

A description was made of the housing conditions in different parts of each area. The services given, facilities for leisure time activities, communications, etc., were also discussed. Information about the population structure was collected. These socio-ecological data will make it possible to study relationships between adjustment and environment.

J. Other data

In the descriptions of some special problems in Chapters 6–13 other data will be presented, which have been collected when the M- and P-groups were in the compulsory school system.

(a) Norm and norm conflicts. Questions about values and behaviour intentions in school, home and peer-related situations. See Chapter 6. M_{15}.

(b) Self-reported delinquency. P_{16}, M_{16} boys.

Attitudes to and knowledge of criminal behaviour and other norm breaks. M_{16} boys. See Chapter 7.

(c) Symptoms, questionnaire. M_{15} girls. See Chapter 8.

(d) Educational and vocational choice, questionnaires

M_{13}, M_{15}, M_{16}, P_{16} (also in M_{18}; P_{19})

Occupational differential M_{13}, M_{15}, P_{16}

Interests, inventory M_{13}, M_{16}, P_{16}

See Chapter 9.

(e) Biological variables, studied on a sample of about 250 children, M_{13}

Brain activity, EEG. Physical capacity

Hormonal activity (catecholamine)

Biological age (ossification) M

See Chapter 12.

(f) Social relations, intensive study of 90 children, M_{11}

Interviews with mother, father, teachers, child

Teachers' observations and ratings

Medical examination

See Chapter 13.

K. Collection of data

The administration of the investigation instruments referring to the students' experiences, attitudes, rating of peers, and the creativity tests, was in the hands of investigation leaders engaged specially for the project. All of these had at least the theoretical education required in Sweden for assistant psychologist, i.e. a B.A. degree. Most of them had some practical experience as teachers. The investigations were carried out during rather short periods. In the total group investigations in the main groups in grades 8 and 9 there were always two leaders for each class.

The investigation was introduced to the pupils orally by the leader of the investigation. The children were then informed that the answers they gave to the questions in the questionnaire would be used to see how things could be arranged in future as favourably as possible for the students in the school. No one in the school, neither teachers nor school-fellows, would know how they had answered the questions, nor would their parents be told. The leader of the investigation also stressed that the questionnaire had nothing at all to do with examinations, tests, or marks.

While the investigation leaders were in charge of the classes, the teachers in grades 3 and 6 rated their pupils. The teachers were informed orally of the purpose of the ratings by the leader of the investigation, who also gave them oral instructions as to how the ratings were to be made. In addition, the teachers were given written instructions. During the data collection there was an investigation leader available in the staff room to inform the teachers about the investigations.

The questionnaire for the parents was distributed by the pupils in closed envelopes with the text "To parents". The pupils were told to bring the questionnaire back, duly filled in, after a few days. In the envelope there was, in addition to the questionnaire, a reply envelope in which the questionnaire was to be put; then the envelope was to be sealed. The reply envelope was addressed to the Psychological Laboratories, University of Stockholm. The written instructions sent to the parents stressed that the information given would be treated as strictly confidential. The reply envelopes were collected from the students by the teachers. The 1971 parent questionnaire was collected by the completed forms being sent by mail to the leaders of the investigations.

The standardized achievement tests were administered and assessed by the teachers, who as a rule do not pass on the results. In this case, however, the teachers who had used the tests made the results available to the project.

Chapter 5
Size of follow-up groups
Problem of drop-outs

It was pointed out in Chapter 3 that it is very important for a follow-up study to concern a group that can be found in the same system during a long period. The research town was chosen on the basis of the view that Örebro, with a well-developed educational system and a diversified labour market, should offer young people such possibilities that they remain in the town during their education and also when they leave school and begin work.

There is, however, always some migration, which over a long period means a loss of subjects that may become considerable. It is also impossible to prevent drop-outs affecting the collection of data. Parents fail to reply to questionnaires, students may be absent on account of illness, truancy or the like, when data are collected. In this chapter an account will be given of how the project managed to obtain data from its follow-up groups and how these groups were reduced by people moving.

A. The main group

In the first place, the situation of the main group, which has been followed from grade 3, 1965, will be described. Of the children in this group, 88 per cent were born in 1955.

Table 5: 1 shows the sizes of the groups that attended the different grades on the first three occasions when the total group investigations were performed on a large scale—1965, 1968 and 1970. It also shows how many of the students in the groups remained on separate occasions or at several of the total group investigations. The increasing numbers are explained by the fact that more pupils have moved to than from Örebro.

Long-term longitudinal studies of the main group can be made in the first place on total groups from one occasion and may then comprise total groups of 1 025 students from grade 3, 1 100 from grade 6 or 1 190 from grade 8. The numbers are given for such combinations as 3, 6, not 8: the children present in grades 3 (M_{10}) and 6 (M_{13}), but not in grade 8.

For most purposes, however, it will probably be most fruitful to start from a group that attended the nine-year comprehensive school in Örebro during the whole period of the investigation, for which data are available

Table 5: 1. Sizes of groups for which data exist for different grades and combinations of grades. Main group.

Grades	Boys	Girls	Total
Total grade 3	515	510	1 025
Total grade 6	543	557	1 100
Total grade 8	600	590	1 190
3, 6 and 8	421	440	861
3, 6 not 8	31	27	58
both 3 and 6	452	467	919
3 and 8, not 6	4	2	6
3, not 6 or 8	59	41	100
6 and 8, not 3	81	65	146
both 6 and 8	502	505	1 007
6, not 3 or 8	10	25	35
8, not 3 or 6	94	83	177

from all—three up to now—total group investigations. From grades 3, 6, and 8, 861 students are registered, i.e. 84 per cent of the original group in grade 3. It must be regarded as satisfactory to be able to follow such a large part of a group over a period of five years in the same system. In some contexts, the follow-up group comprising students for whom information is available from grades 3 and 6 may be relevant. For these, there are 919 students, or 92 per cent of the original population. In other studies, the most interesting group may be the one for which data exist

Table 5: 2. Sizes of groups for which data exist from measurements with different instruments. Main group.

	Grade 3/65				Grade 6/68				Grade 8/70			
	Boys		Girls		Boys		Girls		Boys		Girls	
Type of instrument	N	%	N	%	N	%	N	%	N	%	N	%
Parent questionnaire	501	97	492	96	536	98	542	97	—	—	—	—
Intelligence test	484	94	483	95	540	99	550	99	575	96	576	98
Achievement test	477	92	482	94	460	85	475	85	498*	83	497*	84
Sociometry	515	100	510	100	543	100	557	100	519	87	502	85
Teachers' ratings	475	92	490	96	540	99	557	100	585	98	545	92
Semantic diff.	404	85	431	88	513	94	525	94	—	—	—	—
Student questionnaire	491	95	482	95	513	94	525	94	—	—		
Creativity test	—	—	—	—	447	82	446	80	—	—	—	—
Vocational choice, quest.	—	—	—	—	522	96	529	95	539	90	529	90
Vocational diff.	—	—	—	—	522	96	529	95	537	90	524	89
Interest form	—	—	—	—	522	96	529	95	—	—	—	—
Norm questionnaire	—	—	—	—	—	—	—	—	525	88	533	90
Symptom loading	—	—	—	—	—	—	—	—	—	—	520	88

* Refers to Swedish only.

Table 5: 3. Sizes of groups for which data are available for different grades. Pilot group, students born in 1952.

Grades	Boys	Girls	Total
Total grade 6	486	474	960
Total grade 9	562	546	1 108
Grades 6 and 9	387	403	790

from grades 6 and 8; here a group of 1 007 students can be used, or 92 per cent of the group studied in grade 6.

The description given of the sizes of the groups refers to the total groups registered in the schools. Not all data are available for all individuals. Table 5:2 reports the number of individuals for whom data are available for each instrument. The number of drop-outs is quite acceptable in most cases and in some cases a uniquely high participation can be observed. Thus, for example, a reply frequency of between 96 and 98 per cent is reported for the extremely important questionnaires sent to parents. This is the maximum of what can be achieved when it is borne in mind that some families cannot be expected to answer such questionnaires on account of language difficulties, dwelling at other places for the moment, etc.

Where the frequencies of answers are relatively low, i.e. below 95 per cent, the reason lies in special circumstances which will be commented on. Some of the instruments, e.g. the semantic differential, the creativity tests, the norm questionnaire and some standardized tests, could not be used in a few special classes. In the socio-metric assessments in grade 8 there were

Table 5: 4. Sizes of groups for which data are available from measurements with different instruments. Pilot group, students born in 1952.

Variable	Grade 6/65				Grade 9/68			
	Boys		Girls		Boys		Girls	
	N	%	N	%	N	%	N	%
Parent questionnaire	448	92	447	94	355	63	367	67
Intelligence test	482	99	471	99	—	—	—	—
Standardized test	460	95	457	97	—	—	—	—
Sociometry	486	100	474	100	—	—	—	—
Teachers' ratings	442	91	447	95	—	—	—	—
Semantic diff.	426	87	420	93	—	—	—	—
Student questionnaire	468	96	450	95	—	—	—	—
Interest form	—	—	—	—	445	79	421	77
Vocational choice, quest.	—	—	—	—	448	80	406	75
Vocational diff.	—	—	—	—	447	80	416	76
Self-reported criminality	—	—	—	—	521	93	—	—

certain problems in four classes where some students considered that, for ideological reasons, they could not judge their classmates. They influenced their classmates so that the number of judges in these classes was too small to give values worth using.

Standardized achievement tests are not used so commonly now as formerly, which has led to some loss of data. In grade 8 a whole class refused to write their names on the test sheets. Only the standardized tests in Swedish are included in the table since foreign languages, like mathematics, embrace differentiated tests on account of the different courses taken by different students. In these subjects the tests are not comparable to the same extent over the total material. Drop-outs tend to become more frequent in the higher grades, where students begin to question investigations whose meaning they do not fully understand.

B. Follow-up group from grade 6/65

The group which was in grade 6 when the project was started (P_{13}) has been used for extensive pilot studies and also to try out the instruments, etc. It is in itself a very valuable group for longitudinal studies. Table 5: 3 reports the sizes of the groups.

Of the original group of 960 individuals, there were 790, or 82 per cent, in grade 9 in 1968.

Table 5: 4 shows that both the parent questionnaires and the instruments to elucidate problems of study and vocational choices suffered from considerable numbers of drop-outs in grade 9. In the latter case this was because a whole headmaster area dropped out, for administrative reasons.

Part III
Sub-projects of a total group character

A number of problems which have been the subject of investigations founded on data from the total groups in the Örebro project are discussed in part III. The models that the studies work with, the special data collected for each sub-project and the design of the studies are described. Results up to now are presented in summary form.

The studies discussed here are concerned with:

a) norms and norm conflicts in adolescents,
b) delinquency rate in boys and c) symptom rate in girls, d) choice of line of studies and occupations, e) the role of creative ability and f) the degree and effects of social differentiation in school classes.

Chapter 6
Studies of norms and norm conflicts in adolescents

A. Adolescents and norms

1. *Adolescent culture*

The framework of a society encompasses different sub-cultures, each of which possesses a norm system, which is in part unique. Many regard adolescent culture as such a sub-culture. Davis, as long ago as 1940, pointed out that rapid social development is widening the inevitable gap between generations, and that this has led to different "social contents". He stressed that the longer period of school attendance has increased the possibility of more adolescent contacts and the risk of conflicts between the generations within the small family, as a background to the creation of an adolescent culture.

Mead's (1940) and Riesman's (1950) arguments for the existence of a separate adolescent culture with strong orientation towards peers were other early contributions to the debate, which led to much research around the problem of the parent and peer orientation of adolescents.

A fundamental question is how to define a separate adolescent culture, and a survey of the research work in this sphere (Gottlieb & Reeves, 1963) shows that most workers consider it to be a difference in degree rather than a separate culture. A common opinion was expressed by Coleman (1961): "The adolescent culture is a Coney Island mirror, which throws back a reflecting adult society in a distorted but recognizable image."

In our society, some of the differences between adult and adolescent culture have been encouraged by a teenage industry, which has exploited the differences for profit. This industry has created and sustained certain "teenage symbols", which, in themselves, can hardly be regarded as a sign of a separate culture. It is obvious, however, that the school situation encourages the interaction of people of the same age; they are together in the class and the only adults are the teachers. The school environment provides few possibilities of intergeneration communication, and these communication gaps may provide the conditions for an age-related uniformity in evaluations, actions and norms. The question seems to be whether this uniformity refers only to so-called "teen issues" or whether adolescents in general have acquired standards different from those of their parents.

2. Conflicts between generations

The problem of conflicts between generations is closely related to the discussion of an adolescent culture. In the adolescent process of liberation from dependency on parents, the way to autonomy is often considered to run via strong dependency on the peer group. Adolescents are busily occupied in endeavouring to find and maintain a role in society. Many have to struggle through the crises of earlier years in their search for a new feeling of identity and continuity. But this process of integration implies, among other things, danger of role disintegration, and Erikson (1963, 1968) regards the dependence of adolescents on their peers, and their often cruel rejection of all who are different, as defence against this role disintegration.

The adolescent situation is a phase with often contradictory expectations from peer and parent groups, which, it may be assumed, will easily lead to role and norm conflicts. Adelson (1964) is one of those who consider that the conflicts between adolescents and their parents are exaggerated. Conflicts exist, he maintains, but they are usually at an unconscious level. He regards open conflict as pseudo-rebellion, which is concerned with such trivial aspects as clothes, pocket-money, or hair-length.

During recent years, empirical research has modified the earlier theories of grave conflicts between the generations. Researchers are agreed on the existence of a strong peer orientation and on the notion that conflicts arise in relations to parents, but for most adolescents this is not expected to lead to eruptive solutions. Bealer, Willits & Maida (1969) have compiled empirical research results, which indicate that the theory of a rebellious youth culture is a myth. Younger teenagers tend to follow their parents in more fundamental values.

The literature on the adolescent revolt is generally concerned with older adolescents. Research is needed to elucidate the processes during the early years of adolescence, as a background to later development.

3. The development of independent value systems

Adolescence is important for the development of an independent system of values and standards, not least on account of the rapid intellectual growth, which makes it possible to understand ethic concepts. It has been stressed several times during recent years that the acute value crisis supposed to be present in adolescence refers only to a minority, and that the actual re-evaluation comes later. This problem should be studied in total group investigations. Such studies are reported by Douvan & Adelson (1966) and by Andersson (1969). The present study throws some light on norm development during early adolescence.

4. The picture of the adolescent—extreme or average?

The literature on the adolescent period is full of speculative theories, in which extremes are often unduly emphasized while no attention is paid to "ordinary" adolescents. The myths around the adolescent situation have been analysed by Adelson (1964) who found that two diametrically opposite figures have often been allowed to represent adolescents. One of these he calls "the Visionary", the other "the Victimizer". These two extremes, with their diametrically differing solutions of problems of adolescence, are similar in their opposition to "normal" adolescents, as they appear in studies of normal populations, similar in their extreme independence of the family and in their dissatisfaction with the social order, and in their radical solutions of the problems of adolescence.

The design of the present project with follow-up studies of whole year groups makes it possible to study the total variation in norms in a central Swedish town. We have, however, also chosen, as a second step, to attempt to find different adolescent patterns in respect of norms and study these sub-groups of adolescents from the aspect of adjustment.

B. The concept of norm and the process of adjustment

The concept of norm may be defined as a rule, as what "should" be the nature of something, how one should behave, and so on. This rule is sometimes codified in legislation, sometimes it is a more or less articulated demand on the members of a social group. Norms may refer to behaviour, views or feelings.

Norms may be studied as phenomena at high system levels, e.g. in cultures and subcultures, where they are classified as "folkways, mores, customary law, enacted law and institutions" (Davis, 1966). Norms may also, as here, be studied at the individual level. Here, norms refer to one of the forces in the psychological system that steer adjustment to the surrounding social system. We then speak of an internalized norm, which means that we regard this as a reproduction within the psychological system of a structure within a social system.

The adjustment of an individual can thus be related to his norms. Difficulties of extrinsic adjustment may be regarded as a consequence of lack of or divergent norm internalizing in the individual, a discrepancy between norms in the prevailing social system and the norms within a personality system. Such a discrepancy may also find expression in disturbed adjustment, if the individual modifies his behaviour according to demands made in the social system of which he is a member, at the same time as this behaviour is in opposition to the norms internalized in him.

Many norms have moral qualities. The individual's system of moral rules and moral "theories" pass a process of development, according to Kohlberg (1969) and Kohlberg & Turiel (1971), who described three levels of moral development, each with two stages. Tapp & Kohlberg (1971) have reported a theory of the development of attitudes to law and to norms for delinquent acts. An introduction to the psychological study of moral behaviour is given by Wright (1971). The control of behaviour and the following of norms may be connected with feelings of guilt. This control has been discussed by Aronfreed (1968) in terms of a conscience function.

C. General design of the investigation

A study of norms and norm internalizing may thus be regarded as a central task in research around the extrinsic and intrinsic adjustment of an individual. The studies made hitherto in this domain in the project have been reported by Henricson (1973). They have been restricted to the types of norms that seem to be of prime interest in relation to extrinsic adjustment data, namely norms referring to behaviour evaluated from moral angles, and in which deviations from the norm may be judged as relatively common causes of conflicts between the child and the home or the student and school. The domains of behaviour chosen also make possible certain comparisons with the results of a study made in Finland by Takala (1965).

1. *Investigation dimensions*

Included in the norm is always an evaluation of the behaviour. The norm encourages behaviour regarded as positive. The individual behavioural norms are usually studied in statements of the type, "what one ought to do", thus an evaluation of different types of behaviour.

If we wish to use the individual's statements for prediction, statements of the type, "what one should do", or "what I think I shall do", must be studied. In studies of attitudes (e.g. Triandis, 1967; Fiedler, Osgood, Sto-lurow & Triandis, 1964; Fishbein, 1967) it has also been shown that the combination of evaluations (affective measures) and behavioural intentions (conative measures) gives more certain predictions. Both these types of measure were collected in the present study, as were measures of sanction tendencies and actual breaches of norms.

2. *Transmitters of norms*

The formation of norms in young persons is steered by expectations of different types of behaviour which are transmitted by persons in their surroundings. The transmitters of norms of prime importance are parents, peers and teachers.

The transmission of norms may be studied from the angle of the actual conceptions of norms in the transmitters, and how adolescents themselves interpret the transmitter's conceptions. The present study has been restricted to the latter aspect and is concerned with the students' experience and expectations of parents' and schoolfellows' norms.

The teacher as transmitter of norms has not yet been dealt with in the investigations. Earlier studies have shown that teachers' norms are considered to be very similar to those of parents (Musgrove, 1964; Takala, 1965).

The students' experience of the opinions of the norm transmitters was studied from the same aspects as for the students themselves: *Evaluation, behavioural intentions* and parents' and peers' *sanctions* in case of breaches of norms.

Finally, the present investigation was concerned with certain situations that may be assumed to be of importance for the transmission of norms, in the first place the students' relations to parents and peers.

D. Objectives of the norm studies

The study of students' norms and their experience of the norm climate during adolescence is related to the main objective of the project by its purpose of providing data that may be used in the prediction of various aspects of a person's intrinsic and extrinsic adjustment.

The goal was to study (a) the adolescents' own norms and their perceptions and judgements of their peers' and their parents' norms, and two components of these norms; *Evaluation of behaviour* as well as their own and peers' *behaviour intentions,* (b) the adolescents' perception and judgement of the parents' expectations of their behaviour, and (c) the adolescents' expectations of the *sanctions* from their parents and peers if they violate certain norms.

In a first step the objective was a description of norms among the students in M_{14}, when they had just begun grade 8. Data for this group was supplemented by sample studies in grades 7 and 9. Data from these two grades make it possible to anchor means and measures of deviations for the main group in a developmental trend. The description also promoted the wider purpose of giving some idea of the adolescent culture and of the conflicts between generations present in respect of norms.

Reflections of the sex role patterns existing in society in adolescent norms can also be elucidated by this description, as well as developmental tendencies present during adolescence in respect of norms and evaluations. In addition, the relation between norm dimensions, which are possible to study by means of multicomponent techniques, may be of great interest.

A second step behind the averages must be taken to find sub-groups of adolescents with different norm patterns. These homogeneous groups can later be studied in respect of adjustment during school attendance together with other data from the project. Their further development can also be followed.

E. Investigation instruments

The investigation instruments used in the study of norm conceptions and the formation of norms are aimed at the following types of behaviour:

1. To cheat in an exam or an interrogation
2. To play truant from school
3. To ignore parents' prohibitions
4. To stay out late at night without permission
5. To loiter about town every evening
6. To get drunk
7. To smoke hashish
8. To pilfer from shops
9. To have sexual intercourse with a boy/girl friend
10. To talk to the school medical officer or nurse about a friend with drug problems (to help the friend).

The investigation comprised a questionnaire in three parts: an evaluative rating part, a conative rating part, and a part with items intended mainly to complement the data on the norm transmitters.

1. *Evaluative ratings*

The students had to give, on three separate forms, (a) their own evaluations of each of the ten items of behaviour, (b) how they conceived their parents' evaluations, and (c) how they conceived their peers' evaluations.

The lists were introduced as follows:

(List E)

"Here you shall say what *you yourself* think."

(List F)

"Here you shall say what you think *your parents* feel about adolescents doing different things."

(List K)

"Here you shall say what you think *your peers* think.

(By 'peers' we mean here those whose opinions you care most about, whether they are in your class, in a gang or your best friends.)"

The own evaluations and the perceived parent and peer evaluations of the ten items of behaviour were rated on seven-point scales, where the different steps were defined as in the following example (Item 1, list E).

I think it is

very silly = 1	silly = 2	rather silly = 3	not really OK = 4	rather OK = 5	OK = 6	quite OK = 7

to cheat in exams or interrogations.

The symbol OK was defined as follows for the students in the written instructions which they were to read before beginning to reply to the questionnaire. "By OK we mean here that although you may not consider it really good, it may be acceptable." Thus, the intention was that the scale should extend from a negative or distinctly disapproving pole over a neutral zone to an accepting pole.

2. Conative ratings behavioural intention

The part of the investigation concerned with behavioural intention referred, with one exception, to the same items of behaviour as the evaluative part. One item of behaviour in the evaluative part, number nine, sexual intercourse, was regarded by the advisory group (cf. p. 57) as provocative and was not included.

The task of evaluating behaviour described in general terms of the type "to cheat", "to play truant" would, as a rule, be considered easier than to give behavioural intentions in conjunction with such terms. In the latter case there is often a need to concretize and specify the situations in question. For this reason each question in the conative part was formulated with reference to a description of a concrete situation, involving decision-making from the side of the main person. Thus ten situations, involving possible cheating, playing truant, etc. were described. An example will be given.

"They are going to have an exam, but Gunilla has not had time to prepare herself. It is important for Gunilla to succeed. She has brought a scrap of paper with notes. She hesitates over whether to take up the note and cheat."

After each description of a situation three questions followed, dealing with (a) how the pupil thought the peers would act in the situation, (b) how he himself or she herself would act, and (c) how his/her parents believed that he/she would act. Ratings were made on seven point scales. The following questions were asked for each situation:

1. "If *your peers* found themselves in the same situation as Gunilla, what do you think they would do?

My peers

would absolutely not = 1	would probably not = 2	would perhaps not = 3	I am not sure what they would do = 4

would perhaps = 5	would probably = 6	would most certainly = 7

pick up the notes and cheat."

2. "To be quite honest, what would *you* do in such a situation?"

3. "What do you think your parents think you would do in Gunilla's situation?"

In addition, the question, "How do you think your parents (or your peers) would react if they found out that you had cheated?", was asked. The alternative replies covered the range "would probably not worry" (1) to "they would certainly disapprove strongly" (5).

Finally, the question, "Have you yourself ever cheated?", was asked. The alternative answers were "Never", "once", "2–3 times", "4–10 times", "more than 10 times".

3. *Norm transmitter aspects, etc.*

A number of questions were formulated to specify the transmitters of norms to the students. Some questions, for example, were given to ascertain whether the student thought most of the father's or mother's views when replying to questions regarding parents' evaluations. In the same way, the students were asked whether they had thought most of their classmates in general, or of their companions in the gang, or of their best friends when answering questions concerned with peer evaluations.

A special section of the form dealt with a number of independent items in the questionnaire intended to give information about contacts with parents and friends, methods of sanction used in the home, the student's independence, some aspects of the student's experience of himself, and so on. Finally, an attempt was made, by a number of questions of the type occurring in the MMPI, to detect individuals who were not sincere in their replies.

F. Collection of data

The study of norms in the main group of the project was performed during the autumn term of 1969, when the students of the main group were in grade 8 with a mean age of about 14 years 5 months. The study was conducted by psychologists who were earlier unknown to the subjects. For the data collection the classes were divided according to sex. The students were informed orally that only the leaders of the investigation at the University of Stockholm would have access to the replies, and that they were not to write their names on the forms, which were provided with a code number for each student. To emphasize the confidentiality of the study still further, the students were told to put the form, when filled up, in an envelope, which they were to seal themselves. The introduction stressed how very important it was that the forms were filled in as sincerely as possible.

To permit the study of norm development during the interesting period of adolescence, data on norms were also collected in grades 7 and 9. This investigation was concerned with samples of approximately 100 students of each sex from each grade. The samples were taken randomly.

Data in the main study were obtained for 94 per cent of the students. An analysis of the questionnaires indicated that, on the whole, the students had been honest in their replies.

G. Results of the descriptive processing

A detailed account of the studies of norms and norm conflicts has been given by Henricson (1971), but some results of the basic processing will be given here.

The average ratings of the adolescents' own evaluations are given in Figure 6: 1, where they are compared with their expectations of classmates' and parents' evaluations.

Table 6: 1 gives another aspect. There the percentages are given of boys and girls who have given ratings on the accepting part of the scale, who indicated an active disposition, who judged that their parents expected breaches of norms and who judged an accepting attitude in their parents.

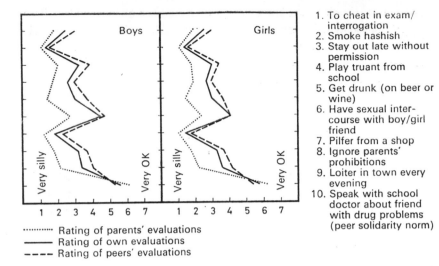

1. To cheat in exam/interrogation
2. Smoke hashish
3. Stay out late without permission
4. Play truant from school
5. Get drunk (on beer or wine)
6. Have sexual intercourse with boy/girl friend
7. Pilfer from a shop
8. Ignore parents' prohibitions
9. Loiter in town every evening
10. Speak with school doctor about friend with drug problems (peer solidarity norm)

············ Rating of parents' evaluations
——— Rating of own evaluations
‒ ‒ ‒ ‒ Rating of peers' evaluations

Figure 6: 1 Profiles showing the average ratings of own, peers' and parents' evaluations, grade 8

1. *Description of adolescent evaluations*

Generally speaking, adolescents are strict in their judgements, and, with two exceptions, the average ratings of their own norms are on the stricter end of the scale.

Adolescents judge such items of behaviour as pilfering and smoking hashish most strictly. Pilfering is a criminal offence, which probably influenced their opinions. As far as hashish smoking is concerned, an intensive information campaign against drugs had just been finished, and this no doubt had influenced the students.

There are two items of behaviour that are more willingly accepted than others by adolescents themselves. One of these was intended to measure loyalty to friends—"to talk to the school medical officer about a friend with drug problems"—but did not function as expected. It seems likely that lack of experience of such situations prevented most adolescents from realizing the conflict such a situation would imply.

The other item of behaviour accepted was "to have sexual intercourse with boy/girl friend". This shows a more permissive sex morality than was earlier considered to exist. Table 6: 1 shows that about 50 per cent of the adolescents in their fifteenth year were permissive in their rating of sexual intercourse. The percentages of permissive evaluations are about the same for boys and girls. Another investigation, of the burden of symptoms in girls (Chapter 8), provides data showing that approximately 22 per cent of the

Table 6: 1. Percentages of adolescents (*a*) who have given accepting ratings of behaviour, (*b*) who state that they would perform the action in question, (*c*) who judge parents' expectations of breaches of norms as accepting and (*d*) who judge parents' evaluations of behaviour as accepting.

Behaviour	(a) Own evaluations		(b) Would act so		(c) Parents' expectations of breaches of norms		(d) Parents' evaluations	
	G	B	G	B	G	B	G	B
Smoke hashish	2	1	7	4	2	1	0	0
Pilfer from a shop	2	3	4	8	1	1	0	0
Cheat in exam./interrogation	8	7	36	37	12	10	0	0
Play truant from school	10	9	24	16	8	3	2	1
Stay out late without permission	10	15	29	31	18	15	0	1
Ignore parents' prohibitions	16	16	55	55	25	22	1	0
Get drunk	21	23	39	41	8	10	1	1
Loiter about town every evening	30	23	35	22	20	9	4	3
Sexual intercourse with boy/girl friend	54	54	—*	*	—*	*	12	17
Speak with school doctor about friend with drug problems	85	80	67	54	—*	*	91	89

* The question was omitted.
Girls N = 533, Boys N = 525.

girls in this year group had had sexual contacts on one or several occasions. The situation in Finland (Jyväskylä) was quite different, with a much stricter rating of sexual intercourse at this age in the study performed by Takala in 1965.

Parents' evaluations, which were judged by their children in general to be very strict, were conceived to be relatively permissive in respect of sexual intercourse (see Table 6: 1). This result indicates an attitude change also in the adult generation, although less marked. This judged parent attitude is remarkable in comparison with the Finnish results reported by Takala (1965), which showed that the sexual relations of adolescents were among the items of behaviour judged most strictly by parents, according to their children.

Still another result illustrated in Figure 6: 1 and Table 6: 1 will be commented on, namely the important role of alcohol, probably mainly beer (3.8 per cent alcohol), in adolescent culture today. About one student in five in grade 8 considered it acceptable to get drunk, and about 40 per cent of both boys and girls stated that they would get drunk in a tempting situation. It will also be observed that when students were allowed to

Behaviour	Grade					
	Boys			Girls		
	7	8	9	7	8	9
Smoke hashish	1.43	1.50	1.89	1.57	1.70	2.32
Pilfer from a shop	2.11	2.01	2.04	1.63	1.59	1.73
Cheat in exam/interrogation	3.46	3.73	3.86	3.56	3.56	3.92
Play truant from school	2.70	2.66	3.08	2.67	2.91	3.67
Stay out late without permission	3.17	3.41	3.94	2.92	3.26	3.69
Ignore parents' prohibitions	4.12	4.44	4.99	3.79	4.43	5.06
Get drunk	3.46	3.71	4.41	2.78	3.49	3.98
Loiter about town every evening	3.28	3.05	3.16	3.22	3.37	2.94
Speak with school doctor about friend with drug problems	4.97	4.54	4.40	5.18	5.02	4.88

Note: Higher values indicate more active intentions.

choose spontaneously what was regarded as "tough" among peers, "to get drunk" occupies a clear first place for both boys and girls.

Norm ratings have also been analysed by the method of latent profile analysis (see p. 40), where different classes of students with different patterns of norms were obtained. Figure 6: 2 shows, among other things, that most of the adolescents belong to a relatively strict norm group, and their views conform largely to those of their parents. By its size, this group can exert a fairly strong influence on the average. Figure 6: 1 and Table 6: 1 therefore give us information from different angles. (Students with accepting ratings "disappear" in Figure 6: 1.)

2. *Sex and age differences in adolescent norms*

It was shown in the previous section that the old sex role pattern, with different expectations on boys and girls, is not generally accepted in respect of sex relations and alcohol, although traces of it can still be observed.

The most consistent sex difference in the material is in respect of pilfering. The boys have a more permissive rating in all three grades, and they have significantly more frequent action intentions in this item. This is also the behaviour which is regarded rather commonly as "tough" by boys. Girls show greater fear of breaches of norms than boys. Another difference is that girls consistently conceived greater acceptance of truancy by parents. This possibly refers to forms of truancy accepted by parents, such as menstruation trouble, nervousness of examinations, and the like.

The sample investigation in grades 7 to 9 shows, above all, a more accepting evaluation and more action intentions for age-related behaviour in higher ages. The results given in Table 6: 2 show that this refers to such items of behaviour as getting drunk, having sexual intercourse, staying out late and ignoring parents' prohibitions.

3. Adolescents' experiences of peers' and parents' norms

a) *Peers.* The adolescents mostly experience peers and friends as more permissive than they themselves are in their ratings. In respect of the sex item they were equally permissive themselves. The friends concerned are the positive norm transmitters ("the friends whose opinions interest you most"), and the results imply that the adolescents are inclined to expect more permissive evaluations of breaches of norms from their peers.

The adolescents may feel a need to give a better picture of themselves than of their peers; a need which, in spite of the protection of anonymity, probably influences the ratings to some extent. If so, peer ratings most likely give a "truer" picture of adolescent values. It is possible, however, that peer evaluations are perceived as being more permissive on the basis of instances of extreme behaviour that has been observed. The ratings imply, too, that it is consistently assumed that peers will commit breaches of norms significantly more frequently than one does oneself.

b) *Parents.* Parents' norms are rated consistently near the strict pole of the scale. It is only in the sexual intercourse item that more than occasional accepting ratings are given. The students are also generally agreed in their judgements of parents' norms. These might, therefore, act with greater force, since they seem to be unambiguous and there is less opportunity to interpret them according to one's own wishes.

In reply to the item regarding the breaches of norms parents expect of their children, adolescents are generally convinced that parents wish to regard their children as "angels". Thus there are remarkably great differences between the behaviour one believes parents expect and adolescents' own intentions, as is shown in Table 6: 1. These differences may be regarded primarily as a sign of lack of information, of a gap in communication between the generations. Especially great are the differences in the item concerned with getting drunk, where 40 per cent of the students say that they would do so in a tempting situation, while only 8–10 per cent of the students believe that their parents expect this of them. Breaches of norms of which parents must have knowledge, e.g. "stay out late without permission", "ignore parents' prohibitions", or "loiter in town late at night" also show great differences. In these cases, however, the ratings of parents' expectations in respect of "breaches of norms" are higher than otherwise.

4. *Relations between own, peers' and parents' norms*

According to earlier investigations (Takala, 1965; Riley, Riley & Moore, 1961), adolescents' ratings of their own evaluations fall between the ratings they make of parents' and peers' evaluations. Boys also expect greater discrepancy between parents' and peers' ratings than girls, and they relate closer to peers in their evaluations than girls do (Douvan & Adelson, 1966; Musgrove, 1964).

It was assumed here that adolescents would rate their own norms more strictly than those of peers but milder than parents'. This hypothesis, with a "compromise pattern", receives strong support, as is shown in Figure 6: 1, where the average ratings of boys' and girls' own evaluations are compared with their conceptions of peers' and parents' evaluations.

Research results from other countries, showing that boys have stronger peer orientation in their own norms and that they experience great conflict between peer and parent norms, were not confirmed by the present study. One reason for this may be a different definition of the reference group in respect of peers. By including only the peers who *really act* as transmitters of norms (instead of an arbitrary group such as "class", etc.), we have probably reduced the norm fiction element in the ratings.

The picture that emerges in Figure 6: 1 also provided a basis for discussions of conflicts between the generations. The items in which differences in evaluations between own norms and parents' norms and between peers' and parents' norms are greatest are concerned with specific causes of conflicts between the generations. As already pointed out, this refers to ratings of sexual intercourse at these ages. The figure also shows that the differences may be very great in such items as "to get drunk", "stay out late without permission", and to a certain degree "to loiter about town" or "play truant". The figure gives the average situation. For large groups there are probably no serious conflicts between the generations. In other groups conflicts are greater than shown in Figure 6: 1, as can be seen in Figure 6: 2, which illustrates the various norm patterns hidden behind the averages.

5. *Peer and parent sanctions*

Those who do not respect group norms are liable to negative sanctions. These may range from vague reproach, disappointment, warnings, loss of prestige or status to a term in prison, depending on the norm broken and in which group or society one lives.

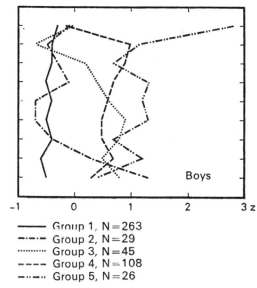

1. Smoke hashish
2. Pilfer from a shop
3. Cheat in an exam/interrog.
4. Play truant from school
5. Ignore parents' prohibitions
6. Stay out late without perm.
7. Loiter in town every even.
8. Get drunk
9. Sexual intercourse with boy/girl friend

Boys

-1   0   1   2   3 z

——— Group 1, N = 263
—·—·— Group 2, N = 29
·········· Group 3, N = 45
— — — Group 4, N = 108
—··—·· Group 5, N = 26

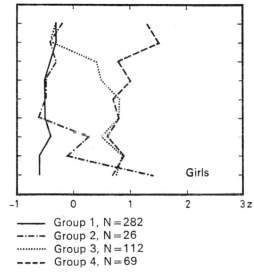

1. Smoke hashish
2. Pilfer from a shop
3. Cheat in an exam/interrog.
4. Play truant from school
5. Ignore parents' prohibitions
6. Stay out late without perm.
7. Loiter in town every even.
8. Get drunk
9. Sexual intercourse with boy/girl friend

Girls

-1   0   1   2   3 z

——— Group 1, N = 282
—·—·— Group 2, N = 26
·········· Group 3, N = 112
— — — Group 4, N = 69

Figure 6:2 Profile groups based on adolescents' own evaluations. The figures are based on the deviations of the different profile groups from the total mean for each variable, expressed in z-values. Boys and girls, grade 8

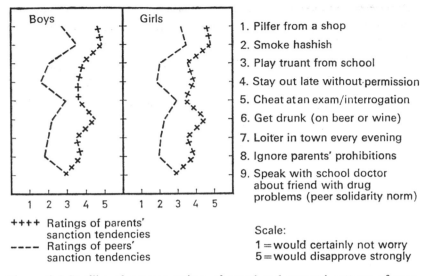

Boys	Girls	
		1. Pilfer from a shop
		2. Smoke hashish
		3. Play truant from school
		4. Stay out late without permission
		5. Cheat at an exam/interrogation
		6. Get drunk (on beer or wine)
		7. Loiter in town every evening
		8. Ignore parents' prohibitions
		9. Speak with school doctor about friend with drug problems (peer solidarity norm)
1 2 3 4 5	1 2 3 4 5	

++++ Ratings of parents' sanction tendencies

———— Ratings of peers' sanction tendencies

Scale:
1 = would certainly not worry
5 = would disapprove strongly

Figure 6: 3 Profiles of average ratings of peers' and parents' patterns of sanctions

No attempt was made to ascertain what types of sanction the students expected to be applied by parents or peers for different kinds of norm breaches. On the other hand, an attempt was made to obtain the anticipated strength of the reaction by the question, "How do you think your parents and friends would react if they found that ...?" (see p. 102). The rating scale ranged from strong disapproval to indifferent reaction. (Thus, positive reactions to some items of behaviour were not measured.) Figure 6: 3 shows that the profiles for expected sanctions by peers and parents differ significantly from each other. On the other hand, sex differences are relatively small.

Parents' reactions are judged consistently as very negative. For the items "pilfer", "smoke hashish", "get drunk" the average is close to the extreme point, "would strongly disapprove". This has an equivalent in adolescents' own strict ratings, except for alcohol, where they have a relatively positive rating and active action intentions. This must, therefore, be regarded as a source of generation conflicts.

6. Summarizing comments on adolescent norms and their relations to the reference groups

a) *Norm aspects.* The differences between the evaluations of the two reference groups shown by the averages in Figure 6: 1 give an impression of different evaluations in peers and parents, but there are still many similarities. When, on the other hand, adolescents rate what they think their friends would do in a tempting situation, the differences in relation to parents' expectations and wishes are much greater.

That the difference reported by adolescents between the two reference groups increases when we come to ratings of action tendencies may be partly explained by the results reported in Figure 6: 3. Sanction tendencies of peers and parents differ greatly there. The parents are expected to stress their evaluations and react strongly to breaches of norms. Peers, on the other hand, are seldom expected to react disapprovingly if these norms are not followed. Thus the pressure from peers to conform is weak in respect of this type of norm.

One might, therefore, draw the conclusion that adolescents express relatively strict opinions when they are asked in serious contexts, but when they are in a concrete situation there is little pressure from friends to make them refrain from breaches of norms. Instead we find that in certain adolescent circles it is considered "tough" to commit breaches of the norms in question.

The difference that adolescents perceive between peers and parents with regard to norms may thus be much greater than, for example, the difference in ratings of the actual norms of the two groups (Figure 6: 1). The parents are experienced as preservers of norms, while the role of peers is in another direction.

The discussion also shows the importance of the multicomponent method in the interpretation of the norm structure of adolescents in relation to the two reference groups.

b) *Relation aspects.* In addition to the rating of norms, the investigation also included a number of problems of relations as a basis for a study of what importance the two reference groups might have as transmitters of norms.

The results did not show extreme peer orientation or strong conflicts with parents as far as most of the adolescents were concerned. This refers, of course, to the conscious level—for we have no data on which to base a statement about unconscious conflicts which may be assumed to have been acute during this period. The answers to the question "Who do you generally feel understand you best—your peers or your parents?" are given in Table 6: 3. The boys seem to be more oriented to parents, but less than half of the girls likewise feel that the peers really understand them better. Another question was: "Do you feel that you and your parents understand each other?" The distributions of answers are given in Table

Table 6: 3 Distribution of answers to the question: Who do you feel understand you best —your peers or your parents? Per cent

Answer	Girls	Boys
My peers understand me best	22.0	11.0
My peers understand me some- what better	21.0	15.0
My peers and my parents under- stand me equally well	37.5	43.5
My parents understand me some- what better	11.5	17.0
My parents understand me best	7.5	13.5

6: 4. Very few of the adolescents think they are not at all understood by their parents.

Peers emerge as an important reference group for these younger adolescents, but for the majority of them relations to parents are not heavily loaded, although different opinions are expressed regarding dress, pop music, times to come home at night and so on.

7. *Relations between evaluations and action intentions*

The study was also designed to allow for a study of norm dimensions. The purpose of this was to ascertain how far the students' ratings agreed with their action intentions, etc. This question is also of importance from the technical aspect of measurement, since several studies of norms have been based entirely on evaluations.

We started from the hypothesis that adolescents are stricter in their evaluations (conform more to parents) than in their action intentions, which are closer to peer control, etc. This hypothesis was clearly confirmed, as has already been shown. In all cases, strong action intentions were significantly more frequent than accepting evaluations. The left two columns in Table 6: 1 illustrate this. Evaluations form only one of the motives behind an action or an intention to act in a certain way. What is

Table 6: 4 Distribution of answers to the question: Do you feel that you and your parents understand each other? Per cent

Answer	Girls	Boys
Very well	26.5	23.0
Pretty well	33.0	44.5
Sometimes well, sometimes badly	29.5	28.5
Pretty badly	7.0	2.0
Very badly	4.0	2.0

found, therefore, is that adolescents are, in several respects, rather elastic in their norms, they stretch their "consciences" when other motives than ethical ones appear. While only 7–8 per cent of the students in grade 8 give a permissive rating of cheating, rather more than 35 per cent say that they would cheat in a tempting situation. Several such examples can be found. Fifty per cent of the students would ignore parents' prohibitions, but only 16 per cent accepted this in their ratings, and so on. Thus, for many students, evaluations do not have any considerable effect on behaviour intentions. There is certainly also a considerable difference between these intentions and actual behaviour.

H. Results from homogeneous subgroups

1. *Individual norm patterns*

Adolescents are often treated as a single homogeneous group. One speaks of one adolescent culture, describes adolescents in terms of total group averages, and so on. We started from the assumption—an obvious one—that adolescents cannot be treated as a homogeneous mass and we wished to study which groupings were to be found behind the often commercialized regimentation.

The students have been classified on the basis of their own evaluations and their action intentions by the help of latent profile analysis, LPA (see page 40). These classes may be said to represent different conditions, norm-regulated situations, different systems of norms.

Figure 6: 2 shows the average evaluations in the profile groups based on the students' own evaluations.

a) *Analyses of evaluations.* In these we have found four to five general ways of acting in respect of the current problems in the population studied.

One large group is consistently strict in evaluations and thus conforms largely to parents (Group L, with low scale values). There is a small group that differs from this pattern, still relatively strict but more permissive in evaluation of sexual relations between adolescents.

Another large group shows what may be called normal adolescent defiance, with acceptance of most items of behaviour except pilfering and smoking hashish, which seem to be the really crucial types of behaviour.

There is also a group (Group H, with high scale values) that accepts everything, in which stronger opposition to parents' culture can be discerned. Among boys this group has two types, dependent on whether the evaluation of smoking hashish is positive or not.

b) *Analyses of intentions.* When, instead, the students are classified according to their action intentions, a similar picture emerges.

There is a large group conforming to parents' norms, with no intention of committing breaches of the norms in question. (The small deviant group cannot be studied, for the question on sexual intercourse was excluded from the intention part.)

Here, too, is a small, relatively strict group, but with a certain deviation. These students seem primarily to intend to get drunk (i.e. a type of behaviour that seems to be fundamental in Swedish "adolescent culture" today), and to ignore parents' prohibitions.

There is also an intermediate group with moderate adolescent defiance and two more oppositional groups of boys and girls who intend to break most of the norms. Both boys and girls form two different constellations, depending on whether attitude to smoking hashish is positive or not.

The groupings of adolescents on the basis of evaluations and action intentions respectively showed satisfactory agreement. This suggests that adolescents' evaluations are related to their intentions, even though we found earlier that the levels differ (consistently more action intentions than what the evaluations themselves would lead to).

2. *Norm patterns and adjustment*

The underlying hypothesis was that the different norm groups would differ systematically in their adjustment to important sectors of adolescent life: to school, in relation to parents and peers, and the like.

On the basis of the conforming group's profile pattern, it was assumed that the strict groups would be more parent oriented in general, and experience less conflict in relations to parents than the other groups— especially the oppositional high groups. Partly as a consequence of this, the strict groups were assumed to be less peer oriented, although the quality of peer contacts need not necessarily be unlike that in other groups. It was also assumed that it would be easier for these groups to adjust themselves to the school situation. Conflicts in relation to the school and to parents were assumed to be more usual in adolescents belonging to a more accepting profile group (own norms farther from parents' norms), because the norms and intentions of these groups are often in opposition to those of the adult generation. In these groups, it was assumed that peers would play an increasingly greater role as reference group. The most accepting groups were therefore to have the most conflicting parent relations, be less school motivated and find relations more difficult than the other groups. They were also assumed to be distinctly more peer oriented.

On the whole, the results confirmed our expectations, but the complexity of the pattern is impossible to describe within this restricted framework. The most comprehensive processing has been devoted to the different intention groups and the work is still proceeding. A study has been made of the adjustment of these groups in the early years at school and in the preadolescent age; they have been followed up during grade 8 in respect of critical adjustment behaviour and in other relevant variables.

Generally speaking, it may be said that our hypothesis on relations to parents received strong support. Some results from analyses of data for the girls are given in Figure 6: 4. There are significant differences between the strict (low) and the accepting (high) groups in the experiences of the relations to the parents. The results given in Figure 6: 5 show the same tendency for girls in some questions about relations to teachers and about the school situation. In questions about sexual problems the high groups express significantly more experience and positive interest than the low group (see Figure 6: 6). The hypothesis on stronger peer orientation in the high groups was not confirmed clearly.

Differentiation in different adolescent patterns is, as shown in Figures 6: 2 and 6: 3, most distinct in respect of the "upper" half of the adolescents among those who express some form of rejection of parents' norms. Another step in the investigation here is to study the "silent" majority behind the parent conforming low pattern. It is probable that different student groups can be found, for example, one group of stressed, anxious and inhibited students, another with strict norms but in which adjustment is otherwise more flexible, and a third group in which it is mostly a question of a response style.

3. Comments

This part of the investigation has shown that it is possible to group adolescents in relatively homogeneous sub-groups with varying evaluation patterns and different action intentions in norm-regulated systems, which seem intimately related to the total situation of the adolescent. These groups have quite different life patterns from their early years, which is possible to show in this project.

To refer to adolescents as a homogeneous group or to use the term "adolescent culture" as a general term is a gross simplification that is made far too often. Measures to meet adolescents' problems in general ways and in the same way for all will inevitably be failures. In forming the school system these results should be considered, so that it can offer good stimulation to all groups.

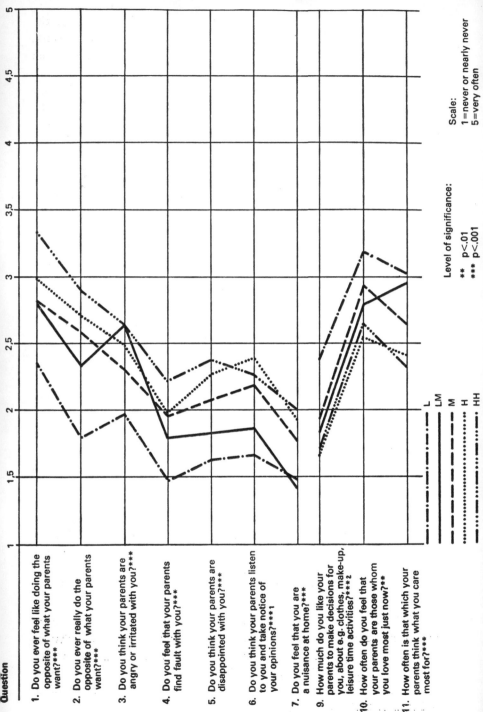

Question

1. Do you ever feel like doing the opposite of what your parents want?***
2. Do you ever really do the opposite of what your parents want?***
3. Do you think your parents are angry or irritated with you?***
4. Do you feel that your parents find fault with you?***
5. Do you think your parents are disappointed with you?***
6. Do you think your parents listen to you and take notice of your opinions?***1
7. Do you feel that you are a nuisance at home?***
9. How much do you like your parents to make decisions for you, about e.g. clothes, make-up, leisure time activities?***2
10. How often do you feel that your parents are those whom you love most just now?**
11. How often is that which your parents think what you care most for?***

L
LM
M
H
HH

Level of significance:

** p<.01
*** p<.001

Scale:

1=never or nearly never
5=very often

Figure 6:4 Comparisons between homogeneous subgroups in experiences of relations to parents. Girls, M_{15}.

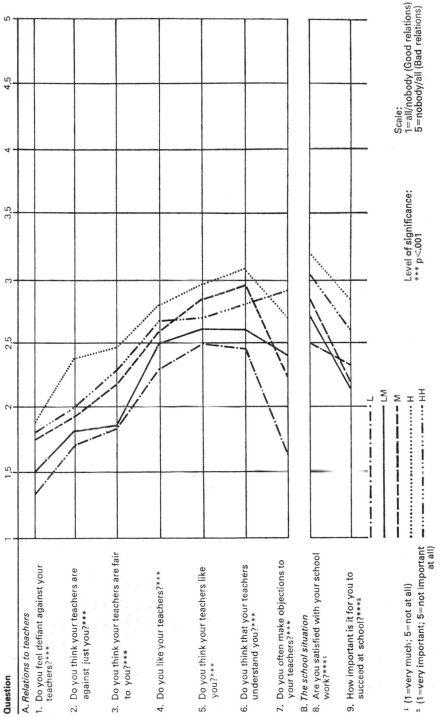

Figure 6:5 Comparisons between homogeneous subgroups in experiences of the school situation. Girls, M₁₅.

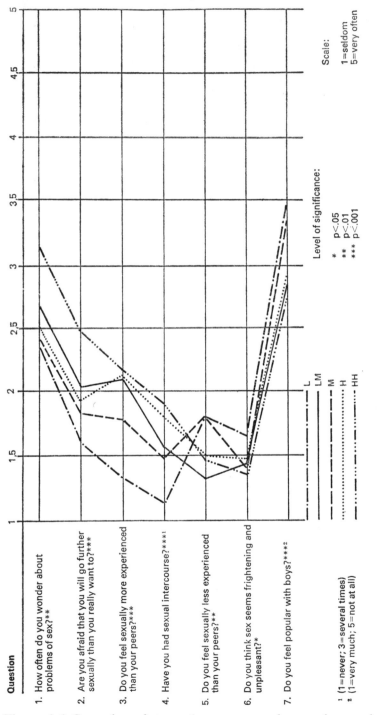

Figure 6: 6 Comparisons between homogeneous subgroups in experiences of sexual problems. Girls, M₁₅.

I. Retrospective view of the investigation

In the interpretation of the results it must be borne in mind that the investigation is based on data obtained from adolescents who have themselves answered the questions. No one—not even their classmates—will know how they have replied. There can be no doubt that the results would have been different if we had had a "public" item, for which, for example, we had said that classmates would be informed of the answers (see, e.g. Bronfenbrenner, 1967, 1969), or if we had allowed a group of adolescents to answer the questions together.

Much of the adolescent behaviour we observed in school and outside is a "gang phenomenon", and a series of group-psychological factors belongs to the picture. That our observations of adolescent behaviour do not always agree with the empirical results of questionnaires may, of course, be due largely to the psychological differences between a single reply situation and a concrete action situation with group psychological components. (One attractive method, therefore, would be to allow groups of adolescents to answer the questions in common. Such an approach would, in practice, imply a number of problems, but it would provide a completely different type of information.)

The multicomponent method gave a differentiated picture of adolescent norms. Rating evaluations separately gave a picture of a very restricted norm climate among the adolescents. When the ratings were compared with intended actions, sanction tendencies and so on, a completely different picture of the norm situation of adolescents emerged.

The division into different norm dimensions showed how important it is to pay attention to sanction tendencies. It also showed how important the conative dimension is. In the action intentions, the ratings were based on an actual situation (attitude to situations might be studied specially), and an essentially different picture was obtained than when the evaluations were studied. Our experience suggests, above all, that the study must be continued along these lines.

The multicomponent method restricted the investigation in another way, too—in scope. Since so many dimensions were studied in respect of the concept of norm itself (evaluations—action intentions—sanctions—actual breaches of norms), and concerning the norms of different persons (own—peers'—parents' norms), only a few norms could be studied. In this respect the investigation had somewhat the character of a model. It would be interesting to extend the scope of the sectors studied to other norm domains, e.g. politics, sex roles, human co-existence, and so on.

The design, with a study of a whole year group, has been both a strength and a limitation. We have obtained information about a total norm varia-tion and, by the second step with LPA-analyses, have been able to study different adolescent groups with different adjustment. It would be valu-able, however, to supplement the investigation with an intensive study, within which more fundamental information could be obtained than is possible by questionnaires.

In the further work, the sub-groups of adolescents we have found will be specifically studied regarding the background information about these students, collected during the whole of their school attendance. They will also be followed in their further development.

Chapter 7
Delinquent behaviour in boys—
a criminological study

A. Background and purpose

One function of a supreme social system, the state, is to ensure conformity to the norms regulating certain types of behaviour in the individual. This is done by laws and measures aimed at individuals. Legislation is intended to reflect values and norm concepts which are shared by most members of society, and transmitted to the young individuals during the process of socialization. Laws give us formulations of demands on the behaviour of the members of the society and are thus a kind of criteria of adjustment and maladjustment.

The steps taken by juridical bodies concern groups of individuals we regard as maladjusted. In the first place, this is a classification concerned with adjustment defined on the basis of the demands made by a social system, thus, extrinsic adjustment. When an individual commits a crime, we may regard this also as a symptom of intrinsic adjustment disturbance. Then the crime is interpreted as a kind of inadequate solution of a conflict, a maladaptive reaction, and treatment should aim at helping the individual to achieve better intrinsic adjustment.

It is obvious that the system of sanctions used by society today against young people in their upper teens and against adults who commit crimes has very little therapeutic effect. Many of the steps taken by society when a crime has been discovered may lead to the individual's developing a feeling of alienation from society and its valid norms, and becoming attached to groups that do not regard crime as wrong. If this is so, the steps counteract the purpose.

The study of the social problems defined by criminal conduct is thus urgent from the aspect of both society and the individual. Juvenile delinquency in particular must be regarded as a grave problem, causing considerable social and individual injury. Between 1920 and 1963 the number of serious crimes committed in the age group 15–20 years increased fourfold in Sweden (Blomberg, 1963). Adolescents are responsible for most of the great increase in crime during recent decades.

Children learn to obey most of the rules and satisfy the demands made on them. They learn the habits of obedience, i.e. habits that do not correspond to any well thought-out system of values of their own. During the period of puberty, young people begin to question the legitimacy of some rules and demand that they must correspond to their own values, which, during a period of development, are diffuse. During this transitional period, which may be expected to be prolonged by the increased period of school attendance, rules codified as laws are broken quite frequently.

But criminality during youth is, to a great extent, a transitory phenomenon. Many adolescents who commit crimes cease their criminal conduct when they become adults, if not before; they conform to the norms of society. Continued criminality in an individual may, as already mentioned, be associated with undesired effects of steps taken by society in conjunction with crime. It is obviously very important to attempt to isolate factors influencing the development of an individual in the direction of conformity or criminality. Long-term goals for the part of the present project presented in this chapter are (a) to make possible early predictions of risk of criminality by studying the etiology of crime and conformity and by strengthening the theoretical basis, and (b) to study the effects of steps taken by society.

If these goals are reached, there will be grounds on which to propose methods of individual treatment that can be more efficient in the prevention of further development of extrinsic and intrinsic maladjustment. The planning of this study has been reported by Magnusson, Dunér & Olofsson (1968).

B. Theories and models in the study of causes of criminality

Criminological theories may traditionally be divided into those which stress mainly biological factors (Kinberg, 1955; Weinschenk, 1967) as causes of criminality, psychological and psychiatric factors (Healy & Bronner, 1950; Abrahamsen, 1960), and sociological factors (Merton, 1968) respectively. These earlier restricted theories have now been replaced by a multidimensional approach, see e.g. Cortes & Gatti (1972).

The simplest model in such an approach is to assume that the different factors expected to influence the individual's development towards criminal conduct are additive and that each factor functions in the same way for different individuals. Attempts have been made to determine, on the basis of this simple model, regression equations, with the help of which risks of crime may be calculated for individuals in an early stage of development (see Glueck & Glueck, 1950; Ohlin, 1951). A certain amount of progress has been made in these predictions (see Blomberg, 1963; Sveri, 1965).

A prediction equation need not be based on the assumption of causal relationships, nor does it immediately give any knowledge of such. Variables with heavy weightings in the equation may lack causal effect and covary with the criterion only by indirect causal chains within the system. From the causal aspect, important variables may disappear from the equation by covarying with other variables in the system which have higher correlation with the criterion.

The simple additive model often seems psychologically unfeasible. Psychological theory makes it reasonable to increase the predictive validity by, for example, the application of moderator techniques. In some situations it is possible, moreover, to test hypotheses of causal relationships by way of models.

Generally speaking, it may be said that more fundamental knowledge of the relations between individual and environmental variables on the one hand and on the other the occurrence of a certain disturbance in adjustment makes it possible for us to plan experiments by which we can intervene in a course of development in order to influence it in a positive direction. The analysis need not then be carried so far that any "definitive" conclusions about the causal situation can be drawn. When intervening in an actual problem situation, one is often aware that factors which are seen as primary causes of the problem cannot be influenced. Nevertheless, even in such a situation it may be possible to influence development by manipulating certain intermediate variables in a causal chain.

The earliest formation of norms may be assumed to be of great importance. According to learning theories, the acquisition of norms may be regarded as a form of avoidance conditioning (see Bandura & Walters, 1965). The most effective way of transmitting norms to children is to teach them to avoid the withdrawal of affection. According to such theories, development depends on both hereditary and environmental conditions. The constitutionally extraverts are more difficult to master, and thus demand a more effective learning situation for a sound development (Eysenck, 1964). Effective learning presumes an emotionally warm relationship between upbringer and child. Thus, according to these theories, extravert children who are emotionally rejected in their families are in the worst situation. Such emotionelly rejected, extravert children are often found in environments where the language is poor (Bernstein, 1961, 1970). Sanctions for breaches of norms and rules, which are unavoidable in children, are more difficult for children to understand since verbal correction is non-existent on account of a barren language.

Children in these circumstances are found more often in the lower socio-economic groups. When such children begin school they may reveal shortcomings in behaviour which lead to treatment that further augments the children's feelings of being excluded from the community of others, of being outsiders in the school. Expectations are created that may steer development in an unfavourable direction (Aldrich, 1967; Johnson & Szurek, 1954).

A general model has been outlined for studies of juvenile delinquency in the present project. Parts of this model have been tested in different phases of the investigation. Figure 7: 1 shows the principal features.

The model is a dynamic development model, in which fragments of earlier theories are included.

A central feature of the model is the congruence between personality and the demands of the environment, possibilities of satisfying demands and so on (cf. Lofqvist & Davis, 1969). Incongruence may lead to several outcomes, for example:

1. Adjustment reactions, which may occur by the individual altering himself or by his changing the situation in the environment.

2. Maladjustment reactions in the form of neurotic solutions of problems.

3. Change of environment to groups deviating from the values of the school or society, which take over the functions of norm transmitters and reference groups. In the cases in which these deviant groups feel rejected by society and develop an anti-social norm system of their own, this solution easily leads to criminality.

The third solution is the one that has become the main interest of the present investigation. Attention will also be paid to the forms which have been found to belong to group 2, neurotic solutions leading to criminal conduct. Social measures to prevent delinquency must be started early in the lives of the individuals in the risk zone. We must therefore learn more about the theoretical basis before we can determine which individuals are risk cases and design both general and individual measures to prevent this form of maladjustment.

The criminological studies in the project are therefore focused on the individual's experience of society and his own relation to it, the outsider attitude in Becker's terminology (Becker, 1963). According to Becker, the central point in problems of criminology is that the individual feels outside society, the family, the school, etc., and instead identifies himself with a group whose values encourage criminal conduct. Identification with such a criminal group may be augmented by the reactions of society to criminal conduct, which is, as a rule, likely to emphasize that the criminal is a deviant individual, that he "is unlike others".

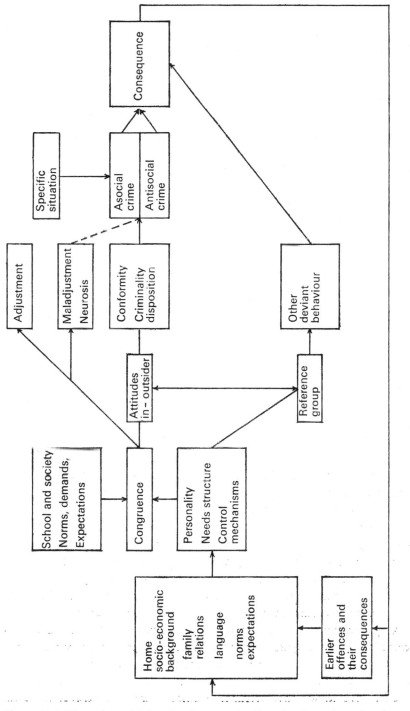

Figure 7: 1 General model for development in the direction of conformity or criminality

C. Mapping criminal conduct in the sub-groups of the project

Special data have been collected for the criminality section of the project. Instruments and methods are reported in this chapter. The total group investigations have also provided certain data which may be assumed to be of interest for the study of the outsider feeling; mainly students questionnaire data and sociometric data. Further, data on the main group have been collected in respect of the formation of norms and experience of the norms of the surroundings which will later be related to the criminological data (see Chapter 6). The data referring to criminal conduct collected within the project make possible the study of the effect of society's measures against single individuals, since they include both detected and undetected criminality.

Data for this study were obtained from P_{16} in 1968 and M_{16} in 1971.

1. *Registered and self-reported criminality*

A study of adjustment disturbance in the form of criminal conduct may be based on official registers of crime or on information given by the individuals themselves. Previous investigations have shown that undetected criminal conduct reported by individuals themselves is very usual, in any case among children and young people (Porterfield, 1946). According to a study of school children 9–14 years old in Stockholm, only 7 per cent of those who had committed a crime were detected or reported to the police (Elmhorn, 1965).

According to current legislation in Sweden, all cases of criminality among children and young people up to the age of 15 years that become known to the police shall be reported to the child welfare authorities. Such reports are also made as a rule when the crime is committed by young people between the ages of 15 and 18 years. The *child welfare registers* may therefore be used as a criterion of known criminality within certain age groups. On condition that the secrecy of the information was respected, the leaders of the project were permitted by the Child Welfare Board of Örebro to study and use the registers and the inquiries made by the board in conjunction with crimes. The information in the child welfare register was complemented by data from the police register.

A questionnaire of self-reported delinquency was used to obtain information on other types of criminal data. The present study was made on P_{16}, when the pilot group was in grade 9 and referred to male students only. Earlier investigation results, like the scrutiny of the child welfare register, had shown that criminality among girls was extremely small.

The problems of social adjustment in girls are, instead, studied from other aspects (see Chapter 8).

A study with a revised version of the questionnaire was made on M_{16} just before this group left the comprehensive school (cf. Figure 3: 2, p. 53).

The data collected in the questionnaire study of 1968 has been processed in relatively detailed analyses together with the basic data collected in 1965. A complete presentation of this first criminological study in the Örebro project is available (Olofsson, 1971). Some of the results obtained are given below.

2. *The questionnaire*, P_{16}

The questionnaire used for P_{16} contains (*a*) items referring to twenty-two different types of crime (examples in Table 7: 1, p. 132), (*b*) items concerned with "less desirable" conduct not of a criminal character, and (*c*) items dealing with peer relationships and the students' experience, if any, of being different from their schoolfellows. Some of the crimes are petty offences, but all involve breaking a law.

The items referring to crime were supplemented by further questions. For each main question of the type "Have you taken money or anything you knew belonged to someone else?" the students were to indicate how many times they had committed the crime (more than 10 times, 3–10 times, once or twice, never). After that they were to answer questions intended to elucidate certain circumstances in conjunction with crime, namely:

1. Number of persons participating in the crime.
2. The time during the student's school attendance when the crime was committed.
3. Whether the student was detected or not.
4. Whether the student was reported to the police for the crime or not.

The non-criminal conduct included in the questionnaire referred to behaviour which was found by a scrutiny of the child welfare board registers to occur very frequently in individuals who had committed crimes, e.g. drunkenness, sniffing thinner, truancy, running away from home. These items of behaviour may be regarded as symptoms appearing simultaneously with criminality (see, e.g. Nye & Short, 1957).

A few questions, concerned with the feeling of being different from classmates, were intended to measure what is called outsider feeling in Becker's terminology (1963).

3. The questionnaire, M_{16}

The questionnaire was revised for use in M_{16}, grade 9 in 1971. In addition, new items were added to cover *attitude* and *knowledge* aspects. Of the 22 items used in 1968, twelve were retained. The new items cover the same domains as the previous ones, and two others, dealing with violence, have been added.

Some of the follow-up questions were reformulated so that more unambiguous results could be obtained. The scale for the number of crimes committed was made more exact. The concept "detected" is measured more precisely by the students' reporting by whom they were detected. In order to obtain a more reliable criterion of conformity, a question was also added to each item to ascertain whether the crime had been committed during the previous spring term.

An important section was added to the study of M_{16} in order to measure the adolescents' attitudes to and knowledge about crime. This attitude and knowledge section is based on six of the items of behaviour in the previous part of the instrument and four other situations. One situation is described in each item, in which the behaviour of a sixteen-year-old, previously unpunished, person is described. The students' task was to say whether they consider the situation described as a crime or not, and, if a crime according to law, how serious it is. After that, they were to state what they thought the child welfare board would do if the person were detected. The answer to a third follow-up question was to say what the student himself thought about what the boy had done by rating on a five-point scale ranging from extremely serious to rather correct. Finally, the students were asked whether they would have acted in the same way.

4. Collection of data

The investigation in 1968 of P_{16} was performed in the middle of May, just before students in the ninth grade were to leave the compulsory school. In schools with many classes in the ninth grade it could be completed in one or two lessons, to prevent the students' being influenced by schoolfellows in other classes who had already answered the questionnaire. The leaders of the experiment were persons unknown to the students. All the leaders were males (with training in psychology) and accustomed to young people. In an oral introduction the students were informed of the purpose of the investigation and that the information given in the questionnaire would be treated strictly confidentially, i.e. only the leaders of the project would see the individual replies. It was also emphasized in the introduction that it is quite common for children and young people to do the things included in the questionnaire.

128

The questionnaires were given code numbers which identified each student in the grade. The students themselves were to put the completed questionnaires in the envelopes, which they were to seal.

The collection of data was performed according to programme without more than one refusal to fill in the questionnaire. The students seemed to be interested in the questionnaire and to rely on the assurances of confidentiality. Of the 549 male students in grade 9 in May 1968, 519 (94.8 per cent) answered the questionnaire. Of the 30 drop-outs, 26 were absent when the questionnaire was administered. The questionnaires of the other four students had to be excluded from the processing since, on account of language difficulties or for other reasons, the answers to the questionnaire showed that the instructions had not been obeyed.

5. Reliability and validity of the data

Self-reported data on crimes committed and other actions subject to a certain norm pressure must, of course, be used with some caution. Some sources of error which may be present in this connection are the following.

a) Erroneous answers may be caused by semantic difficulties. When dealing with an unselected group of young people, one should not, of course, use legal terms which may be assumed to be unknown to some of the individuals in the investigation group. In the design of the questionnaire, advantage could be taken of results of earlier investigations and the questionnaire was carefully scrutinized to ensure that it was clear and easy to understand.

b) The investigation was retrospective and the actions with which it was concerned had sometimes occurred a long time previously. Ordinary errors of memory may be assumed to have a systematic effect, i.e. be in the nature of suppressions. This would mean that the actions associated with the greatest norm pressure are forgotten more often and more thoroughly than others. The mechanism of suppression may also function most effectively in individuals with the strictest norms, i.e. probably the least criminal of them. To sum up it may be said that errors of memory lead to our obtaining too low frequencies of crime in questionnaires and that the underestimation of actual criminality may be systematically related to the character of the crime and the characteristics of the individuals studied.

c) It was presumed that students answered the questions sincerely and endeavoured to give answers experienced as true ones. If this is not so, i.e. if the students did not trust the confidentiality of the investigation, underestimation of the frequency of crime is to be expected. Fear that information given in the questionnaire may lead to some kind of consequence may be present in all students. It is possible that a student who had been detected in conjunction with a crime might be less afraid to mention this in the questionnaire.

d) A feasible reaction to an investigation situation experienced as unusual and possibly unpleasant is a form of flight which may imply an attempt to sabotage the investigation by using some arbitrary principle when the alternatives are marked off, e.g. by drawing crosses for all alternatives or applying crosses without reading the questions.

The validity of an investigation instrument of the type in question here may, in principle, be expressed as veridicality, i.e. as agreement between the information obtained by the instrument and objectively observable phenomena. Since we have few possibilities of collecting data on these objective phenomena, however, the problem of determining the validity of the data cannot be solved quite satisfactorily. We can only study certain situations that may give indications of the veridicality of data.

In the group studied, 36 of the boys had been subjected to investigation by the child welfare authority in conjunction with crime. Agreement between the information given by these boys about themselves and the entries in the welfare register was very good. The register often contained notes on truancy, sniffing thinner, drunkenness, etc., and in respect of these items, too, the students supplied corresponding information in the questionnaire. The results of the investigation thus suggest that at least detected delinquent students answered the questions truthfully. The results may be considered to support the validity of data.

The different crimes mentioned in the questionnaire might be expected to be represented in the investigation group with greatly varying frequencies, from very high frequencies of minor offences to very low ones for serious crimes. If many of the subjects had felt threatened and did not trust the promise of confidentiality, this would probably have resulted in consistently low frequencies and thus poor differentiation. The results here may also be considered to support the validity of data (cf. Table 7:1). The most frequent offence in 1968 was reported by 71 per cent of the students, the least frequent by 1 per cent. The frequencies of other crimes are rather well distributed between the extremes.

The value of a retesting of a group of students as a basis for conclusions regarding the validity of data was judged to be uncertain. It may be assumed that, within a reasonable period of time, one can reply consistently to questions on crimes committed, without the agreement between the information given and the actual situation being particularly high. A test–retest investigation would probably provide information mainly about whether the students had replied to the questions carefully and with due

130

consideration or whether they had answered them carelessly and haphazardly. The reliability of the investigation results in this restricted aspect of reliability may, however, be judged on the basis of data from a single investigation occasion. The design with main questions and follow-up questions presumed a certain consistency and deliberation when answers were given. The results obtained indicate that the students were serious when they answered the questionnaire.

The agreement in frequencies between P_{16} and M_{16}, reported on in section E below, is also an indicator of good reliability, see Table 7: 1.

Finally, the reliability and validity of data can be elucidated by the result of a calculation of internal consistency. In a component analysis based on phi-coefficients for the correlation between questions on different crimes, the answers being dichotomized into the categories "committed a crime once or more"—"has never committed the crime", four groups of crimes were obtained called preliminarily "Petty offences", "Theft", "Fraud", "Serious crimes". The group with most questions, ten in all, was the group called "Theft". Internal consistency calculated as an alpha-coefficient (Cronbach, 1951) for this group was 0.78. Thus, it may be said that there is consistency in the students' replies to the questionnaire.

To sum up, the results obtained by the criminological questionnaire seem to suggest that the students answered the questions conscientiously and that they took their task seriously. How far systematic denial of crime occurred is impossible to determine, but it seems likely that the questionnaire gives far more information on criminality in the investigation group than can be obtained from registers.

D. Some descriptive results

1. *Frequency of crime*

Results will be reported here from the study of P_{16}. For M_{16} only descriptive results are given to make it possible to compare P_{16} and M_{16}. Complete results and analyses referring to data from P_{16} have been reported separately (Olofsson, 1971).

Table 7: 1 reports the percentages of students who stated that they had committed various types of crime included in the questionnaire.

The number of occasions for each crime is, in most cases, one to two. It is only for the most frequent crimes that more than a few per cent of the students stated that they had committed these crimes more than ten times. Sixty-five per cent of the replies implying confession of crime were given for the category 1–2 times, 26 per cent for category 3–10 times, and 9 per cent for the category more than ten times.

Table 7: 1. Percentage of boys in P_{16} and M_{16}, who reported committing different offences.

Offence	Group	Per cent	Of which 0–10 times	More than 10 times
Shop-lifting	P_{16}	65	57	8
	M_{16}	65	53	12
Breaking lamps or windows on purpose	P_{16}	61	53	8
	M_{16}	64	57	7
Driving car, motorcycle or moped when drunk	P_{16}	34	31	3
	M_{16}	42	37	5
Selling or buying something known to be stolen	P_{16}	38	35	3
	M_{16}	41	36	5
Getting money or advantage by cheating others	P_{16}	21	20	1
	M_{16}	28	26	2
Breaking into attic, cellar, shed or parked car	P_{16}	23	22	1
	M_{16}	25	24	1
Assault on peers	P_{16}	—	—	—
	M_{16}	24	23	1
Moped or motorcycle theft	P_{16}	16	15	1
	M_{16}	18	17	1
Breaking into slot-machine, bookstall, shop, flat or house	P_{16}	13	13	0
	M_{16}	13	13	0
Serious assault on school-fellow	P_{16}	—	—	—
	M_{16}	11	11	0
Assault or threats to person with intent to obtain cigarettes, money etc.	P_{16}	11	10	1
	M_{16}	9	8	1
Car theft	P_{16}	5	5	0
	M_{16}	5	5	0
Selling drugs	P_{16}	4	3	0
	M_{16}	2	1	1
Bag-snatching	P_{16}	1	1	0
	M_{16}	2	2	0

There is a surprisingly good agreement between the rates for the two groups P_{16} and M_{16}.

2. *Individual numbers of crime*

In P_{16} only 4 per cent of the students in the investigation group, or twenty students, stated that they had not committed any of the crimes mentioned in the questionnaire. Of the 96 per cent confessing to crimes, the number of types of crime confessed varies between 1 and 21. The median is 5.96 types of crime (Fig. 7: 2).

Figure 7: 2 shows that those who committed only a few types of crime also gave the lowest number of offences per type of crime. Of the 105 stu-

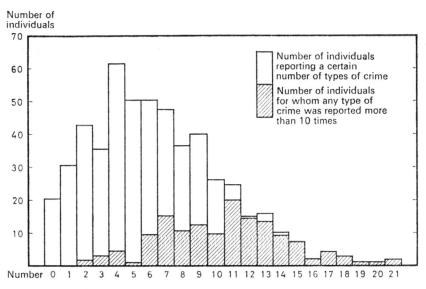

Figure 7: 2 Numbers of students reporting different numbers of types of crime

dents who had committed only 1–3 types of crime, only eight admitted committing any crime more than ten times, and then only one of the types of crime mentioned. These were all petty offences: "entering a cinema or sports ground without paying" or "breaking street lamps or windows". The more types of crime an individual claims to have committed, the more often high frequencies of types of crime occur.

3. Relation between self-reported and registered criminality

Apart from the students' information about their own criminality, information was also taken from child welfare and police registers. Since criminological studies are often based on detected crimes only, i.e. register data, it may be of interest to study how the frequency of detected crime varies with the number of crimes revealed in the individuals' own information. This information may possibly be regarded as an indicator of the true criminality of individuals in the investigation group. The measure of criminality for P_{16} was the number of types of crime among the 22 in the questionnaire that an individual stated that he had committed (see Fig. 7: 2).

Figure 7: 3 gives, too, the individuals who have been subject to measures on the part of the child welfare authorities. The figure shows that detection and investigation occur among boys with high as well as with low criminality. There is, however, a correlation between detection and

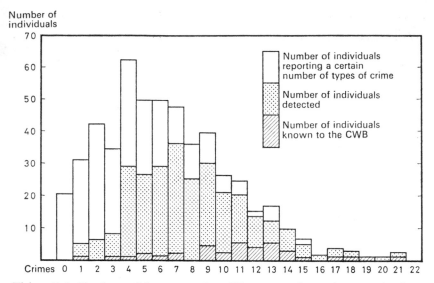

Figure 7: 3 Numbers of boys reporting different numbers of types of crime: (a) total numbers of boys, (b) numbers of detected boys, (c) numbers of detected boys known to the CWB. Observe that (a) is represented by total columns

child welfare investigation on the one hand, and on the other self-reported criminality, as is shown in Table 7: 2. Criminality increases monotonously from the category "Not detected" to the category "Has been the subject of child welfare board investigation".

E. Comparisons between seven groups of boys according to the sequence model

1. *Categorization of the boys according to criminal and conformity behaviour*

As mentioned earlier, some of the analyses in the project were aimed at testing a sequence model. According to this, the boys were characterized in respect of (a) whether they had *committed* crime or not, (b) whether they had been *detected* or not, and (c) whether they had been the subject of child welfare board *intervention* or not. Each of these groups was divided into two groups with reference to whether the members were still criminally active or not. A student who stated that he committed a type of crime mentioned in the questionnaire during the current term was defined as criminally active. This procedure gave seven groups, which are shown in Tables 7: 3–5. There some information is included from P_{16}, which compares the boys in these groups.

134

Table 7: 2. Self-declared burden of crime in students who have not been detected, been detected, and been detected and subjected to investigation by the child welfare board (CWB) respectively. P_{16}.

	N	M	s
Not detected	206	4.48	2.57
Detected	255	7.98	3.53
CWB investigation	36	10.94	4.33
No crime	20	0.00	0.00
Total	517	6.76	3.95

The boys in group 7 were still active after having been reported to the CWB. This group was regarded as a risk group and its situation also in earlier school years is of great interest.

2. *Individual characteristics and adjustment in the middle stage (grades 4–6)*

Table 7: 3 reports results for the seven groups in P_{16} for intelligence and some adjustment variables. In all cases the data are taken from the investigations in grade 6. Group 7 deviates from the other groups in a striking way. These boys have lower intelligence than the boys of other groups. Group 1, the completely conforming group, has a somewhat lower value than the others, which are very similar to each other. The two extreme groups differ from the other groups in adjustment, too. Group 7 was judged by teachers as aggressive, motor disturbed and very tired of school —LPA class II—while group 1 was judged as timid and tense—LPA class III—to a greater extent than the other groups (see p. 81).

Peers have judged the boys in group 7 to be unmotivated, and fewer of them have been rated as confident in their behaviour. Nor was this group as popular among peers as the intermediate groups. Group 1 has also lower average popularity than the intermediate groups, but does not differ from them in motivation.

In the scales obtained from the student questionnaire, too, group 7 has poorer adjustment. These boys felt less satisfied with school, felt the burden of work heavier, and rated peer relationships to be somewhat poorer. The boys in group 1 reported in these variables a better adjustment than any other group. This may be a sign of over-conformity, a tendency to give socially desirable answers to questions of this type.

These results show clear correlations betwen adjustment data from grade 6 and the categorization of boys from criminological data collected in grade 9. The same is true of information from grade 6 referring to the

Table 7: 3. Individual and adjustment data at age 13 for seven groups of boys, categorized according to the sequence model. Means or per cent.

	No crime 1	Undetected		Detected		Reported to police or CWB		
		Conf. 2	Active 3	Conf. 4	Active 5	Conf. 6	Active 7	Total group
Number of boys	11	83	77	62	126	21	46	426
Intelligence	27.6	32.4	31.7	30.1	29.6	29.1	25.3	30.1
Teachers' ratings								
Aggressive, restless % low motivation	28	34	45	42	53	53	79	48
Timid, inhibited, % depressed	36	8	11	9	12	0	5	10
Peers' ratings								
Motivation	3.1	3.2	3.2	3.1	3.0	3.0	2.4	3.0
Confidence	2.9	3.1	3.1	3.0	3.1	3.1	2.7	3.0
Popularity	2.8	3.0	3.1	3.1	3.0	3.1	2.9	3.0
Student questionnaire								
Satisfaction with school	4.3	2.5	3.1	2.4	2.6	2.9	0.1	2.4
Load of work*	6.9	7.9	8.4	8.7	8.6	8.3	9.6	8.5
Peer relations*	7.0	7.9	7.9	8.0	7.8	7.9	8.2	7.9

* High values imply poor adjustments.

social and economic background. Comparisons between the groups on some such variables are given in Table 7: 4.

The boys in group 7 belong, to a greater extent than the others, to the two lowest levels in respect of parents' education. Many of them moved into Örebro during the previous five years, and they seem to have poorer housing conditions, and lower family incomes than average. Like the boys in group 6, a large proportion of these boys belong to incomplete families and have mothers engaged in full-time work outside the home. The table shows that, in some respects, signs of less supervision of the children by the parents are present. The boys in group 7 go to bed later and are more often out late at night. On average, the mothers show less interest in the work of the school by never attending a parents' meeting.

It is important to notice that we have found no signs of correlations between PE and the frequency of offences. This indicates that there is no systematic relation between family educational background and delinquency among adolescent boys. The fact that many boys from the lowest levels of PE belong to group 7 shows that there is a marked tendency for boys with low socio-economic background to be reported to the police or child welfare committee when they are detected more often than other boys.

These comparisons suggest the hypothesis that lack of supervision leads

Table 7: 4. Background factors for the students in seven groups of boys, categorized according to the sequence model. Per cent.

	No crime 1	Undetected		Detected		Reported to police or CWB		Total group
		Conf. 2	Active 3	Conf. 4	Active 5	Conf. 6	Active 7	
PE 6 7 (lowest)	50	54	48	55	54	35	70	54
Lived less than 5 years in Örebro	0	14	15	10	9	12	23	12
Lives in old flat	10	4	7	8	8	5	18	8
Family income below 20 000 kr	20	32	33	29	31	33	47	33
Incomplete family	0	10	7	5	13	30	28	12
Mother working full time	10	8	17	8	19	30	36	17
Bedtime after 10 p.m. at 12 years of age	18	26	26	27	27	15	44	26
Home fewer than 3 evenings a week	0	19	14	14	22	10	38	16
Mother never been to a parents' meeting	0	3	6	4	6	22	31	8

to greater likelihood of a development in the direction of juvenile delinquency.

Also in the results reported in Table 7: 4, group 1 differs from the intermediate groups in the opposite direction from group 7.

In Table 7: 5, the groups are compared with each other in the adjustment critical behaviours mentioned in the questionnaire. Criminality tends to be associated with abuse of alcohol, drugs, vagabondage, truancy, etc. In all respects, members of group 1 were innocent of such behaviour, and the frequency 0 is present for this group. Group 7, on the other hand, has the highest values, in some cases very high frequencies. These types of behaviour are clearly associated with criminality.

3. *Prediction of criminality*

It was shown in the previous section that certain behavioural variables measured in grade 6 were distinctly correlated with group affinity in grade 9 according to the sequence model. Group 7 in particular deviated from the other groups. The members showed signs of maladjustment three years before they answered the questionnaire on self-confessed criminality.

Some of the variables for which data were collected in grade 6 have

Table 7: 5. Adjustment critical behaviour in seven groups, categorized according to the sequence model.

	No crime 1	Undetected		Detected		Reported to police or CWB		
		Conf. 2	Active 3	Conf. 4	Active 5	Conf. 6	Active 7	Total group
Been drunk, %	0	23	40	43	66	38	90	46
Offered drugs to buy, %	0	2	41	23	54	37	81	40
Used drugs, %	0	6	8	5	22	12	61	14
Run away from home, %	0	0	0	5	5	12	35	4
Played truant, %	0	23	47	50	71	75	83	52

been combined in Table 7: 6 to make a prediction table (Olofsson, 1971). Prediction variables were (*a*) the boys' experienced *Load of work,* (*b*) their *Satisfaction at school,* (*c*) their *School motivation,* and (*d*) *LPA-class affinity.* The LPA-classification was founded on teachers' ratings (p. 81). Class II is characterized by school tiredness, aggressiveness, and disharmony.

Table 7: 6 gives results for the high socio-economic group (PE groups 1–5) and the low group (PE groups 6–7) separately as a marked relationship is often found between delinquency and social background (McDonald, 1969).

In the table the students are divided into a high and a low group in respect of the variables, with the exception of profile group affinity. The interesting information in the prediction table is to be found chiefly in the cells in profile class II, the high group in *experienced load of work* and the low group in *satisfaction* and *motivation.* The students there may be said to have the maximum number of negative signs.

In the high socio-economic group, 12 boys belong to sequence group 7; of these 7 are to be found in this cell. In the low PE group we find 20 out of a total of 33 in group 7. Of all the boys with maximum negative factors, 7 of 28 in the high socio-economic group belong to sequence group 7 and in the low group 20 of 48; i.e. 41.7 per cent, belong to this sequence group. Simple measures of behaviour in grade 6 may thus, as far as can be judged from these results, be used as a basis for predictions of the development in the conformity–criminality dimension of a quality that is rare in the behavioural sciences. It will be possible to cross-validate the results when the analyses are continued on the main group. It will also be possible to study the relevance of this complex of different types of adjustment difficulties all the way from grade 3.

able 7: 6. Division into conformity groups of boys in grade 9 from PE groups 1–5 and PE roup 6–7 respectively with different values in teachers' ratings (profile classes I–III), load of work, nd satisfaction in school (scales from the student questionnaire), and motivation (peers' ratings) in rade 6.

Load of work	Satis-fac-tion	School moti-vation	PE groups 1–5 (high) C-group 1	2	3	4	5	6	7	To-tal	PE groups 6–7 (low) C-group 1	2	3	4	5	6	7	To-tal
low	high	high	1	4	2	2	5	—	—	14	2	4	3	3	1	1	2	16
		low	—	—	—	1	2	1	1	5	—	3	—	2	6	—	—	11
	low	high	—	6	7	1	4	2	—	20	—	5	2	4	1	—	—	12
		low	—	3	2	0	4	2	1	12	—	4	3	2	1	1	2	13
high	high	high	—	1	5	—	—	—	—	6	—	1	—	—	2	—	—	3
		low	—	1	—	2	3	1	—	7	—	1	2	2	2	—	1	8
	low	high	—	2	0	1	2	—	—	5	—	1	1	1	2	—	—	5
		low	1	2	2	4	1	1	—	11	—	3	1	4	4	—	1	13
low	high	high	—	—	2	—	—	—	—	2	—	—	—	—	—	—	—	0
		low	1	3	3	2	4	—	—	13	—	4	2	2	6	1	2	17
	low	high	—	—	—	1	2	—	—	3	—	1	2	—	1	—	—	4
		low	—	5	3	5	6	3	—	22	1	1	1	2	10	1	3	19
high	high	high	—	—	1	1	1	1	—	4	—	—	—	—	—	—	—	0
		low	1	1	2	—	5	2	2	13	—	1	3	1	7	2	2	16
	low	high	—	—	1	—	—	—	—	1	—	—	—	—	1	—	—	1
		low	—	3	5	4	8	1	7	28	—	4	5	7	11	1	20	48
low	high	high	—	—	—	1	—	—	—	1	1	—	—	1	—	—	—	2
		low	1	1	—	1	—	—	—	3	1	1	—	—	3	—	—	5
	low	high	—	—	2	—	—	—	—	2	—	—	—	—	—	—	—	0
		low	—	—	1	—	—	—	—	1	—	1	—	—	1	—	—	2
high	high	high	—	—	—	1	—	—	—	1	—	—	—	—	—	—	—	0
		low	—	—	1	—	2	—	—	3	1	—	—	—	1	—	—	2
	low	high	—	—	—	—	1	—	—	1	—	—	1	1	1	—	—	3
		low	—	1	—	—	3	—	1	5	1	2	2	2	2	—	—	9

G. Perspective

The system of norms and the codification of norms into laws determine what is to be designated crime and who is a criminal. In our society, there are several levels of crime. The crimes exemplified in the present work are associated with the common concept of crime. They become more uncommon in adult life than they were in adolescence. Many people adjust themselves to society. This may be due to different causes. In some people the norms become internalized, for many it becomes obvious that the risks and costs of criminal conduct are far greater than the chances of profit. Devotedness to parents, teachers and other adults, whose affection is risked, was at least of the same importance as norms for the decision to act against the norm in an investigation by Hirschi (1969). Such personal costs of transgressions have been discussed also by Piliavin, Hardyck & Vadum (1968). Different causes for conformity in these respects may lead to differences in other types of criminal conduct, which are often not viewed as strictly morally, e.g. false income tax returns, traffic offences and parking transgressions. The degree of supervision, the sanctions, etc., which are part of society, affect criminal tendencies and opinions of different crimes.

In a healthy society there should be a continuous discussion and revision of prevailing laws and norms. This is natural for the younger generation. An intensive involvement in such discussions may polarize opinions and lead to the view that, for ideological reasons, one cannot obey what one regards as an iniquitous law. In other words, one finds it difficult to obey society's rules for the alteration of rules. During such periods of particularly intensive opposition a great increase in different types of criminality may occur. The society is by certain groups regarded as "criminal" (Schur, 1969). There are researchers who study not the individual delinquent to find causes of criminality but the structure of society, which they regard as responsible for the fact that many people become deviants and become the victims of the prevailing system in society (Schur, 1969; Taylor, Walton & Young, 1973). Many crimes typical of adults may in the same way be regarded as conscious defiance in face of the wrongs of society. Tendencies of this kind, which might previously have been vague and related to a specific situation, may be strengthened by the fact that in society there are groups of people restricted to each other.

In the further work in the criminological study of the process of conformity, attention should be paid to the role of society in this context: attitudes, motivation factors behind the development of conformity such as internalizing versus cost–reward speculations. Data for this study have been collected by questionnaires, as already mentioned, and also by other instruments used during the same school term.

For the elucidation of these important problems it is essential for the study to be performed as a longitudinal total group investigation. The whole process can be followed. The first information was obtained in this project when the subjects were in their tenth year, i.e. before the beginning of this type of delinquency for most of them.

However, it is desirable that the total group study of the conformity process be complemented by sample studies of special groups to throw light on problems demanding information which can be obtained only by interviews or other individual methods of investigation.

In the long run, studies of these problems should hopefully make it possible to modify certain situations in the school and society so that it will become easier to adjust to the norms necessary for a social interaction.

Chapter 8
Social adjustment and intrinsic adjustment among adolescent girls

A. Background

The scrutiny of the local child welfare registers that preceded the criminological investigation of boys (Chapter 7) showed that there were six times as many boys as girls registered for crime, and that the crimes committed by girls were usually petty ones. This picture of the differences in criminality between boys and girls agrees with that obtained in earlier, similar investigations. In view of the low criminality, the first criminological questionnaire investigation was restricted to boys. There are also reason to believe that girls show more varied symptoms than boys (Achenbach, 1966).

The interventions by child welfare boards in respect of girls are due in most cases to non-criminal conduct, i.e. conduct that is not punishable according to law. Classifications occurring very frequently in child welfare registers are "out late at night", "vagabondage" and "sexual promiscuity". These are types of behaviour which, although they are subjected to relatively strict norms, do not lead, in Sweden, to intervention by society as far as adults are concerned. The reasons for intervention by society in respect of such conduct in young persons are to protect them from various types of physical and mental injury to which a certain way of life is assumed to lead, possibly also to prevent development in the direction of grave adjustment disturbances, criminality, for example.

The measures taken by society in these contexts reflect differences in behaviour between boys and girls, as well as differences in the conceptions of norms valid for each sex. These conceptions are more strict in respect of girls, above all in the domain of sex.

Thus, it was obvious that investigations of the social adjustment of adolescents should be designed separately for boys and girls. The grave problem of criminality in boys justified the investigation of boys being concentrated on this type of adjustment disturbance. As far as the girls were concerned, a wider attack seemed to be called for.

The types of maladjustment which are the province of child welfare authorities have already been discussed. Other Swedish bodies whose duty it is to investigate and treat the adjustment disturbances of young people are the child and youth mental welfare boards.

Intervention by the *child welfare boards,* which have the right to use various coercive measures, is usually due to reports from the police or private persons of observations of certain types of conduct in the young people concerned. Investigation and treatment by *child and youth mental welfare authorities* are voluntary, except when the child welfare authorities are requested to take such steps. Young people themselves may approach the mental welfare boards, or their parents may do so on their behalf, either on their own initiative or on the advice of the school or a doctor. After an investigation of each case, which usually includes a history of development, an account of the patient's social environment and his parents' personalities and a psychological examination, a plan of treatment is drawn up. This may comprise such measures as change of environment, therapeutic counselling, or a more or less comprehensive psychotherapy.

While intervention by the child welfare board is usually due to conduct opposed to the norms of society, i.e. *extrinsic maladjustment,* the background of action by mental welfare boards is often such disturbed adjustment as is troublesome for the individual himself, i.e. symptoms of *intrinsic maladjustment.* These symptoms may include anxiety, compulsive thoughts and actions, and depression, that is to say, types of symptoms that are common in ambulant general psychiatric treatment. At mental welfare centres are lists of items of behaviour and reactions that are classified as symptoms.

The "symptom population" studied in the present section of the project is those items of behaviour, reactions or states in an individual, which are regarded in the mental welfare board instructions or practice as adjustment disturbances or indications of such disturbances. This list of symptoms also contains some items of behaviour which, according to the child welfare legislation or the criminal code, may be classified as maladjustment.

B. Purpose of the investigation

In the frame of reference outlined in the introductory chapter, the adjustment variables were defined as measures of certain individual–environmental relations, namely relations between an individual's behaviour and the different role demands in a social system, and relations between an individual's needs, attitudes, evaluations, etc., and various reward aspects of the social system. Here we may, if we wish, replace the term "measure" by "symptoms". This use of the concept of symptom may be most natural, perhaps, with reference to an individual's intrinsic adjustment.

The symptoms of an individual's intrinsic adjustment utilized in clinical work are attributed different degrees of importance from the aspect of criterion. Statements about depression, lack of feeling of well-being or the like we are usually immediately inclined to classify as indicators of lack of intrinsic adjustment. We attribute a certain value to this type of symptom: we attempt, for example, to find some measure which may be assumed to improve the person's adjustment and observe the result of the measure in his statements about his feeling of well-being. There are, however, other symptoms to which we do not attribute the same value. We are concerned with variables which covary with other variables of a criterion character but which do not have the character of criteria, e.g. bad relations to parents and other adults. The latter implies that we are not immediately inclined to give a positive or negative evaluation to the situation of an individual in this type of symptom variable.

Some of the variables studied in the present investigation are of such a type that we *a priori* attribute them high criterion values. Other variables have been included in the investigation instrument because, on the background of earlier empirical observations or certain theories, they are considered to indicate adjustment disturbances and are therefore utilized clinically.

The first objective of the investigation was to map the occurrence of these phenomena in a normal population of female adolescents. Such a study has long been needed, for previous knowledge of adjustment disturbance in Swedish teenage girls stems mainly from studies of clinical populations. Knowledge of the frequency of different symptoms in normal populations provides a valuable background for a further assessment of symptoms to which we are often inclined to attach high criterion value.

Another purpose of the investigation was to analyse the covariation of symptoms. Such analyses make it possible to test parts of the theories which originally justified their use in clinical work.

Within the wider framework the investigation is, finally, a phase in the follow-up study of the main groups, for which various adjustment and other data are available from the tenth and thirteenth year of age respectively. The investigation was made with M_{15} during the spring of the school year when the group was in grade 8.

A report on this subproject has been written by Crafoord (1972).

C. Survey of the symptom population

The phenomena studied in this investigation are, as shown earlier, associated with different social and clinical definitions of adjustment and psychological theory. The symptom population in question may be divided according to different principles, e.g. in respect of the situations in which the symptoms appear or according to theories of personality functioning. The survey presented below is based on a functional division. No uniform theoretical model for the division of human functions and symptoms as symptom channels which can be used in this connection has been found in earlier literature in this domain. The division proposed here does not claim to be complete or nonoverlapping. It is, on the whole, a division according to function often used in practical clinical work.

Group A: *Antisocial behaviour.* Disturbances in conscience and morals in the form of socially unaccepted conduct such as (*a*) criminal actions, (*b*) so-called depravity and (*c*) abuse.

Group B: *Disturbances in relations.* Disturbances on the interpersonal level, i.e. in contacts with others, here in contacts with (*a*) parents, (*b*) peers and (*c*) teachers.

Group C: *Physical symptoms.* Disturbances in physical functions such as (*a*) psychosomatic symptoms, (*b*) habitual manipulations and psychomotor symptoms.

Group D: *Emotional disturbances.* Disturbances in emotional life such as (*a*) depression, (*b*) anxiety and (*c*) poor control of impulses.

Group E: *Disturbances in self-esteem.* Disturbances in self-esteem such as (*a*) acceptance of one's own achievements, (*b*) self-evaluations and (*c*) acceptance of sex role.

D. Description of the symptom groups

1. *Group A: Antisocial behaviour*

This category includes items of behaviour contrary to the Swedish child welfare legislation, i.e. different kinds of criminal action, abuse, sexual promiscuity, vagabondage, loitering, running away, truancy, and certain other phenomena in the school situation. When detected, these types of behaviour may lead to intervention by the child welfare board.

One kind of behavioural disturbance considered particularly important in this context is sexual depravity. It has sometimes been claimed in the literature (e.g. Jonsson, 1944) that teenage girls express intrinsic disturbance in this and other ways. Our knowledge of sexual experiences, attitudes to sexuality, experience of own sexual maturity, and norms for sexual behaviour in a normal population of girls in their middle teens is so slight, however, that we have no frame of reference by which to determine what types of sexual behaviour are to be classed as "depravity". This will probably lead to vacillating practice in the activities of child welfare boards. It is, for example, unclear to what extent child welfare officials in practice judge sexual intercourse with girls below the age of fifteen years as a breach of the law, which it is according to present legislation. Two questions about *Sexual experience* and *Attitude to sexuality,* and the relation of the answers to other adjustment variables, will therefore be dealt with separately.

2. *Group B: Disturbances in relations*

This category is concerned with some relations of great importance for young people, namely relations to parents, peers, and teachers.

In relation to *parents,* such aspects as experience of emotional repudiation by parents, lack of confidence in relations, high degree of defiance, aggressiveness against and disappointment in parents, inability to understand parents, and experienced lack of understanding on their side, etc., were considered extremely important. Relations to father and mother were studied separately.

In relations to *peers,* studies were made of feelings of isolation and loneliness in the circle of peers, number of friends, permanence of contacts with peers, experience of self as rejected or unfairly treated, dominance and subjection respectively in peer relations, and lack of identification with peers.

In *teacher* relations, finally, own acceptance of teachers and experience of teachers' acceptance, degree and type of defiance and opposition to teachers were studied, among other things.

3. *Group C: Physical symptoms*

This category included such somatic states as are regarded as physical defence reactions in the organism due to states of emotional strain, as well as psychosomatic symptoms such as thumbsucking, nail biting, tics and stuttering, which are also considered to express or to be results of underlying mental strain.

4. *Group D: Emotional disturbances*

The emotional life of adolescents has received little systematic study. On the other hand, it has often been elucidated in diary studies, analyses of letters and the like. A number of affect dimensions assumed to be relevant from the aspect of symptoms was selected. This selection includes sorrow, boredom and depression; nausea, aversion and discomfort; uneasiness, anxiety and fear; defiance, aggressiveness and irritation of more diffuse types, i.e. not directed against parents, peers or teachers, in which cases the symptoms are attributed to group 2.

5. *Group E: Disturbances in self-esteem*

Self-esteem was defined here as the degree of self-acceptance and self-estimation, i.e. an individual's ability to accept himself as he is, with the situation and the possibilities in which he lives and his emotional evaluation of himself. Important aspects of self-esteem include self-acceptance and positive evaluation of age and current development, of female sex role and the functions connected with it, of current achievement and faith in own capacity.

E. The investigation instrument

Information on the occurrence of symptoms studied in the present section of the project may, in certain cases, be collected from outside observers, in other cases only from the individual herself. For financial and administrative reasons the collection of data was restricted to refer only to information supplied by the students themselves. In view of the great number of individuals in the investigation group (about 500 girls) a written questionnaire had to be used.

The questionnaire items were formulated so as to be as concrete and behaviour-related as possible. Fixed reply alternatives, sometimes with an open follow-up question, were used.

Example: "How often do you feel angry or irritated with your mother?

very often
rather often
sometimes
occasionally
hardly ever
Why?"

The reply categories comprised, as in the above example, statements of frequencies with five alternatives. Intensity ratings might have been possible in many cases, but frequency ratings were judged to be somewhat less influenced by subjective definitions of the scale steps and therefore more reliable. For some of the symptom groups, e.g. *Anti-social behaviour,* and *Physical symptoms,* objective information could be used in certain cases.

The questionnaire was tried out in a preliminary version. On the basis of the results and the experience gained in the administration of the questionnaire, it was revised in some points. Certain ethic views were expressed in the advisory group (see p. 57), which also led to the modification or exclusion of some items. The greatest change was made in some questions concerned with thought disturbances. These questions were deemed to be risky from the aspect of mental hygiene, for they were assumed to be able to trigger mental disturbances, and were therefore excluded from the questionnaire. The final questionnaire, therefore, contained five categories of totally 132 questions. Of these 122 were directly concerned with different symptoms and the remaining ten with certain items of background data and the students' experience of the questionnaire.

F. Collection of data

The field study was made in April 1970. The data collection in each school was finished in a day. Four test leaders with good experience of adolescents were in charge of the collection of data. They succeeded in getting good contacts with the students and were able to motivate them to collaborate. There were very few protests against the investigation. On the contrary, some of the girls were very interested in discussing the purpose and choice of questions in the investigation and volunteered views of their own.

In immediate conjunction with the answering of the questions, a random sample of girls were interviewed individually. Most of these girls showed great interest. One girl refused categorically to be interviewed and another wanted a friend with her. The duration of the interviews varied between 30 minutes and two hours.

The questionnaire was answered by 89 per cent of the girls. Of the dropouts 50 were absent on account of illness; in the other cases (12 Ss) the reason was usually practical vocational orientation.

G. Data processing

1. *Calculation of frequencies*

As has been shown earlier, the distribution of answers for the individual questions is considered to be of great interest as a background to the judgement of different symptoms in cases being investigated clinically. The first step in the processings was therefore to calculate frequencies. The results for some questions in different domains are reported in Table 8: 1.

Within the realm of *anti-social behaviour* are questions which are the same as some of those in the questionnaire on self-reported criminality administered to boys in grade 9, for which some results are reported in Table 7: 1 (p. 132), and elsewhere. The frequencies for girls are con-

Table 8: 1. Reply frequencies for individual items in the questionnaire on adjustment critical behaviour in girls. Percentages. M_{15}.

(a) Anti-social behaviour	Reply alternatives				
Question	never	once	2–3 times	4–10 times	more than 10 times
Have you ever taken things from a shop, etc., without paying for them?	68	14	10	5	3
Have you drunk so much beer, spirits or wine that you felt drunk?	45	14	17	11	13
Have you ever forged another person's signature to gain an advantage, e.g. written a medical certificate or the like?	86	7	4	2	0
Have you been away from school this year without permission (played truant)?	54	16	20	7	3
Have you smoked hashish?	95	3	1	1	0
Have you used other drugs than hashish?	96	2	1	0	1
Have you deliberately destroyed or helped to destroy things not belonging to you (windows, cars, telephone booths, benches, gardens, etc.)?	79	12	6	3	0
Have you avoided paying (e.g.) at a cinema, café, train, bus or elsewhere?	87	8	4	1	0
Have you ever run from home?	91	6	2	0	1
Have you ever annoyed and plagued small children or old people?	82	10	6	1	1

(b) Sexual attitudes and experiences	Description of extreme position	Reply alternatives					Desc. of ext. posit.
Question		1	2	3	4	5	
Do you think you ought to know more about problems of sex?	not at all	13	34	40	11	4	very much more
How often do you wonder about problems of sex?	seldom	22	29	37	12	1	very often
Do you think sex seems frightening and unpleasant?	no	62	25	11	2	1	very much
Have you had sexual intercourse?	no	78	7 (once)		15	more	than once
Are you afraid that you will go further sexually than you want to really?	never or hardly ever	53	22	20	4	2	very often
Do you feel sexually less experienced than your classmates?	never	53	29	14	4	1	very often
Do you feel sexually more experienced than your classmates?	never	60	23	12	2	3	very often
Do you feel popular with boys?	not at all	12	23	47	17	1	very much

(c) Relations to parents	Reply alternatives				
Question	seldom or never	occa- sionally	some- times	rather often	very often
Do you ever feel like doing the opposite of what your parents want?	11	35	38	10	6
Do you think your parents are angry or irritated with you?	33	30	27	8	2
Do you think your parents are disappointed with you?	46	31	18	3	3
Do you and your mother quarrel with each other?	36	25	23	12	5
Do you and your father quarrel with each other?	54	20	17	7	2
Do you wish your mother were different?	44	41	10	5	0

(d) Relations to teachers	Reply alternatives				
Question	(nearly) all	most of them	some	hardly any	none
Do you like your teachers?	9	42	42	6	0
Do you feel defiant against your teachers?	0	2	2	44	52
Do you think your teachers are fair to you?	27	47	21	4	1
Do you think your teachers like you?	9	34	42	13	3
Do you think your teachers are *against* just you?	1	3	15	45	36

(e) Relations to peers	Reply alternatives				
Question	seldom	occa- sionally	some- times	rather often	very often
How often do you feel angry and irritated with your classmates?	11	40	36	11	2
Do you feel shy and uncertain when you are with your classmates?	42	30	22	5	1
Do you trust your classmates?	1	10	31	47	12
Is it difficult for you to make friends?	47	23	21	7	2
Do you think your classmates like you?	0	8	58	31	3
Have you ever done something you would really have preferred not to do only to be together with your friends?	52	35	10	1	0

(f) Emotional disturbances	Reply alternatives				
Question	seldom	occa-sion-ally	some-times	rather often	very often
Do you feel unhappy and depressed without knowing why?	23	26	37	11	3
Do you often feel frightened without knowing why?	55	27	13	4	1
How often are you restless and find it difficult to keep still?	22	33	25	15	5
Do you worry about there being something wrong with your body, that it doesn't function as it should?	34	25	27	11	4
Have you ever felt as if you didn't want to go on living?	31	41	17	8	3
Do you feel tense and anxious together with new people?	20	29	29	16	5
Do you blame yourself for things you know you really cannot help?	30	33	29	7	1
Do you worry about what will happen to you in the future?	15	26	34	17	8
Do you feel alone?	38	28	23	8	3

(g) Disturbances in self-esteem	Reply alternatives				
Question	seldom	occa-sion-ally	some-times	rather often	very often
How often do you think you are no use at all?	25	34	29	10	2
Do you sometimes think that boys are better off than girls?	41	23	25	7	3
Do you accuse yourself of things you know that you couldn't help?	30	33	29	7	1
Do you ever wish you were someone else than you are?	52	23	18	6	1
Do you look forward to having and bringing up children?	10	20	24	23	23

sistently lower, and only part of the differences can be explained by the fact that the girls answered the questionnaire a year earlier than the boys.

Some questions on *sexual attitudes and experience* gave frequencies showing that 22 per cent of the girls had had sexual intercourse one or several times (Table 8: 1 b). According to their answers, most girls do not experience any problems in respect of the behaviour covered by the questions, but a few per cent of them experience sex as frightening and unpleasant, and some girls stated that they think a lot about problems of sex. A few per cent considered that they differ from the majority in respect of sexual experience, and for a few the feeling of not being popular with boys was a problem.

According to the answers reported in section *c* in Table 8: 1, *parent relations* are good for most of the girls. But here, too, the interesting answers are found among those who state that they often experience the disturbed relations described in the questions.

Section *d* gives a picture of *teacher relations*. Students like some or most of their teachers and consider them fair and understanding. The positive judgements are seldom valid for all teachers, however. A few per cent claim that hardly any or none of the teachers qualify for these positive judgements.

Peer relations are described by a few questions in section *e*. Some girls, 6 per cent, feel shy and uncertain when with peers, and about as many consider that their classmates do not like them very much. Nine per cent think making friends is a problem. The majority, however, have not given answers implying any problems of this kind.

Some *emotional disturbances* are touched upon in section *f* of Table 8: 1. While most of the girls do not report symptoms more than once or so, there are 14 per cent who often feel unhappy or depressed without knowing why, 21 per cent who feel stressed and anxious together with new people, and 25 per cent who worry about the future.

Finally, in section *g*, a few examples of disturbances in *self-esteem* are given. Twelve per cent of the girls stated that they often feel fit for nothing. Although most of the girls seem to be without problems in these questions, there are some for whom answers to these questions reveal symptoms in an important sphere.

2. Dimensional analyses

The structure of the symptom population has been studied by factor analysis. Oblique rotation was used, since the factors could not be assumed to be uncorrelated in the symptom population in question. The correlations between factors are given in Table 8: 2. All variables with loadings exceeding 0.30 were assigned to the factors, which left twenty-nine variables not represented in any factor. The greatest perspicuity and interpretability were obtained by a solution with ten factors. Nine of these are interpretable. They are reported below.

Factor 1. *Non-specific anxiety and poor self-esteem*

Twelve variables were included in this factor, most of them psychosomatic symptoms, a number of affect symptoms and self-esteem answers.

Factor 2. *Social confidence and sexual experience*

This factor included thirteen variables concerned with degree of heterosexual relations, popularity among peers of both sexes and some affect answers. High factor points indicate a high degree of sexual experience, popularity and confidence in social situations, as well as a low degree of loneliness and shyness.

Factor 3. *Relations to parents, especially the mother*

This factor was represented by fourteen variables. In addition to variables concerned with relations to the mother, they refer also to relations to both parents regarding respect for parents, criticism of parents, disappointment in parents and degree of defiance against parents.

Factor 4. *Relations to teachers*

This factor included twelve variables, of which some with low loadings refer to acceptance by peers, self-experience and ambition in school.

Factor 5. *Relations to father*

This factor was measured with six variables, all concerned with relations to father; all have high loadings.

Factor 6. *Relations to peers*

All the twelve variables in this factor are concerned with relations to peers.

Factor 7. *Anti-social symptoms*

Eleven anti-social variables composed this factor, all with relatively high loadings. Of the questions within the anti-social domain, there was only one variable "persecution" that did not reach a factor loading of 0.30 in this factor.

Factor 8. *Self-esteem and acceptance of sex role*

The six variables defining this factor are concerned with self-evaluation, sex role evaluations and desire to alter oneself. It thus seems as if the group of questions on self-esteem should be divided into a group designated "negative self-esteem–low self-evaluation" (Factor 1) and a group concerned with lack of acceptance of the current role (Factor 8).

152

Table 8: 2. Correlations between factors in the analysis of structure in the symptom population.

	2	3	4	5	6	7	8	9
1	0.02	−0.17	−0.17	0.21	−0.25	−0.09	0.27	0.28
2		−0.07	−0.03	−0.05	0.24	−0.17	−0.07	0.01
3			0.28	−0.31	0.13	0.25	−0.12	−0.13
4				−0.21	0.08	0.23	−0.03	−0.11
5					−0.18	−0.14	−0.17	0.17
6						−0.04	−0.26	−0.16
7							0.07	−0.05
8								0.18

N = 520

Factor 9. *Depression, introvert brooding*

The three variables with loadings in this factor are concerned with unhappiness, sexual brooding and daydreams.

The intercorrelations of the factors are reported in Table 8: 2. The correlations are rather low.

3. *Extreme group studies*

The groups appearing as extreme groups in any of the domains covered by the questionnaire are of special interest. Such groups will therefore be studied in greater detail. Two examples will be reported.

a) *The extremely anti-social girls,* according to factor scores in Factor 7, Antisocial symptoms (As), reported behaviour implying that they most likely have problems and constitute problems for their relatives and society. This is an example of poor extrinsic adjustment. In order to study these girls, groups were extracted in the following way.

The most extreme cases on the factor scale mentioned were taken as the anti-social group. After that the girls were matched in threes, so that in each group of three one girl had an extremely low load of symptoms, while another had an average load. The girls in each triad belonged to the same PE group and the same school.

Of the investigations of these groups, Table 8: 3 reports a comparison made by means of variance analysis of scores in all factors appearing in this sub-study. It shows that no differences could be attributed to PE or school; all F-ratios were close to 1. On the other hand, the differences between the groups with different anti-social loadings were shown to be significant in respect of all the other factors in the instrument except peer relations and self-esteem. (Parent relations were divided into four factors

153

Table 8: 3. Summary of variance analyses of factor scales as dependent variables, and anti-sociality and PE and school as independent variables.

	Sources of variance			
	Anti-sociality		PE + school	
Factor	F	P	F	P
1. Non-specific anxiety and lack of confidence	3.62	< 5	0.72	—
2. Social confidence and sexual experience	18.14	< 1	0.81	—
3. Relations to mother	8.43	< 1	1.15	—
4. Relations to teachers	23.77	< 0.1	0.99	—
5. Relations to father	3.31	< 1	0.72	—
6. Relations to peers	0.31	—	0.91	—
7. Anti-social symptoms	242.62	< 0.1	1.04	—
8. Self-esteem and acceptance of sex role	2.54	—	1.25	—
9. Depression	4.75	< 5	1.40	—
10. Relations to home	15.06	< 0.1	0.71	—
11. Dependency on parents	3.35	< 5	0.58	—

in this sub-study, instead of two as in the factor analysis reported. The new factors were called *Relations to home* and *Dependency on parents.*)

This is an interesting parallel to the results of the study of juvenile delinquency in boys, showing that the criminal boys also have high loadings in other behaviour that is critical for adjustment. (See Chapter 7.)

b) *Anxious girls.* The other example is a corresponding study of anxious girls, which can elucidate an aspect of intrinsic adjustment. The study is performed on triads of girls with high, medium, and low loadings respectively, on the factor scale "non-specific anxiety and poor self-esteem", called "anxiety" (Anx) in the following.

Table 8: 4 shows that these three groups, too, are distinguished from each other in the other factors. The high anxiety girls (Anx) reveal significantly higher loadings in all factors except *"Social confidence and sexual experience"* and *"Dependency on parents".*

4. *A comparison between anti-social and anxious girls*

The two factors "anti-sociality" and "anxiety", used as independent variables, are interesting to study in parallel, since it is feasible to propose the hypothesis that it is a question of alternative symptoms. Anti-social behaviour is acting-out, anxiety is "neuroticizing". The loading scores should then be negatively correlated.

In the investigation, however, certain similarities have been shown

Table 8: 4. Summary of results of analyses of variance of factor scores as dependent variables and anxiety and PE (social status group) and school as independent variables.

	Sources of variance			
	Anxiety		PE + school	
Factor	F	P	F	P
2. Social confidence and sexual experience	0.37	—	0.37	—
3. Relations to mother	10.62	< 1	1.10	—
4. Relations to teachers	6.99	< 1	1.10	—
5. Relations to father	2.20	< 5	0.81	—
6. Relations to peers	12.76	< 1	0.86	—
7. Anti-social symptoms	4.63	< 5	0.77	—
8. Self-esteem and acceptance of sex role	15.69	< 1	0.66	—
9. Depression	27.60	< 1	1.16	—
10. Relations to home	15.90	< 1	0.38	—
11. Dependency on parents	0.32	—	0.86	—

between the groups with high loadings in the two variables. Two girls have even belonged to both of these extreme groups. The coefficient for the correlation between the two factors was − 0.09. This result does not support the hypothesis about anti-sociality and anxiety as alternative symptoms.

Important differences also appear, however, between anxious and anti-social girls, which make further study desirable.

It is true that both the groups have disturbed parent relations, but the disturbances are much more marked in the anti-social group. There the girls dissociate themselves from their parents more decisively and more emotionally both in questions with given reply alternatives and in the open questions and comments. The anxious girls are often ambivalent, and show much admiration and understanding to complement and modify the usually negative answers given to the questions.

The anti-social girls show, according to the instrument, greater social maturity and have more sexual experience. The anxious group is more heterogeneous in this respect. These girls are characterized more by lack of self-acceptance, introversion and depression, and they have negative peer relations.

The picture of this group can be complemented by analyses of data from other instruments in the project. Some results are shown in Table 8: 5, which reports variables that could be analysed by two-way analysis of variance in the same way as used for the factors in the symptom investigation, and Table 8: 6, where the main results for some other variables

155

Table 8: 5. Comparison between groups of girls who are high, moderate and low in anti-social behaviour and in anxiety. Values from two-way analyses of variance.

Factor	Anti-social behaviour			Anxiety		
	F	P	Effect	F	P	Effect
Intelligence (WIT), grade 8	1.32	—		1.94	—	
Satisfaction, grade 8	25.14	< 1	As$_h$ least	6.37	< 1	Anx$_h$ least
Do my best at school, grade 8	36.75	< 1	As$_h$ least	1.62	—	Anx$_h$ most
Aggressiveness, grade 6	3.53	< 5	As$_h$ most	4.42	< 5	Anx$_m$ least
Motor disturbance, grade 6	7.48	< 5	As$_h$ most	4.09	< 5	Anx$_m$ least
Timidity, grade 6	3.88	< 5	As$_m$ least h + l most	0.14	—	
Disharmony, grade 6	6.47	< 5	As$_h$ most	5.75	< 1	Anx$_h$ most Anx$_m$ least
Distraction, grade 6	1.48	—		4.60	< 5	Anx$_h$ most Anx$_m$ least
Lack of school motivation, grade 6	4.73	< 5	As$_h$ most As$_l$ least	4.71	< 5	Anx$_m$ least
Tension, grade 6	0.35	—		0.42	—	
Self-rating, grade 6	0.79	—		1.34	—	
Popularity, grade 6	0.03	—		1.93	—	
Motivation, grade 6	4.80	< 5	As$_h$ least As$_l$ most	3.21	< 5	Anx$_m$ most Anx$_h$ least
Confidence, grade 6	1.83	—		2.06	—	
Satisfaction, grade 6	0.82	—		2.75	—	
Anxiety for school work, grade 6	0.38	—		5.00	< 5	Anx$_h$ most
Burden of work, grade 6	0.38	—		2.26	—	
Anxiety for acting individually n class, grade 6	0.19	—		4.29	< 5	Anx$_h$ most

As$_h$ = extreme group with high anti-sociality
As$_m$ = group with moderate anti-sociality
As$_l$ = extreme group with low anti-sociality

Anx$_h$ = extreme group with high anxiety
Anx$_m$ = group with moderate anxiety
Anx$_l$ = extreme group with low anxiety

are compared. In no variable has PE group or school class a significant effect. Nor are there any marked differences in intelligence.

In grade 8, the highly loaded groups have the poorest adjustment, and this is especially true of the anti-social group. Members of this group do not consider that they do their best in school work. The norms of the anti-social girls (see Chapter 6) are clearly more accepting than those of the low and intermediate groups. This is not valid for the girls in the anxious group.

Table 8: 6. Comparisons between groups of girls who are high, moderate or low in anti-sociality and in anxiety.

	Anti-sociality	Anxiety
Norms (LPA-classes)	As_h more accepting	insign. diff.
Chosen line of study	As_h less choices of g-line, more practical work	Anx_m more g-line; $Anx_1 +$ Anx_h more practical work
Accepted time for study	As_h shorter time	Anx_m longest time; Anx_1 shortest
Confidence for studies	As_h low	Anx_m highest; Anx_h lowest
Changes of dwelling	As_h most	Anx_h most
Size of dwelling	—	Anx_h least
Mothers work outside home	As_h most	Anx_h least
Income of family	As_h least	Anx_h least
Help with homework from parents	As_h least	Anx_h most
Parents' experiences of education problems	insignificant differences	Anx_h most

As_h = most anti-social group Anx_h = most anxious group
Anx_m = moderately anxious group
Anx_1 = least anxious group

Regarding study choice in grade 8, the girls in the two highly loaded groups choose the grammar line in grade 9 less often than other girls. They also show less self-confidence on questions regarding their entry and success in different types of schools.

The social backgrounds seem to differ in the various groups although this is not the case with level of parents' education. The highly loaded groups have changed dwellings most often during their early years, they live in the smallest houses and their families have the lowest incomes. The mothers of the anti-social girls work more often full-time outside the home while the mothers of the anxious girls work outside the home least often. The anti-social girls get least and the anxious girls most help with their homework from their parents. The parents of the anxious girls report more trouble with the girls than parents in the other groups. This is not valid for parents of anti-social girls, who should have real causes for trouble. The parents of the anti-social girls may possibly be assumed to be less involved and to supervise their children to a smaller extent. In the anxious group, on the other hand, parents are unusually deeply involved with their children and consequently they supervise and take great interest in them.

Data referring to grade 6 show that for anti-sociality and anxiety the high, medium and low groups differed from each other in several respects. The high groups were judged by teachers to be most aggressive, motor disturbed, disharmonious and suffering from school tiredness. Their classmates, too, rated the anti-social and the anxious girls as least motivated. No marked differences in popularity or self-esteem were present.

The answers indicate that the very anxious girls suffer most from their situation. The anti-social girls are observed more, and more attempts are made to help them although they do not, in the same way as the anxious girls, suffer from their unsatisfactory situation.

It is quite feasible that the highly loaded groups are products of different environments. The anti-social girls are from families in which the children are not supervised and are characterized by passiveness and lack of involvement. The very anxious girls are supervised and protected, and the family is characterized by deep involvement. In their extremes these patterns may contribute to the development of the girls' behaviour in different directions.

H. Perspective

Most young people now attend school during the whole of their teenage period. Great problems arise if the normal process of liberation during this period should occur in an unalterable school. Adolescent development is dependent upon the cultural framework and is sensitive to changes, and young people often form the vanguard in the struggle for reform.

If the educational system is to perform the task of helping the adolescents to achieve a sound liberation and a development of personality, the actual situation of the generations must be studied successively. To do this, total groups, not only deviants, must be studied.

It is a remarkable fact that we have found no effects of socio-economic background or of intelligence on the frequency of symptoms. Other home factors seem to be more decisive. It may be in the families and not in the schools that we have the best possibilities to improve the adjustment of children and adolescents.

Other results in the project point to the conclusion that factors in the family life play a more dominant role for the adjustment of the children. Then the measures taken to improve the conditions for better adjustment would be the measures affecting the family life.

The study of the symptom patterns is an endeavour to elucidate the situation of the young people. This is not yet completed; the analyses made hitherto show many problems on which work must be continued. In some cases this may be done with data already collected, in others the problems should be best studied by complementing these data with intensive studies of smaller groups, chosen on the basis of studies already completed.

Two results may be mentioned as examples of knowledge valuable for the further work.

Concerning the total group studied, not so much defiance towards parents is reported as older literature on adolescents might lead us to expect. This may be associated with changes in the cultural pattern. As long as the family group was firmly united, and had a distinct authoritarian character, it was only natural that the process of liberation was directed towards independence from family ties, with defiance against parents as a consequence. Modern views on children and young people have often been accompanied by a more democratic family group. When there are no authorities from which to free oneself, efforts towards freedom are perhaps directed elsewhere, towards the restrictions on the adolescents' freedom of action made by society, and the norms of society are questioned. Defiance is not then aimed at the people nearest, but at an abstract system regarded as imperfect. Then untested alternatives are accepted and many other theories are developed via ideological work in movements that are foreign to the older generation.

Others may seek liberation by imitating adult behaviour. The "symptom load" of the great majority is within the regions of behaviour of which parents have some or great understanding and not in domains that would have been chosen if it had been a question of defiant behaviour.

Another result concerns a group of anxious girls. They appear as tormented and suffering, which might lead to greater social uncertainty and poorer self-esteem. This will tend to increase feelings of rejection, depression, perhaps drive them into themselves. A vicious circle is developed, and one duty of the school is to break this circle. At present this type of disturbance is not observed as much as anti-social disturbances, which probably have a much better prediction. In spite of the fear of contacts in anxious children, which often repels the adults in the school environment as well as peers, active contributions should be made at all stages of the school.

Chapter 9
Educational and vocational choice

A. Choice as an element in the process of adjustment

According to the discussion of the process of adjustment in Chapter 1, extrinsic and intrinsic adjustment in the individual's relations to a social system may be achieved by changes in the individual's psychological system or the social system, but also by choices by which the individual chooses systems and roles or the social system chooses the individuals. All these ways to improve adjustment are relevant as objects of study when we wish to deal with the important problem of achieving good adjustment in working life. The section of the project to be presented in the following is concerned with a study of choice situations in which the individual acts. The ultimate purpose of this study is to find ways of helping the individual to choose "correctly" in different contexts and to avoid choices which will lead to intrinsic or extrinsic adjustment disturbances.

The individual is led towards a position in his working life by a process which includes, among other things, choice of line of education. "Correct", rational choices assume correct perceptions. This means perception of (*a*) one's own possibilities and needs, (*b*) the structure of the educational system, (*c*) the possibilities of, as well as the demands made by the various lines of education, and finally (*d*) the labour market, including demands and rewards in different occupations.

B. Problems of choice in the nine-year comprehensive school

Choices of educational line and occupation take place successively in a continuous process.

At the time of the collection of data for the project, the students in the project had to make three successive actual choices of importance for their later careers: Choice of optional groups in grades 7 and 8, which implied choice of subjects and curriculum for a certain number of lessons a week, and the choice of stream in grade 9, which implied a differentiation of the students in classes with different curricula. The present study was performed in this system. (Later the organization has been changed somewhat for grade 7–9. There is, e.g., now no streaming in grade 9.)

In each situation, the choices may be made in relation to immediate or future goals. Further, the choices may be experienced by the individual as more or less binding in respect of future freedom of action. They may, perhaps, be interimistic, which means that the individual endeavours to postpone binding choices with long-term effects on the future.

However an individual experiences the choice situations in the comprehensive school, they have real significance for later choices. Most choices have the effect of decreasing the number and kind of remaining alternatives to choose among in the next stage. The choices lead to a successive differentiation of students in respect of intellectual capacity and in other respects into different optional groups and streams. In reality, this final differentiation of the students into streams in the last class of the comprehensive school implied that their possibilities of choosing lines of further education were limited. Some streams in grade 9, for example, did not qualify the students for entry into the higher secondary school.

The choice process was studied in the main group in conjunction with choices of optional groups for grades 7 and 8, choice of stream for grade 9, and with choices of type of school and work respectively after the end of the compulsory school. In order to cover as far as possible the circumstances which may influence the choices, the collection of data was made at a point of time immediately after the choice had been made.

The individual passes through different periods of growth. When the series of choices begins he has usually left the fantasy period behind, a period characterized by more or less chance preferences for specific occupations, and is in a transitional period in which difficulties are recognized and knowledge of the problems is increasing. Often the choice of a specific occupation is realistically experienced as too difficult. Instead the individual takes a general education or makes a choice of line similar to the previous one, attempting at the same time to keep possibilities open to attain attitude-steered, diffusely experienced vocational goals. It is probably not until towards the end of the compulsory school that the average student begins to approach a period of relative growth in which he is in a position to judge realistically his capacity and the expectations he has on his occupational activities in relation to what his working life has to give.

C. Models for choice of occupation and choice behaviour

The reality in which the study of occupational choice is carried out is a complicated one. It consists of an open system in the sense that there is an almost unlimited number of feasible potential variables. One way of making progress in such complexes of problems is to work with models.

First the vocational choice process will be viewed from the angle of a model taken from perception psychology (Dunér, 1972).

1. *A simple perception theory: the hypothesis theory*

It has been found fruitful to regard the process of perception as a categorization, a series of hypotheses testings, usually performed rapidly and unconsciously, but sometimes demanding conscious effort, when it is really experienced as a search for hypotheses with subsequent testings (see, e.g., Bruner, 1957).

According to this theory, hypotheses are tested. Hypotheses must always be propounded first. Since it is unreasonable to imagine that all feasible hypotheses can be tested, principles must be designed to restrict the number of alternatives and to decide which hypotheses are to be tested first. In the perception theory such principles may be assigned to three groups.

a) Experience and knowledge. One cannot assume that a stimulus pattern represents something one is unaware of or does not know of.

b) Emotions, needs, evaluations give rise to seeking behaviour aimed at satisfying needs. Very simply, it may be said that one "sees what one wishes to see".

c) Actuality, set, the tendency to perceive what one is accustomed to perceive in a similar situation. This principle can be reduced to the idea that "one sees what one expects to see".

In what follows it will be shown how corresponding principles may be assumed to lead to a limitation of the number of alternatives a person really considers in a choice situation. Whether in respect of choice of line of education or occupation, the final choice is probably made among a limited number of alternatives when in fact, an innumerable number of alternatives may be present.

2. *The hypothesis theory applied to the vocational choice situation*

In a way similar to the process of perception, it is assumed that the limitation of alternative choices of vocation or education is based on three principles.

a) In the first place, one cannot choose between occupations or lines of education of which one is completely ignorant, which one does not know exist. The first limitation, therefore, will be to *known alternatives* (Fig. 9: 1 Areas 1–4).

b) In the second place, there are some occupations one knows of, but which one would never think of choosing for oneself. The reasons, more or less unconscious ones, for this are fundamental attitudes and emotional

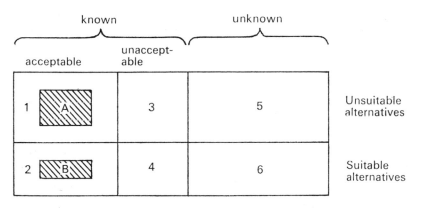

Figure 9: 1 The individual's different alternatives

reactions. Such reasons may stem from sex prejudices or class conscious-ness acquired early (Fig. 9: 1 Areas 3 and 4). The remaining alternatives, therefore, are known and *acceptable* emotionally (Fig. 9: 1 Areas 1 and 2). It may be noticed that certain formerly unknown alternatives may be included in this group simply because knowledge of their existence is com-municated.

c) However, it is still wrong to attack the problem of choice as if the individual chooses among all his acceptable alternatives. The number is most likely far too great for most persons at the time when the choice is to be made. We assume, therefore, that the alternatives tested seriously and consciously in the next phase of the choice process comprise only those which, in one way or another, become of immediate interest. An occupation may become a *current alternative* (Fig. 9: 1 the shaded areas A and B) e.g. because a grown-up acquaintance has the occupation, a voca-tional counsellor discusses it in a context interesting to the person, or an idol is training for it. In some places, certain occupations are always of current interest to practically all (who regard them as acceptable alterna-tives) because they are very common in the place of residence. In this part of the vocational choice model the local labour market aspects are of im-portance.

A further division of the alternatives may be made from the aspect of criteria. Some occupations may be regarded as *suitable* objectively for the individual, others *unsuitable*. If an occupation is to be regarded as suitable it must, according to the criteria used earlier, give extrinsic and intrinsic adjustment. Extrinsic adjustment implies that the individual can satisfy the demands on capacity made by the occupation. This does not mean, na-turally, only intellectual demands, although these may be the most general ones. It may just as well refer to demands on physical condition, robust health, artistic expression, or skill in social interaction. Intrinsic adjustment requires agreement between on the one hand the individual's needs, interests, attitudes and evaluations, etc., and on the other rewards, or, expressed generally, certain circumstances connected with the occupation.

A suitable occupation should also be available in the labour market, now and for a reasonable time to come. In Figure 9: 1, *suitable alternatives* are those in areas 2, 4 and 6.

It must be stressed that we assume here that there are several suitable alternatives for the individual. By way of an adjustment process the individual can achieve success and satisfaction within a group of occupations, different in certain respects and to a certain extent. The characteristics of the individual, as they have developed by interaction of genetic and environmental factors, limit, however, the sphere of occupations that may be regarded as suitable for the individual. These suitable occupations give possibilities of optimum adjustment, give the individual the possibility of taking the role he needs, of leading the life he wishes to lead (Super, 1953).

The last step in the choice situation may be described generally as a matching. Here the individual matches his opinions of his capacity with the different demands made by the alternatives. In the same way, the pattern of experienced occupational needs, vocational wishes, etc., is matched against conceptions of the specific gratification pattern of the occupation. The alternatives dealt with in this matching process are, as shown earlier, the current alternatives (Fig. 9: 1, A + B).

3. *Consequences in the form of measures*

The steps taken by society in connection with the individual's choice of educational line and occupation can be given in conjunction with the model. The limitations of the number of alternatives, which are a consequence of lack of knowledge of the labour market (areas 5 + 6), of prejudices (areas 3 + 4) or of external circumstances (areas 1 + 2 outside the shaded areas A + B) are unnecessary limitations which may at the worst, lead to some alternatives actually suitable for the individual not being included in the matching process. By the communication of information and a certain modification of attitudes, the school endeavours to increase the number of alternatives the individual really tests. At the same time, attempts are made to give the students knowledge of the demands that the different alternatives make and of the situations that may be assumed to be of importance for the satisfaction of needs in different occupations.

The measures reported here are general in nature. Measures are also taken to give the individuals increased knowledge of their capacity and their needs, e.g. in terms of interests. This may be achieved by informative conversations founded on data collected in the school situation or by special vocational aptitude tests. Endeavours are also made to help the individual by giving further information about the alternatives of immediate interest to him and possibly by drawing attention to other alternatives in addition to those which the individual himself regards as being of current interest. The latter may, in the vocational counselling situation, imply that new alternatives are discussed with an individual who sees only occupations already represented in the family as feasible.

4. The choice as a matching situation

Different models can be made to illustrate how the matching of the alternatives is performed. The matching may have the character of a step-by-step sorting of alternatives with successive augmentation of the demands that the alternatives shall be included in the continued matching process. The demand side of the matching problem may possibly be used in a preliminary sorting of the alternatives. The individual then decides whether the alternatives are available to him. This may be easy when it is a question of a choice related to a certain line of studies, namely when admission to the education in question is based on earlier school marks.

The matching situation which, according to the frame of reference presented earlier, leads to a choice of study line, occupation or a certain appointment, may be illustrated schematically in the following way (Fig. 9: 2).

Various models have been designed for the process which, for the time being, we call matching (see e.g. Vroom, 1964; Ziller, 1957). These models include such elements as certain mental dispositions in the individual, e.g. disposition to take risks, and level of aspiration. It is reasonable to assume that some of the mechanisms discussed below under the heading "perceptual processing" also influence the matching situation.

The perceptual process culminating in an experience of demands made by the occupation, own capacity, etc. (shown in Figure 9: 2 by arrows from the areas with broken contours) may be described as four components in the process of perception from object to conscious experience.

a) Distal object. Events and phenomena with which the individual has no immediate contact. This refers to conditions in a certain occupation or line of education, and to features of the psychological system outside the individual's sphere of consciousness.

b) Proximal stimuli evoke processes in the boundary area between the psychological system and its surroundings. This refers to the situation in

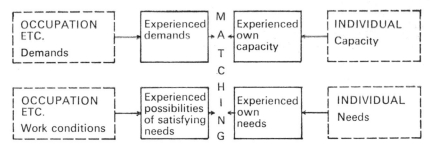

Figure 9: 2 Matching at choice of line of studies, occupation, etc.

which it is possible for the individual to collect information about the distal stimuli.

c) Central communicating processes. Development in the psychological system implying the processing of the incoming information by selection, interpretation, etc. This processing may be conscious or unconscious.

d) Central representations of objects. Conscious conceptions within the psychological system.

How the experience of a certain occupation develops may be described in the given frame of reference by the following model (Fig. 9: 3).

Erroneous conceptions about the occupation may, in this model, be regarded as a consequence of unfavourable circumstances at the individual's contact with the occupation: wrong information, non-representative observations and experiences, etc.; or of distortions in the perceptual processing, due to certain socially conditioned attitudes.

The individual's experiences of his own capacity and his own needs are shown in the same way in Figure 9: 4.

It has been assumed that the individual's contact with situations in which he is confronted with certain demands on performance or which give him the possibility of experiencing satisfaction of needs is the basis of experiences of his own capacity and his own needs. Erroneous or incomplete awareness of this capacity and these needs may be viewed as a consequence of a lack of or a misleading situational experience—on the capacity side incomplete feed-back regarding the quality of a certain performance, on the need side a screened growth environment—or as a consequence of perceptual distortions. An example of the latter could be the social pressure or the expectations that may lead to an individual belonging to a high socio-economic group not accepting his interest in a "practical" occupation, or one belonging to a lower social group, in spite of good prospects, not accepting himself in a "theoretical" occupation, or a young man refusing to accept interest in a "feminine" occupation.

166

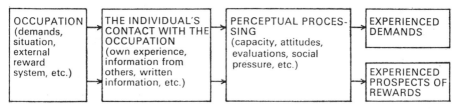

Figure 9: 3 Perception of the occupation

D. Basic data of the project

For a number of variables necessary for the study of the perceptual processes sketched in the above models and of the choice process, data are available from a number of total group investigations at different times (see the survey in Figure 3: 1 and Chapter 4). In some cases, it is a question of variables that may be assumed to be immediately active in the processes in question, in other cases underlying variables which may be assumed to affect these processes by way of the first type of directly active variables.

1. *Variables concerned with the home environment*

Some of the variables of interest in this connection, e.g. the socio-economic status of the home, have, in many earlier investigations, been found to be related to the choice of lines of study and occupation made by young people (Coleman, 1966; Mosteller & Moynihan, 1972; the Plowden Report, 1967; Härnqvist, 1966; Husén, 1969, 1972; Passow, 1971). A replication of these earlier investigations is not of primary interest. The variables in question are most important as moderator variables in the study of other variables whose influence on the process of choice is less well known. In multivariate models an important task is also to study how several variables function simultaneously in the perception and choice process. This type of simultaneous multivariate approach is not well represented in earlier research in the domain of educational and vocational choice.

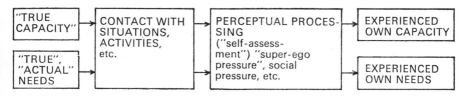

Figure 9: 4 Perception of own capacity and own needs

A large proportion of a child's contacts with the world of work is made in the home. During his years of growth a child gains information about different occupations through parents, brothers and sisters, relatives and acquaintances of the family, etc. This information gives the child both facts and values. By questionnaires sent to the parents, information about parents' education and occupations was obtained in the total group investigation. The questionnaires also contained items concerned with the parents' views on how their children should choose lines of education and occupations and their evaluations of them. All these data can be used as indicators of the students' experiential background in respect of the world of work, thus of proximal stimuli in the perceptions of occupations, and of indicators of such attitudes and values as affect the perceptual processing of the information about occupations the child gets outside the home; at school, for example.

The student's experience of his own capacity and his own needs can also be related to factors in the home environment. True capacity and need variables are determined largely by early environmental influence, and the proximal stimuli in the form of situationally conditioned experiences vary with early environment. Also attitudes and evaluations that influence the perceptual processing of the child's later experiences are determined to a great extent by such early environmental influence.

It should perhaps be pointed out that in studies of the educational and occupational choice process, as in many other connections, much more comprehensive information about conditions in the home environment than that provided by the parent questionnaire would have been an advantage.

2. *Capacity variables*

The results of the tests available in the project may be regarded as expressions of the individual's "true" capacity, the features which, above all others, determine an individual's scholastic achievement. It is, however, mainly by achievement at school that the student can judge his capacity. In so far as results of tests are communicated to the student they may, naturally, act directly as proximal stimuli for the student's experience of his own capacity.

It should perhaps be added that even though the test results are not communicated to the student, the test situation itself may give him stimulus material which may form a base for such experience. But this stimulus material may give the student a wrong idea of his capacity. Since the tests are, as a rule, constructed to differentiate even at high levels of intelligence, it is probably by no means unusual for the tests to give rise to feelings of failure in students at lower levels of intelligence, which may cause them to underestimate their capacity.

The capacity variables are also of importance for an individual's perception of the world of work. The definitions which form the basis of the measurements of intelligence we make in various contexts describe such aspects of the individual's way of functioning as his orientation in the surrounding world, and thus include ability to obtain information about this surrounding world. We may assume that a student with high intelligence, everything else being equal, also has a wider and more detailed knowledge of different occupations than a student with poor intelligence.

3. Achievement variables

The most important basis for a student's assessment of his intellectual capacity is scholastic achievement, about which he obtains information at interrogations in the daily work of the school, by results of written tests and in term marks. The basic data of the project include measures of scholastic achievement, partly in the form of term marks, partly as results of standardized tests. Since the latter are not usually communicated to the students, it is mainly the marks that can be used as a measure of proximal stimuli in this connection.

The other type of measure of achievement used in the project, the measure of over- and under-achievement, may possibly be assumed to express certain motivational circumstances in the individual, level of aspiration and the like, which influence the perceptual processing of the information on own achievements. No definite hypotheses can yet be formulated here, however; this must be postponed until measures of over- and under-achievement have been studied further.

4. Sociometric variables

In contacts with other people, we are often confronted with a stimulus material which gives us a certain basis for an assessment of characteristics of the type "social ability" in ourselves. Our social relations are also important for the formation of our need structure. Positive reinforcements may lead to greater interest in contact activities. Frustrations in contacts may trigger intrinsic adjustment actions causing the development of substitutes for social needs.

It should therefore be possible to relate some aspects of perception in the vocational choice process on both the capacity and need sides to the peer ratings included in the basic data of the project. An expression of the individual's experiences in this context is to be found in the students' self-ratings of their popularity among classmates.

5. Intrinsic adjustment to the school situation

The students' experience of different aspects of the school situation was studied by the help of questionnaires. The answers to the questions may be viewed as expressions of the congruence between the students' needs and rewards that may be present in the school situation. There the students have possibilities of making experiences that probably determine to a great degree their choice of theoretical or practical occupations.

E. Collection of data concerned specifically with the educational and vocational choice process

For the study of choice of line of education and occupation, the basic data are complemented with data specific for this study. It is necessary, for example, to make a survey of the proximal stimuli on the occupational side, e.g. the information that the students have received regarding lines of education and occupations. The final step in the process of perception must also be studied, i.e. the students' experience of the prospects of reward in different occupations in relation to their own needs, as well as the choices in the form of preferences, decisions or actual measures.

By the spring term of 1968 the main group (M_{13}) was in grade 6, and the pilot group (P_{16}) was in grade 9. From this time these two groups have taken part in the investigations of the choice process on several occasions. For the collection of data specifically concerned with this study the following types of instruments have been used.

Vocational questionnaires, to get information about factual choices, the students' motives, experiences, plans etc.

Occupational differential, designed to get information about occupational values etc. The instruments are designed as semantic differentials.

Interest inventories, to get information of the interest structures of the students.

These instruments will be described in some detail below. They were administered to the main group and the pilot group on several occasions. The following survey will show what instruments were used on the different occasions. From the group designations it is also clear at what ages the students in each group answered the questions.

Instrument	Group				
	M_{13}	M_{15}	M_{16}	P_{16}	P_{19}
Vocational questionnaire	1968	1970	1971	1968	1971
Occupational differential	1968	1970		1968	
Interest inventory	1968		1971	1968	

1. *Vocational questionnaires*

The questionnaire constructed for the pilot group in grade 9 (P_{16}) was the most complete one. It was divided into two parts, one concerning *education,* and one concerning *work.* They were used for a preliminary study, the results of which guided the work with the questionnaires for M_{15} and M_{16}. These forms were shorter and together covered the same types of information. Each form was designed to get the information needed about the situation on that specific occasion. First a description will be given of the contents of the questionnaires for P_{16}. Then the special features of the other questionnaires will be commented on.

P_{16} The contents may be described in the terms of the model for limitation of alternatives and matching.

a) *Limitation of alternatives.* Which alternatives, lines of education and occupations, are feasible (acceptable) for the individual? Does the individual consider he has many or few alternatives among which to choose?

b) *Proximal stimuli.* How has the individual obtained information about different alternatives (lines of education, occupations)? Does the individual consider he has received enough information and experience to enable him to judge the demands and rewards in different alternatives?

c) *Perceptual processing.* Experienced social pressure that may affect the perception of the alternatives. The strength of the reference group, internalization of role expectations.

d) *Experience of own capacity.* Which alternatives does the individual consider he can manage?

e) *Matching process.* Outcome of the process, choice made or preference for an alternative. Confidence in choice, difficulty, etc. (Comparison of different components in the matching process, chief reasons for a certain choice or a certain preference.)

f) *Occupational values.* Preferences for activities related to conditions in different occupations, as well as for external reward aspects of occupations. This section of the questionnaire was based on the survey of attitudes to conditions of work made by Herzberg et al. (1957). The thirty-two questions concerned intrinsic and extrinsic factors. A factor analysis (Andersson et al., 1969), of this material gave a solution with eight factors, which have been tentatively designated:

1. Care and contacts
2. Outdoor work
3. Dependence and uncertainty
4. Status

5. Mobility and flexibility
6. Spontaneity and expenditure of energy
7. Aspiration without risk-taking
8. Solitariness and quietness

Factor scores were computed for each individual as a sum of the variables with factor-loadings of at least 0.40. These individual values are used in further analyses, where the factors are related to coming educational and vocational choices.

M_{13} The first vocational questionnaire for the main group covered the same topics as the form for P_{16}.

The form for M_{13} was, however, shorter. The problems of choice which are specific for the grade are fewer in grade 6. The occupational values were covered by only a few questions.

M_{15} The questionnaire for the main group in grade 8 was rather short, dealing mainly with the current situation in the choice of studies after the choice of stream for grade 9. The following problems were touched upon.

Actual choices of future studies.
Change of groups of subjects in grades 7 and 8.
Reasons for different choices.
Experienced knowledge of alternative choices
Experienced difficulty of choosing and conviction that the right choice has been made
Satisfaction at school
Aspiration in studies
Experienced ability to succeed in further education

Finally one part of the form contained questions on the importance the students attributed to certain conditions in occupations. The occupational values represented in the question were:

Contacts and welfare work
Status
Spontaneity and expenditure of energy
Outdoor work

M_{16} In grade 9 the form for the main group was also concerned with the current plans for studies, vocational training or work, as well as long-term plans for work. The questionnaire was designed on the experiences from the pilot study three years earlier.

The replies completed the information on the study choices of the main group through the compulsory comprehensive school and the development of the plans for future education and work. In this way the reasons for the different choices have been registered in conjunction with the actual choice situations.

P_{19} Most of the students in the investigation groups will continue their studies in the higher secondary school (the gymnasium). A considerable proportion of them will also proceed to studies after the gymnasium.

It is also important to elucidate the process of choice during these periods.

Parts of the pilot group was in the last year of the gymnasium in 1970/71. A study in the spring of 1971 had the following aims:

a) to serve as a pilot study for the investigations of the main group three years later,

b) to provide material for studies of the process of choice at the transfer to post-secondary education or training, and

c) to provide basic information for continued follow-up studies of students during further education.

A questionnaire was used to collect information on the same type of questions as for P_{16} but adapted to the level the students had reached. Examples are:

Experiences from the time in the gymnasium

The students' information about university level studies, terms of admission, instruction etc.

The students' information about career goals, conditions of work, incomes etc. in such occupations

Expectations of studies and of vocational activities

Factual plans for study or vocational training: aspiration level, degree of decision etc.

2. Occupational differential

M_{13} and P_{16}

In order to map the students' views of conditions in different occupations, a form was constructed according to the Semantic differential technique (cf. p. 65). The form was designed to measure attitudes to some occupations with respect to the status dimension, preferences for different occupations and notions of the demands and rewards inherent in the occupations.

The form contained ten occupations chosen to give a *vertical* and a *horizontal* representation of the labour market. By the vertical aspects

	Horizontal representation		
Vertical representation Status level	Welfare, contact	Commerce, office	Technique
I high	Doctor	General manager	Chief engineer
II medium	Teacher (secondary school)	Bank clerk	Foreman
III low	Nurse assistant	Shop assistant	Workshop worker

Figure 9: 5 The occupations judged in Occupational differential

is meant here the status level of the occupations in the occupational hierarchy, taking into consideration such factors as duration of training, income, etc. The horizontal aspect refers to branches of occupations that may be assumed to differ with respect to certain types of demands and rewards. The choice of occupations is illustrated in Figure 9: 5.
The following scales were included in the form:

long education	—short education
work with hands	—theoretical work
male	—female
interesting	—dull
low income	—high income
clean	—dirty
difficult	—easy
diversified	—monotonous
working with others	—working alone
hectic	—calm
high status	—low status
make own descisions	—must obey
would like very much to become	—would certainly not like to become

The form also included the main groups of alternative actions available to the students at the end of the compulsory school. They were instructed to give their views of the occupations open to them if they chose the following alternatives:

To begin work at once
To attend a vocational training school

174

To attend the (non-vocational) continuation school
To attend the higher secondary school.

The alternatives were judged on scales corresponding to those given earlier. The scale "long education—short education" was replaced by "is good—is bad".

M_{15} The same system of occupations according to horizontal and vertical aspects as used in the occupational differential for M_{13} was used. In addition, "the job I would like to have most" was also included as a concept. The scales were varied to cover partly other aspects.

The seven-point scales were as follows:

Would not like to be	Would like to be
I am sure I should not be accepted for training	I am sure I should be accepted for training
I am sure I should not manage the work and training	I am sure I should manage the work and training
I am sure I should not like the work	I am sure I should like the work

The occupations were also judged on nine scales covering the same values as in the vocational questionnaire dealing with occupations. These measurements should make it possible to judge the relevance of these values in choice of occupation and the consistency in the students' statements.

3. *Interest inventories*

M_{18} and P_{16}

A study of interest was made with the help of the inventory, "Interest schema—activities" (Waern-Härnqvist, 1962). The form contains different activities, on which the students had to express an opinion. The replies were to be given on a four-point rating scale: "Very interesting", "Interesting", "Dull", "Very Dull". The form contains 160 activities, representing eight spheres of interest:

Aesthetic interests: art, drama, music
Open-air interests: athletics, sport
Domestic interests: home and household, needlework
Office and commercial interests: office work, retail shops
Practical interests: handicrafts, making and mending things
Social interests: interest in contacts with people—teaching, helping, leading

Technical and scientific interests: constructing machines, research
Verbal interests: interest in literary production, languages, use of words
and verbal conceptions.

As has been shown earlier and by the above heading, there is some
overlapping of the contents in respect of interest in certain activities in
the questionnaires referring to occupations and the items in "Interest
schema—Occupations".

M_{16} When the students in the main group were attending the top class
of the nine-year compulsory school it was desirable to survey their interests at this time, too. The form used earlier was considered less suitable for teenagers. Instead, an inventory developed by a research group
in Gothenburg (Olsson, 1970) was chosen. This inventory, "Activities",
consists of 99 items. They describe different activities that may be assigned to one of the spheres of interest represented. The replies were to
express how highly the students appreciated the various spheres. The results
are reported as interest profiles of eight spheres. They are:

1. Interest in superficial contacts
2. Interest in welfare contacts
3. Interest in psychological analysis
4. Interest in dominance activities
5. Interest in technical tasks
6. Interest in mathematical work
7. Interest in domestic activities
8. Interest in artistic activities.

4. Other instruments for P_{19}

In Chapter 4 the instruments which have been used to measure individual,
adjustment, environmental variables etc., were described. For the pilot
group (P_{19}) there are measures taken to complete the information just
discussed for the study of the career process.

a. *Intelligence tests.* As a measure of general intelligence a form of
Raven's progressive matrices was used. It may be described as a logical
reasoning test.

Also a verbal test was used, Opposites, a part of WIT III (see p. 60).

b. *Creativity tests.* Two tests of divergent production was used. They
were similar to the tests of creative ability used for the main group
(see p. 191). *Pukort* is a development of the Purdue Creativity test, form
G (Lawshe & Harris, 1960). The task is to give alternative uses for objects represented by pictures or to tell what pictures represent.

Table 9: 1. Reply frequencies to the question: How long would you be prepared to study after grade 9 to get a job you like? P_{16}.

	Boys		Girls	
	Number	Per cent	Number	Per cent
No reply	30	6.7	22	5.4
Not at all; begin work at once	26	5.8	40	9.8
Study 1 year	26	5.8	48	11.8
Study 2–3 years	198	44.6	151	37.2
Study 4–5 years	78	17.5	81	20.0
Study more than 5 years	87	19.6	64	15.8
Total	445	100.0	406	100.0

Titles is a Swedish version of Plot titles (Guilford, 1967). The task is to formulate titles to fit texts.

c. *Teachers' ratings.* The teachers rated the students of each class at a teachers' conference (cf. p. 83). A rough classification method was used: three students were selected in the class who best fitted a description defining the variable. Only one variable was rated. Aptitude for theoretical studies, ingenuity, flexibility, staying power and other factors influence the complex variable that may be designated *prospects of success in adult life.*

F. Some results

1. Study aspirations and choice of studies

In reply to one question, the students had to say how long they would be prepared to study after the compulsory school to get a job they would feel happy doing. Table 9: 1 gives the distribution of replies.

This question gives information about the study aspirations of the students. These aspirations are probably influenced by many factors, and they are of great importance for the choice of studies.

One of the current problems of the educational society is the difficulty in arousing study aspiration among young people from lower socio-economic strata. To illustrate the prevailing situation, the replies have been related to PE.

In the investigation groups there is significant correlation between intelligence and PE; see Figure 9: 6 (Josephsson, 1967). Intelligence has therefore been included in the analysis as a control variable.

Figure 9: 7 reports the average values of study aspiration for three subgroups with low, medium and high intelligence for the combined PE

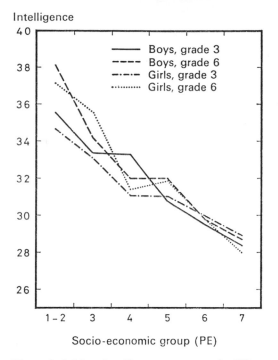

Intelligence

Socio-economic group (PE)

Legend:
- Boys, grade 3
- Boys, grade 6
- Girls, grade 3
- Girls, grade 6

Figure 9: 6 Mean intelligence test scores in different socio-economic groups

groups 1–5 and 6–7 respectively. It shows that aspiration is clearly related to intelligence, but also that students from higher socio-economic groups at all levels of intelligence plan a longer education than students from lower socio-economic groups.

In grade 6 the main group also reported their plans for further education after the compulsory school. Figure 9: 8 shows the percentages of students aiming at higher secondary school studies at the two PE levels mentioned in the previous analysis and for three levels of intelligence. The tendency is very similar to that reported in replies to the simple study aspiration question. At all levels of intelligence, students with parents with a longer education plan more often for higher secondary school studies. Aptitude for studies, expressed in intelligence test scores, has, however, also a great importance for the choice of line of education and study aspiration.

When children from different PE groups, regardless of intelligence, tend to show different degrees of willingness for study it may be assumed to be due to attitudes to education and to different kinds of occupation. Thus there are irrational factors which are important for the determina-

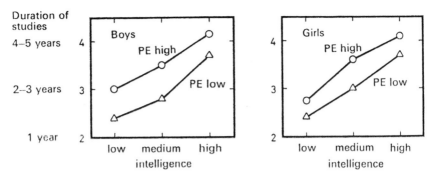

Figure 9:7 Ratings of accepted duration of studies to obtain an occupation one likes. Boys and girls from homes with parents at high and low educational levels (PE)

tion of line of education. The results show that not all students have the same possibilities of obtaining the education that suits them best.

2. Sex differences in preference for status and domain

An illustration to differences in attitude to work between boys and girls and between high and low PE can be obtained by the occupational differential used in the project. One example may be given from P_{16} with replies to the item if one "wishes to be". Figure 9:9 reports the means of ratings on this scale for nine occupations included in the instrument and representing three status levels—with differences in education length —and three vocational domains. Boys and girls are reported separately as are two groups with high and low PE. It will be seen that boys very consistently choose occupations of high status, while girls choose according to vocational domain.

As a matter of fact, the three high status occupations are rated highest by the boys, who then rank the three medium status, and finally the three low status occupations. There are no exceptions to ranking according to status in any of the PE groups. This tendency is most pronounced in the high PE groups, however.

The difference between the means for high and low status occupations is greatest there, as is shown in Table 9:2. In high PE groups status seems to be of greater importance for the preference of occupations than in low PE groups.

The girls rank occupations in respect of what they would like to be according to vocational domains, with a first preference for welfare work, followed by commercial and—with one exception—technical work. Status is of relatively little importance, even though girls, to a certain

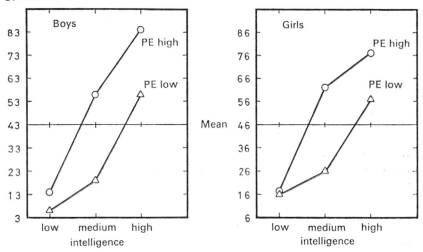

Figure 9: 8 Percentages of students who, in grade 6, say that they intend to continue at the higher secondary school (gymnasium) after the compulsory nine-year school. Division according to sex and parents' education (PE)

extent, take this aspect into consideration. Here, too, status seems to be of somewhat greater importance for girls from high PE than for those belonging to the low PE groups.

From the aspect of choice of occupation it may be regarded as good strategy for students to aim at a theoretical education, but the very marked bias on the status aspect at the expense of interest, which seems to be behind the boys' ratings, does not favour realistic choices of studies and occupations.

3. *Intrinsic adjustment and choice of subjects*

Personal characteristics affect choice of studies and occupations. This complex problem has not, however, been studied much as yet. Analyses based on the data for the main group of the project have been made to elucidate the correlation between adjustment and choice of subjects and streams on the upper level of the comprehensive school (Dunér, 1972).

At the transfer to grade 7 the students could choose between five groups of optional subjects in addition to the compulsory subjects. The alternatives may be regarded as more or less theoretical and in the present work they are divided into three groups, called theoretical, moderately theoretical and practical. The greater part of the students chose the

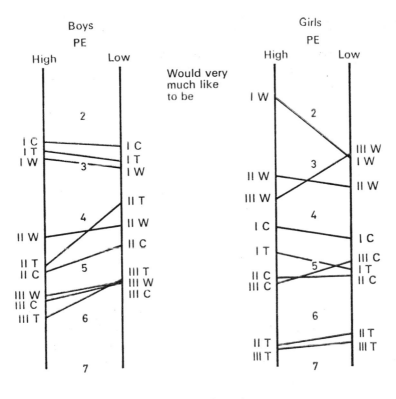

Figure 9:9 Preference for nine occupations in boys and girls from high and low levels of parents' education respectively

theoretical groups, which give the greatest possible freedom in future choices.

At the transfer to grade 9 the students could choose among nine different streams. These, too, have been divided into three groups in the same way as the groups of subjects in grade 7. A large proportion of the students chose the most theoretical streams.

According to this classification, nine different groups of students were obtained. Table 9:3 gives the sizes of the groups. Groups choosing more theoretical studies in grade 9 than in grade 7 are called rising mobile. Groups that chose less theoretical streams in grade 9 are called sinking mobile.

Table 9: 2. Differences in mean ratings of preferences for high and low status occupations and between occupations in different vocational domains. P_{16}.

	Difference high–low status occupations		Difference highest–lowest domain	
	Boys	Girls	Boys	Girls
High PE	3.03	1.67	0.29	3.10
Low PE	2.45	0.59	0.19	2.85

The averages of the adjustment variables measured by means of a student questionnaire in grade 6 have been calculated for the various groups. The averages of two of these scales, *Satisfaction with school* and *Anxiousness in school work,* are reported in Table 9: 4. The scale values are transformed so that the poorest adjustment in any group is designated 0; higher values imply better adjustment, that is better satisfaction and less anxiety. On account of this separate transformation for boys and girls comparisons can not be made between sexes.

For testing of the significance, the differences between the means were calculated in such a way that the averages for the small mobile groups were compared with an average for the large immobile groups, adjusted to refer to the same level of intelligence. The procedure is described by Draper and Smith (1966, p. 21). Significant differences are marked in the tables.

The results show that the differences between groups with theoretical or moderately theoretical choices for grade 7 are rather small in respect of

Table 9: 3. Sizes of groups. $M_{13}/_{16}$.

		Choice of stream for grade 9		
		theoretical	medium	practical
Choice of subjects for grade 7	theoretical	B 136 G 178	B 47 G 65	B 4 G 7
	medium	B 8 G 7	B 67 G 62	B 20 G 17
	practical		B 15 G 14	B 28 G 12

theor., the most theoretical group of subjects in grade 7 and stream in grade 9 respectively
med., the moderately theoretical groups
pract., practically inclined groups and streams respectively

Table 9: 4. Satisfaction and anxiousness in grade 6 in students taking different lines through the upper level of the comprehensive school. M_{13}.

(a) Satisfaction

		Girls				Boys		
		Choice of stream, grade 9				Choice of stream, grade 9		
		theor.	med.	pract.		theor.	med.	pract.
Choice of	theor.	42	37	0*	theor.	64	65	31
subjects	med.	52	37	20*	med.	72	49	0*
grade 7	pract.	—	39	5	pract.	—	59	35
	M = 40; S = 50.				M = 50; S = 53.			

(b) Anxiousness for school work

		Girls				Boys		
		Choice of stream, grade 9				Choice of stream, grade 9		
		theor.	med.	pract.		theor.	med.	pract.
Choice of	theor.	37	33	13*	theor.	49	49	2**
subjects	med.	31	16	0*	med.	61*	28	4*
grade 7	pract.	—	11	3	pract.	—	0	13
	M = 28; S = 29.				M = 35; S = 40.			

* The value deviates significantly from that of the immobile comparative group ($p < .05$).
** Sign deviation ($p < .01$)

satisfaction and anxiousness. The practically inclined group seems to be markedly but not extremely less well-adjusted than the other two.

On the other hand, there are great differences between the rising mobile or immobile groups and the sinking mobile ones. This is especially true of the groups moving to a practical stream in grade 9 from a more theoretical stream.

The intrinsic adjustment in grade 6 is thus correlated with the students' way through the higher level. When satisfaction is low it is very likely that a choice of theoretical subjects for grade 7 will be followed by a fall in the theoretical aspiration level later at school.

G. Perspective

1. *Possibilities and limitations*

A year group of students has been followed for six years in the nine-year compulsory school, and another during an equally long period up to the time when some young people began studying at university level. There is much information, given in the fourth chapter of the present work, about these groups. This information refers to aspects of the process of adjustment, the formation of norms, conformity and relations to other people, and so on.

The groups of students are, according to the present plans, to be followed through their further education and later during their working life.

The varied information gives unique possibilities for further research. The strength of this project contains, however, also restrictions.

In order to be able to study total groups in as many aspects as possible, it was necessary to use group methods and questionnaires in the collection of data. Answers to questionnaires are liable to many sources of error.

There are also weaknesses, especially regarding information about the family, its current situation and the situation during the early years of the child. For most of the students, however, questionnaire data are available about the students' relations to their parents.

In many contexts, the whole of the child's home background will be represented in analyses with the variable PE. This gives some control of certain background conditions, but is naturally far from precise. The scale does not differentiate well at the extreme ends of the continuum. In some contexts it is these extreme values that may be relevant for a problem.

2. Problem domains

The models outlined in this chapter focus interest on problems pertaining to two steps in the choice situation.

a) *Freedom of choice.* One problem domain is concerned with the factors limiting the number of choice alternatives: attitudes, prejudices, attitudes to role, etc., and the situation in which they arise and are allowed to function in school and society.

There is not the same degree of freedom of choice for all students, when they are to decide line of studies at their first choices in school. According to the hypothesis theory, a limitation of alternatives occurs before the conscious choice. A student with an all-round intelligence, with many interests but less prejudices, and with the necessary material qualifications, can choose among a large number of alternatives, while a student only moderately gifted or with strong action-disposed attitudes or family traditions, is steered towards a more limited number of alternatives: he has little freedom of choice. A handicapped student may have no freedom of choice at all, a single alternative may appear to be the only practical possibility. Students who leave school before, at, or shortly after the end of the compulsory school have, as a rule, little freedom of choice.

It is not a primary interest to study attitudes as causes of a certain choice behaviour, as independent variables. Attitudes may be regarded primarily as intervening variables, i.e. the center of interest is the factors of relevance for the formation of attitudes and the conditions that preserve them or affect them. In this, a distinction must be made between attitudes as pronounced evaluations and as action dispositions. In the latter case attitudes may differ in relevance in different situations. They may be of influence in one situation, e.g. a choice during the period of compulsory school attendance, but in a subsequent choice sequence they may not be relevant, and thus no longer steering.

b) *The conscious choice* has been described as a matching between the current alternatives which the individual experiences as acceptable and his perception of himself. This demands a realistic conception of oneself and of the alternatives. Such factors during different ages and developmental stages as may improve this perception, form another important problem domain. Perception of lines of education and the world of work requires knowledge and experience, but is also affected by attitudes.

Of special importance will be the grouping of students according to career through the comprehensive and higher secondary schools. Thanks to the versatile design of the project, there is much information about such groups, about the situation of the young people and about their background and development from their tenth year. This should make it possible to elucidate such problems as those mentioned, and make possible a better formulation of problems for other types of research.

c) *The changing society.* It is not possible to regard the career process as finished when the individual enters his first occupation. The labour market is continuously changing, jobs become unnecessary and disappear and other types of work become usual. It is necessary to calculate with changes of occupation and recurring education or training during the whole of life. The career process during the period now studied can be influenced by this insight, other choices might have been made if a stable labour market was expected.

3. *The role of the school*

The school plays an important role in the student's attitudes to the future. It is in the school that the first choices are made. Even though the Swedish educational system has been transformed to prevent these early choices being of dominant significance for the direction of careers, it cannot be denied that they are still of great importance, which means that certain lines of study at the upper level are followed very regularly by certain streams in the upper secondary school; the choices are actually even if not formally irreversible.

The students come to school and gradually to choice situations with varying value systems, the causes of which can ordinarily be traced to the social background in the home environment. Thus, the school has possibilities during the first six years of compensating and influencing students from an environment which leads to restrictions on the freedom of choice and to unrealistic perceptions of oneself and the world of work.

Of permanent importance in adulthood are such basic attitudes and values, not least in relation to oneself, as are influenced by the school. These attitudes will probably continue to function and strengthen themselves. The school provides society with an opportunity of allowing children to experience themselves, and not only those who are highly intelligent or who, already in the home, have had opportunities of training their social ability and self-confidence.

The persistently strong correlations between social background and interest in theoretical studies, and the great numbers of theoretically uninterested students who do not feel happy in school and leave as soon as possible with few possibilities of choice, provide evidence that much remains to be done to make the school a good environment in which to grow up. It is probably the case that equal evaluation of different types of work and positive attitudes to practical occupations, for which we are striving, cannot be achieved in a school that for the first six years is concerned seriously with only theoretical subjects, devoting little attention to other spheres of interest—only in the form of hobby-like activities.

Chapter 10
Creativity and adjustment

A. Background

In the frame of reference given for the project (see Chapter 1), the individual variable known generally as creativity is of great interest in a number of contexts. Our changing society is getting more and more complex. From this follows that a certain creative ability is necessary for all people to make the individual adjustment process easy (Mooney & Razik, 1967). The prospects of creative work at school and the possibilities of producing a favourable climate for creative solutions have attracted the interest of researchers and school administrators (see Taylor, 1972).

In the light of the conception that creativity is an individual feature which can be traced back to the influence of education and upbringing (see e.g. Gowan, 1967, 1972), the role of the school has come into the focus of interest. It has been asked whether, and if so to what extent, it encourages or discourages the development of creativity in the students. It has been claimed that the creative aspects of a students' personality are not allowed for in conventional intelligence tests or in tests of knowledge now used to measure progress, and that creatively gifted students easily become frustrated when their solutions are not accepted (see e.g. Torrance, 1959). The reader is also referred to Vernon (1970) and for further references to Stievater (1971).

1. *The concept of creativity*

Many attempts have been made to define what is meant by creativity. The discussion of this concept is reminiscent of the debate on intelligence at the beginning of the century.

One of the most detailed attempts was made by Jackson & Messick (1965). On the basis of a logical analysis of creative products and the aesthetic and emotional responses to them, they gave a description of the creative person's characteristics and prevailing cognitive styles. According to Jackson & Messick, the creative products are characterized in the first place by unusualness. Corresponding to this is the creative person's characteristic originality and the cognitive style to tolerate incongruence and lack of coherence. In the second place, the product must fit into its context. The creator of the product must then have sensibility and an analytical cognitive style. The creative product implies in the third place a transformation of material and ideas into forms that overcome social and conventional obstacles. The creative person must then be flexible and accessible to new ideas. The last criterion of the creative product is that it shall give many ideas from new angles. A person who can produce such products is described as poetic and spontaneous.

Most of the aspects that are usually stressed in definitions of creativity can be fitted into Jackson and Messick's system. An essential item in practically all definitions is the emphasis of originality in solutions.

2. Creativity—intelligence

A primary question is whether creativity is a dimension separate from intelligence on the same level of abstraction. If this is so, the correlations between different measures of intelligence and measures of creativity must be low.

A number of studies have not given this expected outcome (see e.g. Getzels & Jackson, 1962; Cline, Richards & Abe, 1962; Cline, Richards & Needham, 1963). Flescher (1963) reported average correlations of 0.04 between measures of creativity and intelligence quotients, but at the same time the average correlation between different measures of creativity was only 0.11.

Wallach & Kogan (1965) discussed the negative results of attempts to confirm creativity as a dimension of its own. They emphasized that an important side of the creative act is relaxation and playfulness, and pointed out that the importance of the test situation had been neglected in earlier studies. The measurements had been made under far too achievement-centred conditions. The measurement situations should be designed to give optimal conditions for a relaxed and playful attitude to the tasks set. Support for such an idea was given later in a study by Boersma & O'Bryan (1968), in which the correlation between measures of intelligence and creativity sank when the instructions were altered in the direction proposed by Wallach & Kogan.

On the background of the views reported, Wallach & Kogan made a study of a whole year group of students in the fifth grade of a suburban school, seventy boys and eighty-one girls. The average correlation between five tests of creativity was 0.40 and the correlation between ten conventional sub-tests of intelligence was 0.50. The correlation between measures of creativity and an individual index based on intelligence tests was 0.10. The results were thus in agreement with what should be obtained if it is to be meaningful to speak of creativity as something other than an aspect of intelligence.

In Guilford's personality model, based on factor analysis, there is a factor, Divergent Production (DP), which seems to correspond closely to the

188

creativity dimension in many respects (1967). Guilford holds the view that low intelligence seems to covary with low DP-values, while high intelligence may be regarded as a necessary but insufficient condition for high creativity values. Thus when level of intelligence is high, the DP-values may be expected to have low correlation with measures of intelligence. As reported by O'Sullivan (1967), it will be seen from the manuals for the tests used by Wallach & Kogan that the subjects were, almost without exception, over-intelligent children with individual values above the seventy-fifth percentile. The low correlations between measures of creativity and intelligence in this group are then in good agreement with Guilford's hypothesis.

3. *Creativity and adjustment*

Wallach & Kogan had still another purpose with their study, namely to seek psychological correlates to individual differences while paying consideration to creativity and intelligence. Their results in this part of the study have immediate bearing on the problems in the Örebro project.

Two observers in the Wallach & Kogan study became acquainted with the children before the tests were administered, and rated the children in eight variables defined to describe different aspects of adjustment; attention-seeking, hesitant, confident, sought as company, seeks company, deprecates own work, inhibited in class, concentration in school work, and interest in school work.

As a basis for the analysis of these judgements, the groups of boys and girls were divided into four sub-groups each according to the results of the intelligence and creativity tests. The boundary line was drawn at the total median, which resulted in groups of approximately the same size for both boys and girls. Thus four groups were obtained for each sex, designated (*a*) high intelligent–high creative, (*b*) high intelligent–low creative, (*c*) low intelligent–high creative, and (*d*) low intelligent–low creative. These groups were compared in respect of the ratings collected. Only intelligence effects were reported for the boys, while the differences between the groups of girls could be attributed to intelligence and creativity and interaction between the two variables. One interesting outcome was that the girls in the group "low intelligent–high creative" had poorer relations with peers and a tendency towards more rowdy, slovenly, and disturbing behaviour in the classroom than the average. The interaction between creativity and sex was in no case shown to be significant.

The results reported by Wallach & Kogan in this context are interesting in a discussion of the forms of work at school. Lieberman writes, for example: "A particularly poignant picture is drawn of the high creative–

low intelligent youngster. To have the existence of such a child brought to our attention is a needed contribution to understanding individual differences in cognitive functioning. The obvious malfunctioning of such a boy or girl in a purely academic setting can be readily understood" (Lieberman, 1968, p. 149). Results of this kind may have significance that makes it imperative to confirm the results by further studies under varying conditions. One such study has been made in the present project, and others are being planned.

B. Purpose of the present investigation

The investigation was planned with the same dual purpose as that of Wallach & Kogan; to ascertain whether creativity, measured in the way it was, differs from intelligence measured with conventional intelligence tests, and, if so, to study the adjustment of a normal group of Swedish children on the background of the interaction between intelligence and creativity.

The design differs in some respects from that of Wallach & Kogan. In the first place, the experimental group was not selected, but may be said to be a normal group of children (grade 6, with an average age of about 13 years). In the second place, creativity was measured without such far-reaching steps to ensure a relaxed test atmosphere. Among other things, a certain time limit was applied. The creativity test was, however, given after the presentation of questionnaires in which the replies were personal opinions, and therefore no "right answer" was to be given, and in which achievement was not judged, which may have produced a favourable atmosphere.

In addition, other instruments have been used to measure creativity. The dependent variables studied also differ in some respects from those of Wallach & Kogan.

In the analyses of the data not only sex but also socio-economic background—as indicated by parents education—were controlled for. Data were analyzed for the total group and for boys and girls separately. Also interactions between creativity and sex and parents education were studied.

Data for this study are taken from the main group, M_{13}.

C. Independent variables

The material was divided into groups on the basis of scores on instruments for the measurement of creativity and intelligence.

1. Intelligence

The composite sum of scores from the six subtests described on page 59 was used as measure of intelligence.

2. Creativity

Creativity was measured with two tests, Consequences, and Divergent figures, designed by Larsson & Sandgren (1968).

a) Consequences (Co) is a verbal test. In fluency scoring (frequency replies) it represents most closely the factor Divergent Semantic Units (DMU) in Guilford (1967). The test contains five items of the type: "What do you think would happen, what would be altered and what would follow if water could burn?"

b) Divergent figures (DF) is a type of test called "doodles". It contains ten items. In Wallach & Kogan's study it has an equivalent in "Pattern meanings", which consists of similar visual stimulus material. The type of test may, in a comparison with Guilford's "Divergent Production Test", be assigned to the factor Divergent Figural Implications (DFI). It is related to Guilford's "Possible Jobs".

Both tests were evaluated in respect of number of replies given, so-called "fluency scoring". The raw scores on both tests were added together to make the measure of creativity.

On an average, the girls have higher scores than the boys, and the sex differences are significant ($p < 0.001$). Reliability, calculated as internal consistency measure with α-coefficients for each sex and test, varies between 0.84 and 0.88. The reliability of the total scores on the creativity test was 0.91 for the boys and 0.92 for the girls.

D. Dependent variables

The dependent variables studied in the first place were scholastic achievement, subjective experience of the school situation, and classroom behaviour.

Results of standardized tests were used to measure scholastic achievement (see p. 60). Factor scores for three scales referring to experience of the school situation, namely *Satisfaction in school, Peer relationships,* and *Anxiousness about school work,* were extracted from the student questionnaires (see p. 62). The measures of classroom behaviour were teachers' ratings on all seven rating variables: *Aggressiveness, Motor disturbance, Timidity, Harmony, Distraction, Lack of motivation,* and *Aspiration.* A smaller special investigation studied popularity, measured as peer status (see p. 69) and self-rating, measured by rating the concept *I* in the semantic differential technique (see p. 65).

E. Moderator variables

1. *Sex*

Great differences have often been observed between boys and girls in relation to the variables studied. The results obtained by Wallach & Kogan show that data on boys and girls should be processed separately. As Cronbach (1968) has shown, it is also necessary to analyze the interactions between sex and creativity. Therefore sex was used as a moderator variable.

2. *Social background*

Since, in the variables studied, there was reason to suspect that role expectations play an important part, it was deemed necessary to keep social background under control to a certain extent by processing data for different PE groups separately and by studying interactions between social background and creativity.

It was necessary for the continued processings to reduce the number of PE groups to two. When the groups were combined, the original groups 1–5 were classed as "high level of education" (high PE) and groups 6–7 as "low level of education", (low PE).

The moderator variables formed a basis for a division into four moderator groups: boys, high PE; boys, low PE; girls, high PE; girls, low PE.

F. Extreme-group design

Four groups were chosen within each moderator group for study. These groups were chosen on the basis of the individual results of the intelligence and creativity tests. The four groups within each sex/educational group were:

1. low creative and low intelligent (ci)
2. low creative and high intelligent (cI)
3. high creative and low intelligent (Ci)
4. high creative and high intelligent (CI)

The divison into 4×4 groups is illustrated in Figure 10: 1, where the final group size and border values are given in raw scores.

A division into groups according to the principles applied by Wallach

Sex	Creativity	High PE *Intelligence* low	high	Low PE *Intelligence* low	high
Boys	low 0–33	ci N=16	cl N=30	ci N=45	cl N=17
	high 42–117	Ci N= 8	Cl N=51	Ci N=12	Cl N=22
Girls	low 0–33	ci N=17	cl N=18	ci N=35	cl N=15
	high 42–117	Ci N=13	Cl N=65	Ci N=16	Cl N=34

Figure 10: 1 Division into groups and size of groups. Moderator variables sex and parents' education. Independent variables creativity and intelligence

& Kogan met with great difficulty. A division according to the total median results in groups differing considerably in size, owing to the girls' higher scores on the creativity test and owing to better achievements on both intelligence and creativity tests for children from families with high PE. If, on the other hand, each sex and level of education had been divided according to its median, comparability would have been lost as well as the possibility to pool data. The study was therefore designed as an extreme group investigation. The boundaries for the selection, which are given in Figure 10: 1, were the same in all four moderator groups. Even with this mode of procedure the sizes of groups varied.

Owing to the correlation between intelligence and creativity, there was reason to fear that the implications of the concept low creative was not the same in high and low intelligent groups. The differences between the mean values of creativity (or intelligence) in the pairs of groups with the same intelligence (creativity) were tested for significance. They were small, and significant in only one case out of eight in each sex.

Choosing the extreme group method we lose part of the generality which a total group investigation can give. Analyses of the total material with the use of regression analysis are therefore planned.

G. Statistical processing

The statistical processing of the four-fold tables was performed in principle by analysis of variance.

On processing-technical grounds it was deemed that t-tests would be simpler than the calculation of F-quotients. The tests have a consistent degree of freeedom in the numerator in four-fold tables and are therefore equivalent to a t-testing. The number of individuals included in the different analyses varies between 81 and 209 in the moderator groups, and the degree of freedom has been regarded as infinite. Within-cell variances were calculated by pooling of the variances in the different cells.

As Cronbach (1968) has pointed out, there is a risk in a moderator design that differences in a pattern of significances will be interpreted as differences between sexes (or PE:s) even if there are no tests of interaction effects. Analyses within moderator groups also cut down the number of degrees of freedom, which may give results that are difficult to interpret.

From such reasons analyses have been performed not only in the four moderator groups, but also (a) in the total group, (b) in the group of boys, and (c) in the group of girls.

H. Creativity and intelligence—separate dimensions?

The correlation between the scores on two creativity tests was 0.59 for the boys and 0.64 for the girls. Thus, for the boys, the two tests had approximately 35 per cent common variance and for the girls about 38 per cent.

The correlation between total scores on the two tests of creativity and the total scores on the intelligence tests was 0.30 for the boys and 0.26 for the girls. The common variance for boys for the tests of creativity and the tests of intelligence was thus about 9 per cent and for the girls approximately 7 per cent.

Of interest in this context are the correlations between the two measures of creativity and intelligence on the one hand and measures of scholastic achievement on the other. The coefficients for the correlation between scholastic achievement and intelligence were 0.78 and 0.77 respectively for boys and girls, and for the correlation between scholastic achievement and creativity the coefficients were 0.34 and 0.33 for boys and girls respectively.

The results are consistent and on the whole of the same size as those obtained by Wallach & Kogan. They support the assumption that creativity may be regarded as a dimension separate from intelligence, conventionally measured and they are consistent with Guilford's (1967) hypothesis that high intelligence is necessary to develop high creativity. This hypothesis has found support in the results of Smith (1971), and it is of interest in the interpretation of the results from the present study.

Table 10: 1. Mean values in scholastic achievement, girls. Raw scores. M_{13}.

	High PE		Low PE	
	i	I	i	I
c	92	175	92	150
C	132	186	119	181

Significant effects:

Intelligence	Intelligence
	Creativity

I. Adjustment in groups with different combinations of creativity and intelligence

As was the case in Wallach & Kogan's investigation, the greatest effects of grouping according to creativity and intelligence were found in the group of girls.

1. *Results for girls*

Significance testings of individual effects were made on a large number of tables. A complete report of this material is in preparation. Two tables are given as examples of the testing of specific variables and a summarizing tabular compilation of the results for the group of girls. In all tests the significance level was 5 per cent.

Table 10: 1 reports the average scholastic *achievement* in the form of standardized tests for the groups of girls studied.

The intelligence effects imply that the high intelligent girls in both the PE groups are superior to their low intelligent peers in respect of scholastic achievement, which was expected.

The creativity effect in the low PE group means that the high creative students achieve better than the low creative. The same tendency is found in the high PE group, but is not significant there.

Table 10: 2 reports the means in the variable *Satisfaction at school* measured with a student questionnaire (see p. 62).

It is remarkable that in this material intelligence and satisfaction at school were not correlated. On the other hand, creativity and satisfaction are correlated in both educational groups in so far as low creative students feel less contented at school. The interaction effect in low PE groups implies that low intelligence in combination with low creativity leads to poorer satisfaction at school, while low intelligence combined with high creativity gives the better satisfaction. The same tendency is present in the high PE groups, but is not significant there.

	High PE		Low PE	
	i	I	i	I
c	8	8	8	10
C	12	10	12	10

Significant effects:

    Creativity   Creativity

                                Interaction

Table 10: 3 gives a survey of the results of all the thirteen analyses made. Significant effects ($p < 0.05$) of *Intelligence, Creativity,* and inter-action between these two variables are indicated by S for each of the two PE-levels. When an effect is significant in one PE-group, a nonsignificant difference with the same sign in the other is indicated by +. All the significant differences are in a direction implying poorer adjustment for low intelligent and low creative girls respectively. The table shows, among other things, that the low creative girls, compared with the high creative girls, are characterized by the following:

a) poorer achievement

b) poorer adjustment to school

c) more anxiousness for school work

d) less school motivation

e) lower aspiration level.

2. *Results for boys*

A number of significant differences appeared between high and low intelligence in the groups of boys. Apart from these, only the following three variables gave effects of creativity and/or interaction.

1. *Aggressiveness.* In the group from homes with high PE, a significant effect of creativity is present, implying that low creative students were rated as more aggressive than high creative.

2. *Timidity.* In high PE groups a significant interaction effect is present. This means that the teachers judged the low intelligent and high creative students to be the most timid. The non-significant tendency in low PE groups is in the opposite direction.

3. *Lack of motivation.* In addition to significant intelligence effects in both the PE groups, there is also an effect of creativity in the groups with low PE. Like the low intelligent in relation to the high intelligent, the

Table 10: 3. Summary of effects of Intelligence, Creativity, and Interaction (I × C) on thirteen variables, girls. M_{13}.

Dependent variables	Intelligence		Creativity		Interaction	
	high PE	low PE	high PE	low PE	high PE	low PE
Achievement	S	S	+	S		
Adjustment to school			S	S	+	S
Peer relations, subj.					+	S
Anxiousness	S	S	S	S	S	+
Aggressiveness	+	S		S		
Motor disturbance	S	S				
Timidity	S			S		S
Disharmony	S	S				
Concentration difficulties	S	S	S	+		
Lack of motivation	S	S	S	S		
Aspiration		S	S	S	S	
Popularity						
Self-assessment						

S = the effect is significant.
+ = the effect is not significant but has the same sign as the other PE group.

less creative children are judged to be less interested in school work than the more creative.

3. *Sex/creativity interaction*

In one respect the same pattern of significance emerges in this study as in that of Wallach & Kogan. We find significant effects in the group of girls but not in boys. Therefore it is necessary to study the interactions with the moderator variables. The data for the moderator groups were pooled in combinations to study the effects of *Creativity* and its interactions with *Intelligence, Sex* and *PE*. A summary of the results is presented in Table 10: 4.

In the case of only one variable there is a case for interpreting the results as a difference between boys and girls. Low-creative girls indicate more anxiousness at school than their high-creative peers, while such a relation is not to be found in the groups of boys.

As regards the other variables in which we have found significant effects in the groups of girls but not in boys, the interactions involving sex are not significant. For most variables the effects are significant in the total group when they are so in the group of girls. In *Aggression* and *Disharmony*, effects of *Creativity* are indicated in the total group, whereas they are not significant in the moderator groups.

The relationships between creativity and adjustment variables are thus

197

Dependent variable	Creativity effects			Interactions		
	Total group	Boys	Girls	C × Sex	C × I	C × PE
Achievement	S	—	S	—	—	—
Satisfaction	S	—	S	—	S	—
Peer relations	—	S	—	—	S	—
Anxiousness	S	—	S	S	S	—
Aggressiveness	S	—	—	—	—	—
Motor disturbances	—	—	—	—	—	—
Timidity	S	—	S	—	S	—
Disharmony	S	—	—	—	—	—
Distraction	S	—	S	—	—	—
Lack of motivation	S	S	S	—	—	—
Aspiration	S	—	S	—	S	—

S = Significant $p < 0.05$

more clearly described in the analyses of data from the total group than from those from the smaller moderator groups.

No interaction effects involving PE are significant. Thus the socio-economic background of the students has not been found to influence the importance of creative ability for school achievement or adjustment.

J. Comments

A sex difference emerges in this study of the same kind as in the investigation by Wallach & Kogan, referred to in the introduction. In both cases the girls show a much clearer and more systematic correlation between creativity and adjustment variables than boys. But there the similarities cease. In the American study, the group low intelligent–high creative proved to have the poorest adjustment to school. In the Swedish group of school children, poorer adjustment is found in: (*a*) the low creative group compared with the high creative, and (*b*) the low intelligent–low creative group compared with the low intelligent–high creative. These tendencies indicate that in the Swedish school environment studied, creativity is an asset which contributes to possibilities of adjustment and personal development in school. The positive effect is strongest in girls but the sex-differences are not significant.

The sex differences in strength of relations may possibly be attributed to different norm expectations for boys and girls regarding adjustment and achievement. The boys may still feel more compulsion to attain achievements demanding intelligence and efficiency, while for girls creativity may be more highly appreciated, in spite of the fact that it is not as valuable for a conventional career.

It has been suggested above that expectations varying with social background may be responsible for certain differences in tendencies observed in different groups. We found no support for this. Creative development may, however, be more influenced by patterns of relations and the emotional climate in the family than by socio-economic status. It seems justified to state a warning not to draw conclusions from single, cross-sectional studies about the relative adjustment of creative children in the school and about the possibility of the school to stimulate or hinder a creative development of individual children.

Such problems will be considered when the divergent thinking dimension is followed up in the investigation to study the development of creative persons and the predictive validity of the tests. Cropley (1972) found with his test battery a satisfying and encouraging validity over five years.

Chapter 11
Social differentiation

A. Background

In the school class an individual is forced into a social system. In the Swedish school he or she may belong to this social system for nine years, during which period the composition of the class may remain largely the same. The character of this social system decides to a great extent what experiences the individual will have during this important period of development.

It seems reasonable to assume that knowledge of other people, of their way of thinking and feeling, their attitudes and systems of values will to some extent be influenced by the interaction with classmates. Rokeach (1967) asserts that allround social interaction has a profound influence on forming an open or a closed mind. There are essential differences in e.g. values (Kockeis, 1970), language (Bernstein, 1970), and perceptions (La Belle, 1971) between socio-economic strata. If the class is very homogeneous, the experiences will be restricted and one-sided. Many students lack sufficient contacts outside the school to compensate for such one-sidedness.

In an educational system where students are grouped early according to an estimated ability for theoretical studies, the composition of the school classes will be systematically different in respect of qualifications for study and interests. Since theoretical courses dominate in all classes, this may also imply systematic differences between classes regarding feeling of satisfaction at school, experience of meaningful work and so on. This may be accompanied by important differences in conduct, order, and conditions for effective work. The result may be a circle effect, with growing differences in attitudes between different classes and greater one-sidedness in the experiences of the students.

Under such circumstances students from different social levels will, on account of differences in intelligence, be placed in different classes, which will thereby become relatively homogeneous in respect of social group affinity also. This will further reinforce the one-sidedness of the experiences of the students.

One objective of the educational system today is to give everyone possibilities of an all-round development and an education suited to his capacity. To reach this goal the school may initiate measures of different kinds, among them the creation of school environments that are all-round in respect of the representativity of different groups.

One important feature of an educational system is its degree of differentiation or homogenization in grouping the pupils into classes. Is the effect of homogenization regarding conditions for study positive and essential? When is the optimal time to begin with differentiation? Svensson (1962) summarized the results of a number of studies on this problem. He himself made a follow-up study of a sample of school children from grade 4. During the sixth to the ninth year at school the students were in different school environments. From his results, Svensson concluded that, in the long run, no differences could be demonstrated in the school environments studied, in which both differentiated and completely undifferentiated schools were represented. An experimentally designed study of the same problem was made at the University of Uppsala (Sjöstrand, 1966). Dahllöf (1967) analysed the material from the two investigations and concluded that certain positive effects exist in homogeneous grouping.

The studies mentioned were focused on achievement and cognitive functions. A system with heterogeneous classes was motivated in the first place by the need of personal and social development of the students and the demand for equality and versatility in the educational environment. Such aspects were elucidated by Johannesson & Magnusson (1960). Johannesson found differences in the school environment in respect of attitudes and in sociometric variables. Magnusson found that students in heterogeneous classes had somewhat higher self-esteem than students in homogeneous classes.

The problem of grouping at different ages were studied in Great Britain in projects at the National Foundation for Educational Research (NFER), among others the Plowden Project (1967) and the Constructive Education Project.

In Sweden the classes formed in grade 1 are now not broken up during the first nine years of school. The students have the same classmates during this period so that they will experience the school as a secure place of work. This means that a school class retains, on the whole, the social structure it has at the start.

When classes are formed at the start of school, attempts are made to see that children from the same dwelling area are placed in the same class. They then have a possibility of spending their leisure time with their classmates and of forming groups which may develop good unity.

For many reasons towns and large population centres are built so that the same type of dwelling dominates an area. In large towns, such homogeneous regions are often of a considerable size. Modern building methods have led to an increase rather than a decrease in this trend during recent years.

Since different types of dwellings have widely differing costs, homogeneous dwelling areas will create rather far-reaching homogenization of the social structure of the areas. Town plans cause a social differentiation which, in very large towns, may be described as segregation.

By the application of the neighbourhood principle and then the principle of retained composition of classes, dwelling differentiation will lead to social differentiation in school classes. This has been observed and has led to a lively debate. In conjunction with this, some attempts have been made to estimate the extent of this social differentiation in Swedish towns. Such a study was made in Malmö (Swedner & Edstrand, 1969), in Gothenburg (Andersson, Ekholm & Hallborg, 1970), in Örebro (Nygren, 1970 a) and in other places.

These investigations indicate that this social stratification is more marked in large towns, but that it does not, in Sweden, become so marked that the designation segregation is justified.

Measures to counteract differentiation have already been initiated. If more far-reaching steps are considered, the results they may lead to should be elucidated. A few studies have shown effects of a more far-reaching segregation. The aspirations for further studies have been related to the socio-economic background of the majority of parents of the children in different schools by Wilson (1959). The results indicate that the immediate social milieu has considerable effects on the aspirations of American high school students. Negro students in an integrated school had significantly higher aspiration than a control group in a segregated school, according to a study by Abramson (1971). De Lacey (1970) reported that aborigines with contact with European children in Australia performed on a par with these white peers while aborigines without such contacts lagged far behind.

On the other hand Duncan, Featherman & Duncan (1972) found surprisingly small effects of school differences in applying causal models on the problems of socio-economic background and its importance for school achievement. Within the normal range of variation there seem to be only small effects to be expected of one of the school components, segregation. In Passow (1971) results are presented which indicate that schools in the United States with bad buildings and bad equipment give their students, who are often from disadvantaged home backgrounds, an inferior education with unsatisfactory achievements. School factors may therefore be expected to have less influence in the Swedish educational system, where differences between schools in equipment are small. Analyses of achievements in science and reading comprehension in the countries studied in the IEA project indicated that differences between schools are least in Sweden. The Swedish schools are thus more homogeneous than those of the other countries in this investigation (Husén, 1973; Comber & Keeves, 1973; Thorndike, 1973).

Some investigations are working with comparisons of extreme groups. Children from high social groups attending classes in which their classmates have the same social background are compared with children from high social groups most of whose classmates are from lower social groups. In the same way, children from low social groups are compared in classes of varying structure.

Such investigations are complicated by the fact that the groups of students compared with each other may be systematically different even in the initial situation when they are assigned to classes. The reason why a high status student is placed in a class of mainly low status students may be found in the situation of this student or his family and the effects of social differentiation may be confounded with effects of this situation. Controls of the child's intelligence and a more thorough study of the social backgrounds of the groups are required if the results are to be interpretable.

The purpose is here to study the extent, the causes and effects of the social differentiation in school classes.

B. Design of the investigations

1. *Investigation groups*

The experimental groups studied were the M and the P groups. The main group was followed from grade 3 to grade 8, and the pilot group from grade 6 to grade 9. Owing to conditions affecting the composition of special classes, only normal classes were studied.

Since the social composition of the class is the independent variable to be studied, the investigation has been restricted to classes which, for a long period, remained unchanged in their structure. Individual students who have moved to other classes have also been excluded.

2. *Method*

An experiment would be the best way of studying the effects of social composition on development in the class to which a child belongs. Students would, at an early stage, be randomly assigned to classes with systematically varied social composition. The subjects could be matched for similarity in the independent and other relevant variables. After a number of years in different social environments, groups of subjects could be compared. Differences might be attributed to the systematically varied condition, the social structure of the class.

It is not possible, for many reasons, to perform such an experiment. Instead the problem must be studied in existing situations in a way as similar as possible to the experiment that cannot be made in practice. Such a mode of procedure is possible in longitudinal investigations, where experimental group data from at least two points in time are available on the variables one wishes to study and variables which may be relevant.

In such situations, students who have, for one reason or another, been placed in classes with different social structures can be compared with each other after a certain period of time.

A possible procedure would be to match students on relevant variables and then follow them for some years in different types of classes. Differences between the matched group in variables measured on a later occasion could then be attributed to the only variable known to differentiate the groups: the social composition of the class.

The matching procedure is, however, complicated and usually gives rise to a large proportion of drop-outs. Instead the same result can be achieved by regression analysis. Control variables measured on the first occasion are inserted as regressors and in this way it is possible to check whether the groups to be compared really had the same initial situation, and if not, adjust for differences.

a) *The data level of analysis*

When a study is made of certain relations within the individual-school environmental system, consideration must be paid to the fact that each individual belongs to a definite class, within which certain factors function and are of influence in a way different from other classes. Such factors, which may be unknown or in any case are not measured in the investigation, may then cause statistical dependence between observations valid for students in the same class. To avoid correlated errors which would disturb the analysis with the individual as unit, the data level used was the means for groups of students in one and the same class. It should be noted that in some cases results pertaining to aggregated data cannot be assumed to hold for interpretations on the individual level (see, e.g. Blalock, 1964). However, in the present studies this was not judged to invalidate the interpretations of the results. No consideration was paid to the fact that numbers of individuals in such groups vary somewhat, and that the means actually have somewhat different mean errors.

b) *The regression analytical model*

A regression analytical model was used to study the means of a number of variables in the groups mentioned. With the simplest model linearity is assumed to exist in the correlations between the regressand and each individual regressor studied. Further, it is assumed that the form and strength of the correlations are not dependent on the values of the other variables.

3. *Variables in the analyses*

a) *Regressor.* Interest is focused mainly on the effects of social differentiation. The social composition (SC) of the classes is, therefore, the principal regressor in the analyses. The percentages of children from homes where the parents are on a low level of education, PE groups 6 and 7, were used as measures of SC.

b) *Regressors as control variables.* The variables subjected to analysis may, in certain cases, be dependent on other characteristics of the individuals, which must be controlled in the analyses. This is done by adding them to SC as further independent variables. The correlations studied between SC and the respective dependent variable will then, in the form of partial coefficients of regression, express the correlation at constant values in the controlled variables. These variables were:

Intelligence, measured with the DIA test (Härnqvist, 1961). This variable may have been affected to some extent even before the first measuring occasion, which occurs in grade 3 or grade 6 in the two groups studied. As a rule, SC was the same in grades 1–3 and grades 4–6 respectively. A probably slight overcorrection may therefore be made.

Achievement at the beginning of the period studied, measured with achievement tests.

Level of education of parents measured on the seven-point scale described on page 86.

c) *Moderator variables.* In this series of analyses, sex and parents' educational level (PE) were used as moderator variables.

As shown earlier, PE also has another important function in the design of the investigation. Comparisons are to be made between class majorities and minorities in this respect. Hypotheses may be formulated in terms of different outcomes in high and low PE groups.

C. Studies performed

1. *Mapping of social differentiation*

A mapping of the social differentiation in Örebro was performed (Nygren, 1970 a). It showed that the differences between classes are smaller than reported from other large towns.

2. *Analysis of causes of social differentiation*

It is also interesting to study whether the causes of the differences found between the structure in different school classes are due only to the application of the principles the school administration had to follow, or whether other types of measures, such as pressure brought to bear by parents, have been of importance, as is implied by some research workers (Swedner & Edstrand, 1969).

A similar analysis was made by Nygren (1970 a), who showed that there is no reason to assume that any other factors have influenced systematically the placing of students in different classes. New students have not been placed in classes in such a way as to increase the social differentiation, nor have classes that have had to be divided at the transfer to a higher level with larger classes been altered in such a way.

3. *Effects of social differentiation*

As a first step a preliminary study with the extreme groups method has been made within the project. The variables which may, in the first place, be expected to have a disturbing influence on the comparability between the groups have been studied, but no control measures were used (Dunér, 1970). Some results are reported in Table II: 1.

The most distinct tendency is that low status children in high status classes seem to be influenced by the majority in their classes to choose a more theoretical line in grade 9 than low status children who constitute the majority in their classes. But this effect, which may be interpreted as higher study aspiration, does not continue in actual choice of school attendance or occupation at the end of the compulsory nine-year school. The social structure of the class does not influence the flow of students from the lower social groups to higher schools according to this pilot study.

Otherwise some variables referring to the problem of choice of studies and occupation were studied with the hypotheses that majorities influence the minorities. In most cases the tendencies were in the direction of the hypotheses, but were not significant. In addition, there were differences between the extreme groups in respect of intelligence, which showed the

Table 11: 1. Students' choices of stream in grade 9 and of type of school after the compulsory school. Division into groups according to the individual's PE (parents' education) and the PE of the majority of the students in the class. Per cent.

	Social class composition	PE of the individual	
		high	low
(a) Stream in grade 9			
To theoretical stream in grade 9	high	54	10
	low	32	19
To the semi-theoretical stream	high	41	68
in grade 9	low	39	44
To a practical stream in grade 9	high	5	22
	low	29	37
(b) Type of school after grade 9			
Higher secondary school	high	54	9
	low	37	11
Continuation	high	29	18
school	low	5	25
Vocational school	high	17	73
(or work)	low	58	64

necessity of continuing with analytical methods, allowing for effective control of certain variables.

Such a study has been made, in which the effect of the level of the social structure of the class was studied (Nygren, 1970 b). The correlation between the composition of the class and achievement at given intelligence and PE-level in grade 6 was calculated for four groups: boys and girls and two levels of education (PE) of the students' parents. The results, which are reported in Table 11: 2, reveal no significant effects of the class structure. According to the hypothesis that the minority of the class is influenced by the majority, significant partial regression coefficients should have appeared, with negative signs for high educational level and with positive signs for low educational level. For the high and low PE groups the signs agreed with this hypothesis, but the differences between the negative value for high PE and the positive for low PE were not significant. For low PE, the improvement in achievement due to stimulus from the majority with high PE in the class was quite negligible.

In another study of the same student group, the effects were studied on intrinsic adjustment, as revealed in scales from student questionnaires (Bagge, 1971). Nor could these satisfaction aspects be shown to have significant correlations with the social composition of the class.

Table 11: 2. Correlation between achievement and social composition at given intelligence and PE for each of the four categories of students, for averages for sex and educational groups, and totally.

Sex	PE	Regres. coeff.	Standard error	Significance test (t)
Boys	high	−0.231	0.186	−1.239 not sign.
	low	+0.042	0.108	+0.389 not sign.
Girls	high	−0.072	0.124	−0.580 not sign.
	low	−0.023	0.112	−0.200 not sign.
Boys	total	−0.095	0.109	−0.872 not sign.
Girls	total	−0.048	0.084	−0.571 not sign.
Boys +	high	−0.152	0.112	−1.357 not sign.
girls	low	+0.010	0.079	+0.079 not sign.
Total		−0.071	0.069	−1.029 not sign.

The very important problems connected with the effect of attitudes and evaluations in conjunction with choice of studies and occupation have been dealt with by Dunér (1972). Some questions studied were as follows: How difficult is it for students to choose, and how confident are they that they have made the right choice? How strongly do students experience influence by peers and parents respectively?

Attitudes to a sample of occupations were measured by semantic differential technique. Hypotheses were propounded that class majorities—according to PE—influence class minorities as regards such attitudes. They were in some cases confirmed by the results in respect of the direction of the differences, but few differences were found to be significant.

D. Perspective

For many reasons it is desirable to give children in the compulsory school as all-round an environment as possible, thus providing opportunities of experiences of different kinds. One of the conditions for this is that the group—the class—to which children are assigned is not restricted in its composition by, for example, factors related to social background.

In Chapter 9 on the sub-project dealing with problems in connection with the students' choice of studies and occupations, it was maintained that students should be given possibilities of obtaining diversified experiences in order to develop their ability to choose among given alternatives so that they will not later be too restricted in their freedom of choice of occupations.

In the report of the criminological sub-project in Chapter 7, the importance of contacts with different people for the formation of norms, the development of personality and adjustment to a social system was discussed.

The analyses made hitherto suggest that a social differentiation of the magnitude occurring in Örebro has no systematic negative effects on the students with regard to the variables studied. This result is important for the question of retained composition of classes.

Other types of group differentiation occurring in the school are probably of greater significance. In the first place there is differentiation according to age, which is almost total in the school. The student groups are differentiated wholly according to age, with great restriction of their prospects of obtaining versatile experience, and with a strong effect on the formation of norms, which may be very specific in a group with limited experience.

The structure of dwelling areas gives rise to social differentiation. This may be a more important problem in the living areas than in the school classes.

Part IV
Sample investigations

For special problems data are needed which have not been collected with the group-administered methods used in the total group investigations. In a few cases such data have not been taken for the total group for economical reasons. Certain biological investigations are too expensive to perform on the total group. The urgent problem of the background of disturbances in social relations has also necessitated an intensive study of a sample of students.

Chapter 12
Biological investigations

A. General purpose of the investigations

Chapter 1 discussed two subsystems in the individual, the psychological and the biological. It cannot be denied that psychological research in general has studied variables in the psychological system without paying much attention to the biological system. This is true not least of the study of such differential and social psychological problems as are dealt with in the present project. It may be assumed on good grounds, however, that the way the biological system functions—as a basis of and in interaction with the psychological system—plays an important role for the total adjustment of the individual, both intrinsic and extrinsic. Important information on the process of adjustment can probably be obtained by a simultaneous study of the two systems. We have therefore deemed it to be an essential phase in an all-round study of the process of adjustment to study measures of the way the organism functions biologically.

In the long run, variable measures in the biological system may feasibly contribute to the attainment of the main goal of the project, by making predictions of behaviour and adjustment more certain and increasing knowledge of the chain of causes leading to various types of maladjustment.

Biological variables are studied parallel with psychological variables for exploratory purposes in the first phase of the project. The data bank of the project provides, in some respects, good possibilities for a study of the covariation of these two types of variables.

Three main domains of the way the organismic system functions have been chosen for study: *hormonal activity; electrical activity of the brain (EEG)* and *general physical performance capacity.* In addition, measures of *biological age* have been collected.

The first of these investigations was made for M_{12-13} during the school year 1967–68. Ossification measures as expressions of biological age were collected for M_{15}.

B. Investigation group

When planning the physiological investigations, limitations were necessitated by the resources of the laboratory. The maximum number of subjects that could be dealt with by the EEG laboratory, in addition to its ordinary work, amounted to about 250 persons during the academic year. Resources for hormonal analyses, like those for studies of physical performance capacity (bicycle ergometry), were limited to about the same extent. Examinations of rather more than 100 students of each sex were considered sufficient in view of the exploratory purpose of the biological investigations.

It was necessary, therefore, to restrict the investigations in grade 6 to about 250 students from normal classes. The investigation group had to be formed in such a way that it did not differ in any important respect from the total year group. The same sample was drawn for all the biological investigations.

Natural units when drawing samples of students from a year group are the class and the school. The various school districts were judged to have socio-economic differences. This had to be allowed for when samples were taken. According to earlier results, there is considerable systematic covariation between some of the variables in the project and the socio-economic background of the students.

The main alternative in the drawing of samples was either to take a number of students from each class in the grade or to take a number of complete classes. The first mode of procedure would ensure the best representativeness of the samples but there were strong economic and administrative reasons against this, particularly as regards the hormonal investigations. The purpose of these was to study the students' reactions to stress in the ordinary school environment, a test of mathematics, for example. The investigations, therefore, had to be made with complete classes. In the other biological investigations, too, the smallest possible number of classes implied clear administrative advantages.

For these reasons, it was decided to make the investigations in nine complete classes, which gave the desired sample of about 250 students. The choice of classes was made with consideration paid to certain differences between the school districts in order to balance, as far as possible, the investigation from socio-economic aspects. In addition, classes were chosen whose members had, to as great an extent as possible, taken part in the total group investigation.

C. Examination of brain activity (EEG)

1. *Background*

Early attempts to relate various indices of electric cerebral activity to such personality traits as intelligence met with great difficulties. Not least, variations in registration technique gave rise to difficulties of interpreting research results and of integrating the outcomes of many small studies. An example of other difficulties is that changes in blood sugar content may result in marked changes in the EEG (Ottoson, 1970). The investigations were also made on different clinical groups which were difficult to define objectively.

Correlations between intelligence and EEG indices of different kinds have been studied in a large number of published investigations. The results have been collected and integrated by Vogel & Broverman (1964, 1966). They summarize their views as follows:

"... while EEG is related to test intelligence, the relationship will be more or less demonstrable depending upon (a) the controls which are instituted for relevant variables, such as sex and age, (b) the means employed to assess intelligence, (c) the conditions of EEG administration, and (d) the EEG indices employed as dependent variables" (1966, p. 99).

Such relationships seem to be clearest in children, mentally retarded and immature individuals. However, Vogel & Broverman (1966) hold the view that such a relationship has been demonstrated also in normal groups of adults.

Differences in the interpretation of research results seem to be caused not least by the fact that abnormal EEG is present rather frequently among persons without clinical symptoms of deviant behaviour. It is present in about 15 per cent of neurologically normal control subjects. Ellingson (1966) scrutinized research results to ascertain whether and if so how normal variations in the EEG phenomenon are related to normal variations in intellectual achievement. He came to the conclusion that no relationships can be regarded as demonstrated for adults, and as far as children and mentally retarded persons are concerned the relationships are contradictory and inconclusive. EEG abnormality and impaired intelligence are, he considered, both effects of organic cerebral trauma and tend to be related for this reason.

Studies of the relation of other personality traits to EEG for normal groups have been rendered difficult by problems of measurement. Better techniques, have, however, made it possible to attack such problems. Broadhurst & Glass (1964), contrary to the results of earlier experiments, have shown that introverted experimental subjects had higher percentages of alpha-activity and alpha-amplitude than controls. The experiment was made on normal individuals. Also extraversion and neuroticism measured with a personality inventory were related to EEG parameters.

Theta-waves are considered to have a relation to emotional responses. They appear when a child shows anger or displeasure. Maulsby (1971) puts the question if differences in personality may explain why certain children react with theta-waves on pleasure, others with theta-waves on displeasure.

2. *Data collection and coding*

The EEGs were taken by the regular personnel at the EEG-laboratory of the Örebro hospital during the school terms with a rate of two pupils a day. The recordings used a conventional technique with 21 electrodes placed according to the 10–20 electrode system with the customary longitudinal and transverse bipolar derivations. The recording occupied 15 minutes with the subject at rest and 3 minutes with the subject overbreathing. The resulting biochemical shifts when the subject voluntarily blows off CO_2 may not only bring forth a characteristic EEG-pattern but also trigger a certain type of convulsive disorders. Other activation procedures, as for instance drowsiness, have not been applied though a different group of convulsive disorders may be triggered into revealing themselves by sleep activation than by hyperventilation. Nor has intermittent photic stimulation been carried out owing to situational factors. No medical man was available to supervise all performances and therefore one could not run the risk of some individuals getting extremely activated. Patterns were registered with an ink-writer and later on visually examined by a neurologist with wide experience from clinical work with the ages in question and the code used. The records have been evaluated with consideration paid to deviations outside the normal boundaries for the age and these deviations are expressed in a code with six positions. The six positions give information on: (1) degree, (2) extent, (3) location, (4) static type, (5) dynamic type, and (6) condition when a deviation is observed. The first digit of the code gives a value on a continuous scale from 0 to 6, the other digits designate categories only.

3. *Preliminary results*

The distributions of the deviations for the 223 children (105 boys and 118 girls) are presented in Table 12: 1.

In the sample about 44 per cent of the records show some degree of deviation. For the boys there are deviations in 36.1 per cent, for the girls in 49.1 per cent of the records.

The frequency of observed deviation under different conditions is given in Table 12: 2.

The condition "at rest, but awake" is coded for about 60 per cent of all the subjects with deviations (boys 56.4, girls 63.8). About 33 per cent of the deviations are coded for the condition "at rest, but accentuated

Table 12: 1. Distribution of degree of deviation (code position 1) from normal EEG.

| Group | Degree | | | | | | | | Sum |
| | No deviations | | Very small deviations | | Rather small deviations | | Moderate deviations | | |
	N	%	N	%	N	%	N	%	N
Boys	66	63.9	25	23.8	10	9.5	4	3.8	105
Girls	60	50.8	41	34.7	9	8.5	8	5.9	118
Total	126	56.5	66	29.6	19	8.5	12	5.4	223

at hyperventilation". The conditon "only at hyperventilation" has evoked deviated records in only about five per cent of the subjects in question.

The deviations are in most cases anterior-temporal in location and according to a static description they consist to 75 per cent of types of delta/ theta of higher amplitude than the base activity. In a dynamic description they may be designated episodic, not bilaterally synchronized in 44 per cent of the cases and as sporadic in nearly 25 per cent of the cases.

A group of special interest in the study of relations to behaviour is composed of children in categories characterized by paroxysmal activity. To this group belong 23 per cent of the students with any recorded deviations.

The base rhythm—alpha frequency per second—has been measured. The range is for boys 7.0–11.5 and for girls 8.0–12.0. Distributions are given in Table 12: 3 for boys and girls and for groups with and without recorded deviations.

Work is now in progress to study the relations between EEG-patterns and behaviour correlates.

D. Investigation of physical performance capacity

This investigation was performed on a test bicycle. The students pedalled at the rate of 50 strokes a minute with a braking resistance of 1.5 kp,

Table 12: 2. Percentage of records with deviations from normal EEG under different conditions.

	At rest, awake	At hyper-ventilation	At rest, awake, accentuated at hypervent.	Accentuated in drowsiness
Boys	56.4	5.1	35.9	2.6
Girls	63.8	5.2	31.0	—

Table 12: 3. Alpha rhythm – base rhythm. Averages and standard deviations.

Groups	Average	Stand. deviation	Number
All boys	9.68	0.77	105
All girls	9.86	0.84	118
Boys with no EEG-changes (code 0)	9.68	0.64	66
Girls with no EEG-changes (code 0)	9.78	0.76	60
Boys with EEG-changes (code 1, 2, 3)	9.68	0.96	39
Girls with EEG-changes (code 1, 2, 3)	9.95	0.93	58

which gives a load of 450 kpm/min. The study was made under optimal conditions which were standardized as far as possible.

The students had been kept physically inactive before the trials, which were performed for all students at the same time in the morning, in an optimal climate with the students dressed for gymnastics.

The students did not eat anything during the hour prior to the test, nor were they allowed to smoke. The work lasted for six minutes, and the pulse was taken every minute, by timing thirty pulse beats. The pulse values finally registered were the means of the pulse values during the fifth and sixth minutes. If the difference between the two pulse values was greater than four, the test was continued for another minute. This was necessary in only a few cases.

Two tests were made with an interval of one week between them. The coefficients of correlation for the stability of data were 0.87 for boys and 0.84 for girls.

The height and weight of the students were also measured in conjunction with the tests.

The maximum oxygen absorption capacity, which is essential for the measurement of physical capacity, is usually determined at maximum load. It may, however, also be calculated from work intensity and working pulse. Thus, it is possible to calculate maximum oxygen absorption capacity from the data collected on submaximal working pulse.

E. Biological age

In most cases the behaviour of the students was judged according to their chronological age. Achievement was assessed according to norms for age classes; different aspects of adjustment, e.g. emotional expressions, were judged as if all the members of a year group were at the same level.

Table 12: 4 Distribution of age at menstruation début for girls in the main group

Age at début	Number	Per cent
Before 10	5	1.3
10–11	35	8.9
11–12	90	22.7
12–13	167	42.1
13–14	81	20.4
After 14	18	4.6
Total group	396	100.0

An especially quick or slow biological growth process leads, therefore, to a student being regarded as unusual. This may give rise to difficulties of adjustment to, for example, peers at another level of maturity.

The problem is *partly* whether biological age as such is a more suitable measure of age than chronological age when judging students' behaviour, *partly* whether deviations in respect of biological age from the group which the student has been forced to join have had a disturbing effect on the development of personality.

For the samples taking part in the other medical investigations, a relatively simple X-ray technique was used to obtain a measure of biological age. The course of ossification in the wrist was the basis of these measures.

As a complementary measure, use is made of data on the sexual maturity of girls obtained in the questionnaire on symptom patterns (Chapter 10).

The distribution of ages at menstruation début in the main group is given in Table 12: 4.

The biological development is to be related to the simultaneous development of norms, symptom patterns, adjustment to peers and to the earlier adjustment to school from and including grade 3.

Adjustment has been compared for three subgroups: one with early menstruation, one with normal, and one with late menstruation début. The general pattern of adjustment indicates that the best adjustment is found in those girls who have their menstruation début at the same time as most of their peers.

F. Studies of hormonal activity: investigations of catecholamine

1. *Background*

Problems concerned with biochemical correlates to behaviour have come into the focus of interest of researchers during recent years. Certain endocrinal functions, primarily the secretion of catecholamines, i.e. adrenalin and noradrenalin, have been found to be suitable for experimental investigation on human beings.

Adrenalin and noradrenalin occur normally in small amounts in blood. Several stimuli, including physical and mental strain, cause a great increase in either one or both hormones. Most of the adrenalin in the circulation is secreted from the adrenal gland. Noradrenalin, too, is produced by the adrenal gland, but most of it originates from the sympathetic nerve endings, where noradrenalin is secreted as transmittor substance. Adrenalin and noradrenalin can be measured in both blood and urine by fluorimetry (Euler & Lishajko, 1961). Urine analyses provide a simple method of measurement that can be used on large groups of individuals.

The role of adrenalin for the efficient functioning of organisms in emergency situations has been well known ever since Cannon's studies during the first half of the present century. The significance of noradrenalin for the homeostasis of blood pressure was elucidated by von Euler and others during the 1940's and 50's. The importance of these substances, particularly adrenalin, for psychological functions was observed early, but it was not until recent years that these problems were studied systematically. A research group at the Psychological Laboratory, University of Stockholm, led by Frankenhaeuser, has, in a series of studies, investigated primarily the relation between the volume of catecholamines excreted on the one hand, and on the other the intensity of simultaneous mental processes. These studies have demonstrated the existence of a systematic relationship between amount of adrenalin and the intensity of the experience. Another important result is that a relationship also exists between amount of adrenalin excreted and cognitive functions under stress conditions (Frankenhaeuser, 1971).

The psychological significance of noradrenalin must, for the time being, be considered less clear. Some relationships between the excretion of noradrenalin in children and variables in the home environment have been obtained in different investigations, however (e.g. Lambert et al., 1969).

2. Purposes of the investigation

The present investigation of the excretion of catecholamines in the Örebro project has mainly an exploratory character. The purposes of the investigation may be formulated as follows.

a) To compare measures of the excretion of catecholamines in children under passive and active conditions in the school environment. The excretion of the two hormones is assumed to increase during the active period.

b) To relate the excretion of catecholamines to measures of achievement obtained in the active period. Achievement is assumed to have a positive relationship to the excretion of adrenalin.

c) To relate the excretion of catecholamines to the adjustment data on the students collected earlier.

3. Collection of data

The investigations were performed in January 1968, in each class in the way described below.

Prior to the investigation the students were given oral and written instructions by their teachers. These instructions were concerned with times for meals, certain articles of food, physical strain, etc., immediately before the investigation. The intention was to minimize the effects of irrelevant factors on the excretion of catecholamines. The study was made during the first three lessons of the day. Two leaders of the experiment, one male and one female, were in charge of the investigation. The teacher was also present, but remained passive.

The first part of the investigation, concerned with the excretion of catecholamines under relaxed, inactive conditions, was an ordinary educational film, "The Iron-ore of Lapland". During the second, active phase, the students were occupied with a test of mental arithmetic, the final results being written in the test booklet. During the test the students were told every third minute to mark in their test booklets how far they had got. This test requires great concentration and the test situation might be experienced as somewhat straining.

Samples of urine were collected after each test. The students were also instructed to empty their bladders before the first item. To facilitate the passing of urine, each student was given a small amount of water before each test. The samples of urine were taken in the school lavatories.

The samples of urine were acidified with hydrochloric acid and frozen within half an hour after they were taken. They were then stored at a temperature of $-18°C$ until they were analysed by means of a fluorimetric method developed by Euler & Lishajko (1961). The reliability of the method of analysis, expressed as the correlation between two independent series of analyses of halved samples, is between 0.80 and 0.90 (see e.g. Pátkai & Frankenhaeuser, 1964).

Achievement during the test of mental arithmetic was registered as (a) the number of tasks performed, (b) the number of correctly solved tasks, and (c) the proportion of correctly solved tasks. In addition, two measures of the course of achievement in time were registered: number of tasks performed during the first half of the test minus achievement during the

221

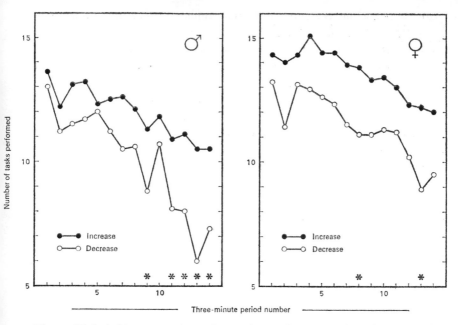

Figure 12: 1 Achievement curves for students whose excretion of adrenalin increased and decreased respectively from passive to active conditions. An asterisk indicates that the difference in mean values is significant at the 5 per cent level at least. From Johansson, Frankenhaeuser & Magnusson 1973

second half of the test, thus a measure of change in achievement during the second half of the test.

In the nine classes chosen there were, at the beginning of the spring term, 252 students, 240 of whom were present during the days when the catecholamine investigation was performed. Of these 240 students, 177 handed in complete sets of tests. For the other 63 students, only one or no catecholamine values were obtained, due to the inablility of the students to pass water on one or several occasions (53 cases), menstruation, which made sampling impossible (6 cases), or technical complications when analysing the samples (4 cases).

4. *Some results*

An account of the investigations has been given by Johansson, Frankenhaeuser & Magnusson (1973). Some results are given below.

a) The excretion of adrenalin was found to be significantly higher during the active period, while the excretion of noradrenalin was somewhat lower. When the subjects were subjected to the strain of mental arithmetic, the boys excreted more of both the hormones than the girls did.

Table 12: 5. Coefficients for the correlation between the excretion of noradrenalin (NA) and adrenalin (A) under passive (p) and active (a) periods on the one hand, and on the other cognitive variables.

	Boys				Girls			
	NAp	NAa	Ap	Aa	NAp	NAa	Ap	Aa
Intelligence								
General intelligence (DIA)	.03	.17	−.03	.10	.27*	.17	.23*	.35**
Creativity	.09	.18	.03	.05	−.03	.05	−.18	.02
Achievement								
Standardized tests								
Swedish	−.03	.11	−.05	.02	.07	.02	.25*	.22
Mathematics	.07	.26*	.03	.09	.15	.12	.15	.28*

* $p < 0.05$
** $p < 0.01$

b) Changes in the excretion of catecholamines between the passive and the active phases are of importance for achievement. Figure 12: 1 shows that students whose excretion of adrenalin increased during the arithmetic test were more persevering in their work than the students whose excretion of adrenalin declined or remained constant. For the girls, the magnitude of the changes was related to the quantity of the achievement.

The amount of excretion was not unambiguously related to achievement. A hypothesis of positive relationship between level of adrenalin and achievement was not verified. For girls there was a significant relationship between level of noradrenalin and achievement.

Table 12: 6 Coefficients for the correlation between the excretion of noradrenalin (NA) and adrenalin (A) during passive (p) and active (a) periods on the one hand and on the other seven teacher-rated variables. All the variables included in the table were transformed by classes into standard scores before the coefficients were calculated.

	Boys				Girls			
	NAp	NAa	Ap	Aa	NAp	NAa	Ap	Aa
Aggressiveness	−.07	−.08	−.13	−.25*	.08	.08	−.22	−.22
Motor disturbance	−.18	−.04	−.21	−.34**	.13	.06	−.26*	−.30*
Timidity	.10	−.09	.10	.12	−.05	.00	.08	.02
Harmony	−.04	−.01	−.17	−.22*	.06	.12	−.12	−.15
Distraction	−.21	−.29*	−.17	−.23*	.14	.07	−.14	−.22
Lack of school motivation	−.07	−.16	−.19	−.12	.06	.09	−.11	−.19
Aspiration	.13	.24*	.11	.09	.01	−.07	.13	.27*

* $p < 0.05$
** $p < 0.01$

c) Positive relationships were obtained between the excretion of both catecholamines and intelligence and achievement. Table 12: 5 shows that these tendencies are most distinct for girls. There seems to be a tendency towards a positive relationship between changes in excretion between passive and active periods and intelligence.

A relationship between excretion of catecholamines and "desirable school behaviour" was also demonstrated (see Table 12: 6). The "high excreters" tended to be less aggressive and motor disturbed and to have better ability to concentrate.

All the relationships reported are relatively low, in no case exceeding 0.40. The structures of the relationships show in some cases distinct differences between boys and girls.

Several results from this investigation of a natural everyday situation agree with results of earlier laboratory investigations.

Chapter 13
Intensive study of social relations

A. Background

Interaction with others often brings us face to face with demands on adjustment of behaviour at the same time as it makes it possible for us to satisfy fundamental needs. During our growth we acquire, in the various groups to which we belong—family, school class, peer group, etc.—different patterns of behaviour and reactions which become of importance for our later adjustment to the role demands made in various social systems, and to our satisfaction of needs in them. Various research workers, among them Roff & Sells (1968), have reported results suggesting that relations to peers during the period of growth are important for the individual, not only for the current but also for future adjustment. Especially difficult is the situation for children who are not only isolated from their peers but also bullied by them. This problem of mobbing has been investigated by Olvaeus (1973), whose results indicated that the prognosis of the mobbing children was still worse than that of the mobbed children. In a follow-up study, Robins (1966) found that only children with aggressive behaviour developed what she called sociopathic personalities as adults. Fraser (1973) reported a study of children caught in violence and suggested measures to help such children. Roff, Sells & Golden (1972) showed in a longitudinal study that peer rejection is a very general characteristic of a child, whose problems cannot be solved with current educational offerings and group activities, which focus on symptoms. The problems of social interaction in schools were also treated in Yee (1971).

Data from the total group investigations give some possibilities of studying peer relations. A further study of the background of differences in peer status has also been made. It was planned and performed as an intensive study of extreme groups. A detailed account of this study has been given by Adebäck (1969).

B. General model

1. Peer status and extrinsic and intrinsic adjustment

Figure 13: 1 illustrates the general model on which this sub-study is based. Peer status, the indicator used to cover the concept of peer relations, has been seen as an aspect of adjustment.

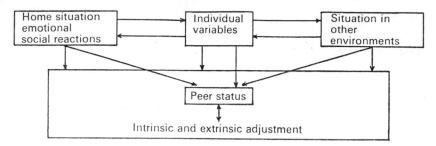

Figure 13: 1 Model of factors affecting peer status

According to the general frame of reference of the project, peer status is primarily an aspect of the extrinsic adjustment of the individual, a measure of how well his behaviour corresponds to the demands on social interaction made in the group of peers. Adequate interaction in the class is regarded as a goal of adjustment. That the individual has not reached this goal may indicate that it will be difficult for him or her to establish satisfactory social relations even later in life, at work, for example.

On the assumption that the gratification of the social needs—the need for appreciation, emotional response, etc.—from the other members of the groups to which we belong are of fundamental importance, the peer status measures may also be looked upon as indicators of intrinsic adjustment. Low peer status may imply that the individual is frustrated and feels rejected and uncomfortable in school. Low peer status may, therefore, be associated with other types of disturbance in intrinsic and/or extrinsic adjustment.

2. Peer status and individual variables

Another goal of the study is to endeavour to isolate the factors in the individual himself in his early environment and in his general current situation that may contribute to the rise of disturbances in his relations to peers.

As a rule, however, the features in an individual that are important for his social acceptance by peers are regarded as products mainly of the earlier process of socialization. The significance of early childhood for the establishment of patterns of behaviour is generally recognized. The emotional climate in the home and the pattern of sanctions form the foundation of an individual's socialization process and emotional maturity. The pattern of social relations prevailing in the family—both relations within the family and relations to people outside the family circle—have great influence on the later behaviour of the child. Several studies have elucidated various aspects of these relationships, see Mussen, Conger & Kagan (1970), Sears, Maccoby & Lewin (1957), Bandura & Walters (1965), Baumrind (1967), Jonsson (1967), and Cox (1966).

3. *Peer status and prevailing home situation*

The home environment is of importance for a child's adjustment, not only as a basis for "explanations" of the child's characteristics and more permanent patterns of reaction. The prevailing situation in the home influences the student's total possibilities of adjustment at a given point in time. Temporary disturbances in the home environment may therefore be expected to influence different aspects of adjustment to school, including adjustment to peers.

4. *Peer status and other environmental variables*

In a similar way, the situation in other spheres of the child's environment outside the home may influence his adjustment to the peer group in school. It should be emphasized here, as earlier, that an attempt must be made to determine which features of an individual are primary for the rise of disturbances in relations to peers and which are secondary in relation to these disturbances. A child's current relationships to persons outside the school environment, in the home or in other contexts, may also influence adjustment to school and be influenced by the situation in the school environment. A model including interaction between variables is therefore necessary.

C. Purpose of the intensive study

In the intensive study it was possible to get more complete information about a small group of children than was possible with the total group. The restriction of the size of the investigation group also makes it possible to attempt to measure the rather diffuse factors designated home situation. One purpose of the intensive study was to find factors that may contribute to disturbances in social relations in (*a*) the individual himself, and his early environment, (*b*) the prevailing home situation, and (*c*) the school situation. Another purpose was to elucidate how peer status covaries with other aspects of the child's adjustment and behaviour and to describe how rejected children experience their situation. A third purpose was to investigate and develop the model.

The relations marked by arrows in Figure 13: 1 may be regarded as preliminary hypotheses of correlations to be tested. For the time being, these hypotheses are only vaguely formulated. One aim of the investigation may be said to be to specify some of these hypotheses. This may lead to more exact definitions of a model needed for the construction of a theory and of testable hypotheses in connection with such a theory.

D. Investigation groups

The students in this sub-study belong to the main group of the project. The special data collection was made when the students were in grade 5. The groups consisted of students with extremely high or low peer status, and a control group of students with ordinary peer status, as follows:

a) 30 students with extremely low peer status   15 boys (B −)
                                                       15 girls (G −)

b) 30 students with ordinary peer status   15 boys (B n)
                                                       15 girls (G n)

c) 30 students with extremely high peer status   15 boys (B +)
                                                       15 girls (G +)

1. *Criteria of peer status*

The selection of experimental groups was based on sociometric data obtained earlier on the main group (grade 3, in 1965), as described on page 69.

To control the stability of peer status a new sociometric measurement was made in grade 4. The stability proved to be good between grades 3 and 4. This is favourable for the use of peer status for diagnosis of adjustment. It is obviously a relatively stable characteristic, typical of the child during a large part of his period of growth.

The final selection of children for the experimental groups was based on three criteria:

1. Sociometric ranking, grade 3 (see page 70).

2. Sociometric choices, grade 3 (see page 70). Each student was to choose the three classmates of their own sex they would prefer to play with during their breaks and leisure time.

3. Sociometric choice, grade 4. Each student was to choose three classmates of their own sex with whom they would prefer to play during breaks.

2. *Matching*

As indicated in the division into groups, the sexes were kept separate. The variation associated with class affinity was controlled by matching. This was done by forming groups of three students, one with high, one with low and one with ordinary peer status, from the same class. Such factors as personality of teachers, peer constellation, size of class, size of schools and their situations in different types of residential areas, etc., may be assumed to influence measures of peer status. Not all these factors can be measured and controlled statistically.

Further, essential information for the elucidation of the problems under study was obtained from teachers. By the matching system, the same teacher always judged the same number in each status group. The effects of the various frames of reference, etc., in the teachers was thus eliminated.

3. *Selection of the groups*

For each selection criterion, the students were first divided into three categories; two extreme groups and one intermediate group. Endeavours were made to ascertain that students who belonged to the same category according to all three criteria were assigned to the experimental groups.

It was most important to obtain a purely low status group. For this reason, the low status member of each triad was selected first. Fifteen boys and fifteen girls were chosen in this way; one boy and three girls were included, who, on one criterion, did not belong to the extreme group, but who were near the boundary.

For the high status group, the matching procedure came to imply that deviations had to be made more often from the demand on affinity to the extreme group in all three criteria. In all such cases, however, the students chosen were very close to the boundary of the correct extreme group.

The normal status students were drawn by lot from the students in the classes in question with intermediate status scores in all three criteria.

4. *Control of the sample*

In order to be able to interpret differences that may appear between the experimental groups, the sample was controlled by comparing the groups in respect of PE, intelligence and scholastic achievement.

Careful statistical testings were made of group differences in PE distribution compared with the distribution in the total population—the whole cohort in the comprehensive schools of Örebro. No significant differences were observed.

The high status groups of both sexes had higher intelligence than the low and intermediate status groups, but only for girls was the difference significant.

In the variable over–under-achievement, i.e. scholastic achievement in relation to expectations according to intelligence, the high status boys were found to over-achieve significantly in comparison with low status boys. Otherwise no significant group differences were found.

The above results are the only ones from the numerous control calculations to which attention need be paid in the interpretation of the analyses of the differences between the groups in the investigation variables.

E. Investigation methods and variables

For the experimental groups, data were available from the total group investigations described in Chapter 4.

This information was supplemented by especially interesting information about the groups to elucidate the problem of peer relationships. These supplementations mainly comprise information that could not be collected by questionnaires or group assessments. Individual methods were used to obtain information on the home situation and the child's situation in school.

a) Interview with mother	Home and school situation, peer and leisure time situation
b) Interview with father	Same contents as *a*
c) Teachers' observations	School situation
d) Teacher interviews with ratings of behaviour	Home and school situation, peer and leisure time situation
e) Student interviews	School situation, peer and leisure time situation
f) Medical examination	Current state and earlier interesting phenomena in physical variables and health

1. *Design of the interviews*

The contents of the interviews were largely determined in advance by deciding the variables in which ratings were to be made. The interviewer kept to the main items given in the interview form, but was also to register and discuss other information which emerged and which might be judged to be relevant in individual cases.

2. *Interviews with father and mother*

The interviews with the fathers and mothers were made independently of each other. All the interviews were performed by one person with long and varied experience of this kind of work.

In this way the difficulties arising from different interviewers' frames of reference, values, ability, etc., could be avoided. It is quite possible that an interviewer's specific value structure can influence his ratings and as a consequence the results of the study. It seems, however, not plausible that the influence of values has had a significant effect in this case, as the interviewer took no part in the planning of the investigation. He did not know the criteria for selecting children to the different experimental groups, he did not even know after all the interviews that the problem of the project was that of children with disturbed social relations. Most of the parents were co-operative and interested. 162 interviews were made. There were, however, some drop-outs. Two mothers and three fathers categorically refused to participate. Another thirteen persons could not be interviewed on account of divorce, death, etc.

In home interviews it may be assumed that great problems in establishing the necessary contacts may arise. The interviewer was therefore allowed great freedom to adapt himself to the situations, devote time to establishing contacts and concentrate the interview to domains with high priority. After the interview a number of variables were rated.

The interviews were made in the form of a conversation. No notes were taken during the interview.

Main variable scales contained the main information on which the interview was focused. For some of these variables ratings were made for all individuals. These scales referred to situations in which it was deemed desirable to make interindividual comparisons. The rating scales were graphic scales with their extremes defined verbally in rather great detail. Other scales were concerned with spheres in which it was considered possible to dispense with the information in case this was necessary on account of difficulties in the interview situation.

To concretize and make the interpretation of the main variables less subjective, *sub-scales* were designed to some of the main scales. When rating a main scale, the interviewer should pay attention to sub-scales, but no mathematical weighting procedure was used.

Each main scale was accompanied by a *confidence* scale on which the interviewer put + if he felt confident about his rating, 0 if he felt neither particularly certain nor uncertain, and − if he felt uncertain.

The variables referred to relations between family members in general, between each of the parents and the child, and between members of the family and people outside the family circle.

Main variables	*Sub-scales*
a) Relations in general within the family	Home atmosphere

b) Relations between parents and children	Permissive—dominating practice
	Absence of restraint, active conscious practice
	Consistency
	Differentiation in upbringing
	Upbringing difficulties
	Accepting
	Child centered
	Involvement
	Anxiety in the upbringer
	Protection
	Emotional restraint in upbringer
	Experience of corporal punishment
	Use of corporal punishment
	Attitude to corporal punishment
c) Mother's or father's attitude to role	Attitude to self as upbringer
	Wish to change working situation
	Experienced fatigue
	Satisfaction with work situation
d) Relations between parents	Attitude to other parent as upbringer
	Use of corporal punishment by other parent
	Relations between parents
	Parents' agreement in problems of upbringing
	The other parent's emotional restraint
e) Relations between members of family and people outside the family circle. External factors	External status of family
	Well-being mindedness of family
	Attitude to dwelling
	Attitude to surroundings
	Child upbringing problems in

	the dwelling area
	Relations to neighbours
f) The child's adjustment to	The child's adjustment to
different situations	school
	The child's leisure time
	interests
	The child's relation to peers
	The child's adjustment
	symptoms
	The child's reactions in con-
	nection with mother's work
	outside the home
g) The actual interview situation	The interviewer's contacts
	with parents
	Assessed reliability of the
	information given

Some items were discussed with the mother only.

3. *Teachers' observations*

Judgements by the teachers were invaluable when more detailed information was required about the relations of the investigation subjects to their peers in school. Ordinary judgements may, however, tend to reflect a general attitude to the student rather than a judgement in a specific variable. To obtain more useful information about certain important items of behaviour, an observation programme was drawn up. Each teacher had to observe the children in the class belonging to the experimental groups. They did not know on what principles the students had been chosen. The observation period was one month, and the following ratings referred to this period only. Thus, the behaviour observed was that in an entirely natural school environment, and the students had no idea that they were being observed. All the teachers participating were interested in the experiment. They were carefully instructed in the technique of observation.

The observations were concerned with two types of natural social situations.

a) Situations in which no collaboration was required on the part of the teachers. The observations were made in the school-yards.

b) Situations in which collaboration by the teachers was required. The observations were made in the classrooms.

Two types of peer behaviour were observed and rated by the teachers:

a) The student's behaviour towards his classmates.

b) The classmates' behaviour towards the student.

The teachers rated several items that represent each type of behaviour on five-point scales.

4. *Teacher interviews*

The teachers have many possibilities to observe the interaction of their pupils and get to know the individual child. Apart from the direct observations, the teachers also contributed information in an interview. The degree of structurization was the same in this interview as in the parent interviews.

a) *The contents of the interview.* The following domains were covered during the interview with the teachers.

Summary of the teachers' knowledge of the home.

Teachers' contacts with parents.

How troublesome the child was perceived by the teacher in school.

Personality traits in the student.

Behavioural problems, cheating, lying, disobediance, sexual offences, theft, truancy, vagabondage, running away, arson, smoking or sniffing.

The teachers' opinions of the student's situation in respect of peers.

What the teacher thought was most characteristic of the student.

The teacher's own ranking of the student with respect to his preferences for them.

b) *Ratings of behaviour.* Only a small number of behaviour items could be observed by the teachers. The frequency of some other important items could be rated at the interview. These ratings, therefore, are dependent on the teacher's earlier opinion or memory of the student's behaviour. In many cases the observations made have contributed towards a clearer conception.

As in the behaviour observed, two types of social situations were considered, those in which collaboration with the teacher was required, and those in which such collaboration was not required. The items of behaviour rated also referred to the student's behaviour towards peers and the behaviour of peers towards the student.

Behaviour towards peers in which the collaboration of the teacher was not required comprised:

Verbal and physical aggressiveness

Defiance against verbal and physical aggressiveness

Verbal, positive behaviour

Friendly, helpful behaviour

Persecution, physical or verbal

Negative leadership
Opportunism.

The behaviour of peers towards the student in situations in which no collaboration by the teacher was required:

Verbal and physical aggressiveness
Persecution.

Items of behaviour in situations in which the teacher collaborated were:

Active and passive behaviour, respectively, at work
Will to collaborate.

The ratings were made on five-point numerical scales.

5. *Student interview*

In order to obtain information on the students' own experiences of their relations with peers and teachers, and on their social situation at school, we performed an interview with each pupil in the experimental group. The interview was designed with the same degree of structurization as the parent and teacher interviews. Rating scales determined what information was to be sought. Also unexpected information could be collected, when considered sufficiently interesting. The interviewer endeavoured to obtain as much information as possible in a free conversation, the character of which might be different for different students.

The rating scales comprised four *main scales,* on which ratings were always to be given, and less abstract *sub-scales* to help to make the ratings on the main scales as objective as possible. The scales were chosen to correspond to some of the scales used in the parents' and the teachers' ratings.

Main scale A: Student's relations to his classmates.

Main scale B: Student's relation to peers in general.

Main scale C: Student's relations to teachers.

Main scale D: Student's attitude to the school situation in general.

Confidence in ratings was also judged for each scale. The rating scales were five-point graphic scales.

As aids in the student interviews, drawings of TAT-type were shown to form a basis for the conversations. These were justified for several reasons. In the first place, such a starting point would create a good and natural contact between inverviewer and interviewed. It was considered that it would be an easy way of starting a natural conversation and of inducing the student to talk, while an interview of the cross-examination type could be avoided. This was assumed to be most true of shy students.

In the second place the pictures would illustrate types of situations that

Figure 13: 2 a Specimen of stimulus material in interviews with students

most of the students might be expected to have experienced in some role in relation to the school, teachers and peers. They would therefore serve to structure a certain type of situation and activate the students' memories of their own experiences in relevant contexts. At the same time, the drawings should be so unstructured that they fit into the student's own personal experiences in similar situations.

The students were asked direct questions about their own reactions to such situations as those shown in the drawings, unless they described them spontaneously. Some cautious interpretations of students' behaviour when confronted by the drawings, e.g. signs of the suppression of strongly negative feelings, were possible in these interviews.

The drawings represented eight different situations, which were shown in one version for each sex. Examples are given in Figures 13: 2 a and b.

6. *Medical examination*

With the help of the school nurse, information was collected from the students' health cards regarding different kinds of earlier states. The school

Figure 13: 2 b Specimen of stimulus material in interviews with students

medical officers made new examinations of the students to determine the current state of health.

The choice of variables was made partly on the basis of the assumption of what might be relevant in this context and partly on the basis of the types of data collected regularly on the students' health cards.

F. Data processing

Numerous data on a limited number of individuals were available. The variables may be divided into two groups:

1. Variables describing how individuals function in various contexts, stress being laid on relations to peers and adults.

2. Variables which may be underlying—"causal"—factors for the development of a certain type of relationships to others.

The experimental groups were studied in their natural environment, that is, in an open system. It is then impossible, on the basis of a few data, to establish positive proof of causal relationships. A systematic processing should, on the other hand, make it possible to arrive at plausible interpretations of a causal character.

The situations studied are complex. A number of variables, covering many different aspects considered especially relevant to a variable, relations to peers or more specific peer status, have been isolated from an individual environmental system. Not every variable can feasibly be expected to function in this system in such an isolated way as the measurement results show. They interact with each other, and are important only when certain other variables assume definite values.

These assumptions of the way the system functions make it necessary to draw up a systematic programme for data processing, in which the whole or continuous parts of the system can be considered at the same time. Several methods must be used, for there is no single method that can elucidate this type of complex system. The following three methods were used primarily.

1. Methods of correlation and regression. Correlations between variables from a certain instrument or from different instruments give basic knowledge of the material, which is necessary for the interpretation of the other types of data processing. It is obvious that these measures of correlation must not be given causal implications.

2. One-way analysis of variance and t-testings. Knowledge of how each individual variable has differentiated between the groups studied is also essential in the continued interpretation. The F-ratio from an analysis of variance shows whether the three groups differ significantly from each other in a variable, while the t-test of pair-wise differences can show whether an extreme group differs significantly from one or both of the others. The normal group may be expected in some cases to assume the same value as one of the extreme groups, which may indicate a curvilinear regression between the variable and peer status.

3. Multiple discriminant analysis. This is very suitable as a principal method for the multiple-dimensional attack in investigations designed as extreme group studies. This method assumes that the groups are given. The linear functions which discriminate maximally between the groups are determined, and significance tests are made to ascertain whether real differences are present between the given groups. A linear function may be described as a joint weighting of the original variables. Derived variables are obtained, "new characteristics", which may be interpreted as orthogonal factors.

The number of variables that can be tested simultaneously in multiple discriminant analysis is limited. To achieve the purpose of elucidating whether the variables studied differentiate the three groups and to obtain indications of which of these variables seem especially important for the discrimination, the data processing was performed in several stages.

In the first of these, the variables were combined on logical grounds into groups, each covering a domain. Multiple discriminant analysis was performed, as well as univariate testings. On the basis of the information obtained, certain variables were judged to be essential for the problem studied. Other variables were regarded as less valuable for one reason or another.

In the following stages new groupings of variables were made, followed by analyses, permitting a successive concentration to the important factors.

Since the experimental group, like the other subjects in the main group, will be followed up in many respects relevant to this problem, the follow-up data should, in certain cases, lead the way to further tests of the probability of the interpretations that can be made.

Finally, the necessity of cross validation of the results obtained must be emphasized. The groups are so small that mean errors may be expected to be considerable, and a successive grouping of the variables may be expected to be influenced by errors of measurement.

G. Results

1. *Relations between peer status and some home environmental variables*

Different groups of variables describing the home environment have been studied in conjunction with peer status. For three such groups of variables Figure 13: 3 gives a summary of the results. In the general home atmosphere and child-rearing practice, in parents' experience of their roles at work and as upbringers, and in variables concerned with relations between parents, the low status group differs negatively in all cases from the other two groups.

Normal and high status boys also differ significantly in respect of home atmosphere and in parents' experience of their roles as workers and upbringers, according to assessments made in interviews with the mothers. No differences appear for girls between the normal and high status groups. It seems clear, however, that the results support the assumption that the home situation has a bearing on the development of peer-contact disturbances.

After analyses of different groups of variables in the parent group, the variables with the most distinct differences between the peer status groups were dealt with in a summarizing discriminant analysis. Table 13: 1 reports these variables and a rank order between them according to their

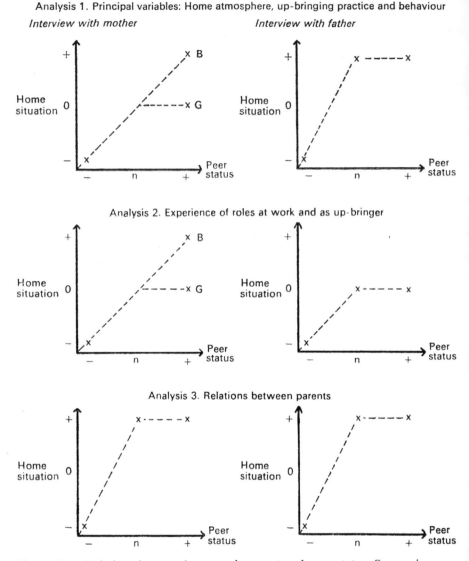

Figure 13:3 Relations between home environment and peer status. Summarizing presentation of the results of three discriminant analyses

ability to differentiate between the peer status groups as this is expressed in their weights in the discriminant analysis. It must be emphasized, of course, that this relative importance of different aspects of the home environment refers to the experimental group and that, until cross-validation has been performed, it must be interpreted with great caution.

Interview with mother

Variable	Multi-variate *p*-value	Rank order according to importance
Boys		
1. Home atmosphere		9
2. Permissive–Dominating upbringing		10
3. M's wish to change working situation		4
4. M's experienced fatigue		1
5. Upbringing difficulties		11
6. M's attitude to herself as upbringer	0.0018	3
7. M's emotional restraint		2
8. M's attitude to corporal punishment		5
9. M's anxiety		8
10. M's attitude to dwelling		6
11. M's attitude to the child's friends		7
Girls		
1. Home atmosphere		12
2. Laissez-faire-active, conscious upbringing		8
3. M's differentiation		10
4. External status of home		5
5. Upbringing difficulties		9
6. M's attitude to corporal punishment	0.0013	3
7. M's acceptance		11
8. Child in centre		6
9. M's anxiety		7
10. M's attitude to her child's friends		2
11. M's encouragement of friends		1
12. M's satisfaction with situation at work		3

Interview with father

Variable	Multi-variate *p*-value	Rank order according to importance
Boys		
1. Parents' agreement in questions of upbringing		10
2. F's attitude to parents' involvement as parents and upbringers		1
3. Upbringing difficulties		8
4. How often F uses corporal punishment		7
5. How often M uses corporal punishment according to F	0.0064	6
6. Relations between parents		9
7. Attitude to surroundings		4
8. Relations to neighbours		5
9. F's attitude to the child's friends		3
10. F's encouragement of friends		2
Girls		
1. Parents' agreement in questions of upbringing		4
2. Upbringing difficulties		3
3. F's experience of feelings of guilt		6
4. F's attitude to corporal punishment	0.0031	2
5. F's acceptance of the child		7
6. Relations between parents		5
7. F's encouragement of friends		1

The following essential aspects may be taken as examples.

For low status children the home atmosphere is more characterized by conflicts, disharmony and irritation among the members of the family. Well-being, and satisfaction with life are said to be poorer. Association between the members of the family is more restricted in time.

Relations between the two parents are also characterized by more conflicts in the low group. The parents state that they have poorer emotional contact. They disagree more, also in questions pertaining to child upbringing. They express more dissatisfaction with the other parent as upbringer. They feel, too, that they have more upbringing problems with the child. The mothers of the rejected boys are dissatisfied with the father's lack of involvement in the upbringing.

Relations between each parent and the child are characterized by less acceptance, more anxiety and overprotection (referring mainly to the boys), more dominance (stricter demands on obedience) and more inconsistency in upbringing.

The parents are less satisfied with themselves as upbringers of the child, and state that they frequently resort to corporal punishment. They have a positive attitude to such punishment, and admit that they often lose control of themselves in their associations with the child (this refers primarily to the mothers of rejected boys).

The mothers report that they are dissatisfied with their working situation, and wish more than others to change it.

The parents do not feel that it is very important for the child to have social contacts with other children and do not state to any great extent that they encourage and support the child in his attempts to obtain such contacts. They also state that they are rather dissatisfied with the child's friends.

There are no important differences between the groups with respect to parents' education, dwelling situation, the mother's work outside the home, and divorce.

2. Students' peer behaviour according to teachers' observations

Teachers' ratings after observations lasting for one month referred to the conduct of the students in question, as actors towards their classmates. The differences between the groups in the rated variables are reported in Figure 13: 4. It will be observed that the low status group deviates greatly from the other groups in these data, too, while normal and high status groups are somewhat more similar to each other.

The teachers judged the behaviour of peers towards the children in the experimental groups. These children are here regarded as stimuli.

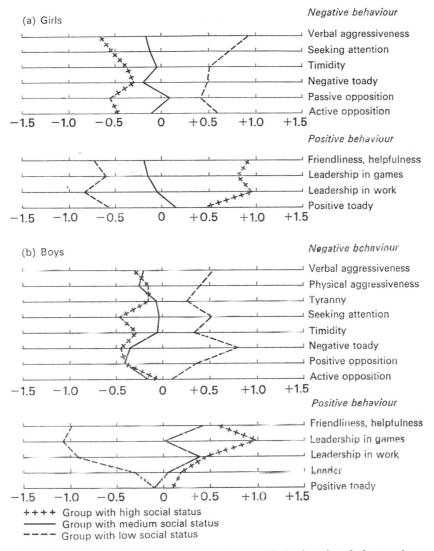

Figure 13: 4 Teachers' assessments of the students' behaviour in relation to classmates

The results, which are summarized in Figure 13: 5, show that the situation for the low status groups is not promising. They seem to be exposed to behaviour from their classmates which may be expected to impair the development of their social ability. They are in a vicious circle.

It may be said that poor relations are characteristic of the homes in which low status children grow up. When they come to school with poor

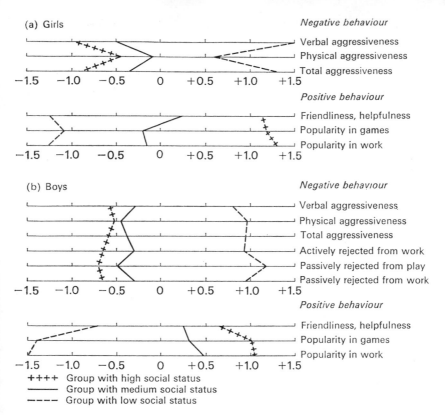

Figure 13: 5 Teachers' assessments of peers' conduct in relation to the students in the experimental groups

or bad patterns of relations and low social ability, they find themselves left outside the world of positive interactions with peers.

H. Perspective

1. *Circle effect?*

The results reveal strong correlation between home environment and adjustment to peers. By inheritance and environment, some students will be socially handicapped. These students also have a socially negative stimulus value for both teachers and peers. The social situation seems to be a grave one, which may have enduring consequences for adjustment and development of personality.

Only contemporary data have been analysed hitherto. It seems, however, to be of great interest to follow the development of these students,

244

for it appears likely that they are in a vicious circle, and that their situation will deteriorate further. Treatment of and conduct towards a person are of great importance for the development of a conception of self, and such groups as the family, teachers and peers are particularly important. The negative expectations of and treatment by these persons may lead to more fixed negative behaviour, which serves to confirm and strengthen the opinion held in the environment. Such a circle effect may lead to disturbed adjustment, which spreads to other domains, and, with the student's conception of himself, may spread to other groups.

2. *The role of the school*

If some students come to school with handicaps, it is the duty of the school to help them, by individual measures. This refers also to students with social difficulties. It is the task of the school to contribute towards breaking the circle effect mentioned above. The analyses made cannot answer the question whether and if so to what extent this occurs during the first years of school attendance, for we know very little about a child at the start of school, nor in how many situations an improvement has occurred. When the extreme groups studied are scrutinized, however, the school does not seem to have had a positive effect. The teachers' views on the students were very negative, and it is possible that, by the way they treat these students, they strengthen the circle effect instead of working consciously to counteract it.

If so, they contribute towards impairing the stimulus value of these students, their conception of themselves and the development of their personality. Then they also strengthen the behaviour of classmates against these students. This must be regarded as injurious for the classmates, too, for they, according to the aims of the school, should be encouraged to develop their social skills so that they can associate with others including those who are handicapped. A solution of the problem of social training in school also implies the solution of the problem of mobbing.

Chapter 14
Concluding remarks

Whole cohorts of children in one town have been followed through their primary and secondary schools. On a number of occasions attempts have been made to catch the situation for each child and get information about the actual environmental circumstances and about how he or she experienced and handled the situation. For about a thousand children of the main age group it is now possible to give a rather good description as regards individual and environmental variables of importance from their tenth to their eighteenth year.

Some of the main problems of the project have been discussed in this book and some results have been given in summary. Not until now, however, has it been possible to use the benefits of the longitudinal design fully. Hitherto mostly cross-sectional data have been reported but the plans are to continue the project with the purposes (a) of following the students to adult life in order to use adjustment in professional life as a criterion in studies of the predictive value of different kinds of early behaviour, and (b) of using the data for longitudinal elucidation of the essential problems of the project.

Characteristic of the project is that a common base of information can be used to study different kinds of problems. The character of the project also makes it possible to attack problems as and when they become of current interest with the advantages of a longitudinal design. Some good examples of this can be given from the project.

Throughout the project much time and effort has been devoted to cooperation with all parts: parents, students, teachers and headmasters. Extensive information has been given directly to these groups and through a very helpful press also to the community. These efforts have resulted in a small number of drop outs and full cooperation in all data collections, including postal questionnaires to students who have left school. In a collection of data by postal questionnaire to the students of the P-group two years after they had left the gymnasium, about 90 per cent sent in replies.

Examples of current problems

The present work can concentrate more and more on problems in which the longitudinal design is necessary. Causal factors behind certain behaviour disorders can be studied most effectively by penetrating cases, in which the situations of individuals have been changed. The importance of such changes in the environment for the development of present and future adjustment can be investigated.

Too little is known about the actual importance for the future of certain behaviours in children in the school situation about which adults are often anxious, e.g. motor disturbance, aggressiveness, shyness, anxiety, disturbed social relations, or psychosomatic symptoms. Such problems can be studied in two ways:

a) Groups of individuals who show symptoms of bad adjustment in their teens or later can be studied through earlier data in order to find patterns of early behaviour which can be used for prediction. Such a study has been performed on delinquency in the P-group of students and reported in chapter VII. In this group the most delinquent boys were more than usually tired of school, were less motivated for school work, found the school work too hard and were more aggressive and motor disturbed in the classroom. If a boy had these characteristics in grade 6 and came from PE-group 6–7, he ran a more than 50 per cent risk of belonging to the group of boys in grade 9 who had committed a crime during the last semester in spite of having been detected and charged on earlier crimes. The strategy of the project with successive age groups makes it possible to cross-validate the actual predictive power of these variables. The calculations on these problems are now being made and will be reported in the near future. If the results from the P-group are verified in the data from the M-group the next important step will be to find adequate therapeutic and prophylactic measures in order to break a disastrous developmental process for the boys in the risk zone without marking them as deviants.

b) The second and more effective way is to study the development of groups of children, who early show specific behaviours which may represent symptoms of serious disturbance of predictive value with regard to adult adjustment. Data are now processed in order to study the prognosis for children who showed motor disturbances, aggressiveness, withdrawal, too high ambitions, or bad peer relations or some of these behaviors in combination with each other or with other behaviors at the age of ten.

Under-achievement may be regarded as an aspect of bad adjustment. It means that an individual does not use his potential resources in achievement. Problems connected with under-achievement have been dealt with by other researchers and they will be considered in this project. With longitudinal data it is possible to study individual change in relative achievement as the dependent variable, which might be an effective way towards elucidating the interaction of influencing factors behind under-achievement. This work is going on.

Less attention has been paid to over-achievement in earlier research. When at the focus of interest it has mostly been regarded as an expression of extremely good adjustment and something which is desirable. However, there are good reasons to believe that over-achievement in the long run can have negative effects for the individual, sometimes of a disastrous nature. Connected with this problem is the question whether what might be called "over-adjustment", continuous adjustment to norms, rules and expectations of the social environment, is good for the individual. Does it cost him too much in the long run? The possibilities of elucidating this problem in the project are good since both psychological and biological data are available for the individuals studied. Detailed planning of a study of this problem is now being done.

Recently an integrated secondary school with vocational as well as theoretical lines was introduced in Sweden. In an analysis of the school system the problem of drop out at the secondary school level has arisen. At the moment studies are being made in the project of groups of individuals who left the secondary school during their first year without finishing their course. Intensive studies have been made to find out the causes of the drop out and an analysis of project data will be made in order to study possible environmental and individual factors in the process.

Changes of the factor structure of intelligence and achievement over age are of interest from a theoretical as well as from a practical point of view. The question of the differentiation or integration of abilities has been of special interest in the discussions of streaming and of the structure of comprehensive schools. Studies on this problem are going on.

New ways to higher education have been opened and the possibilities of choices have increased. During a period of high unemployment there has been a change of interest in theoretical studies. More teenagers want to go directly to a vocational training. They can do so without being locked out from further education if they want to change their mind later—the irreversibility of the educational system is to be decreased by liberal demands of competence for admittance to universities. There will also be increased resources for adult recurrent education. The intention of the project is to describe the students' perceptions of this situation, their own educational plans and actual choices as well as factors that prevent them from obtaining such training or education as they want.

The adult life which young people are now looking forward to is different in many important respects from that of earlier generations. Predictions are difficult for reasons discussed earlier. The youngsters cannot expect and prepare themselves for a place on a stable labour market in a stable society. One of the ultimate purposes of the project is to follow the subjects through education to the labour market in an attempt to study some of the problems connected with these circumstances.

Thus many questions have their answers in the future, which motivates further data collection. This will follow two main lines. Some problems will be studied by total group investigations. With the present system for national registration it is easy to find any person living in Sweden. Information by questionnaires can be collected for the total groups. Studies will also be performed with information which can be obtained only by personal contacts. Such investigations will be carried out on samples of subjects with specific characteristics of behaviour in early school years.

References

Abrahamsen, D., *The psychology of crime.* New York, 1960.

Abramson, E. E. Levels of Aspiration of Negro 9th grade males in integrated and segregated schools. *Psychological reports,* 1971, *29,* (1).

Achenbach, T. The classification of children's psychiatric symptoms: a factor-analytic study. *Psychol. Monograph,* 1966, *80,* 7, No 615.

Adebäck, B., *Sociala relationer i skolan. (Social relations at school.)* Örebro project, special study 6–7. Stockholm: Psyk. inst., 1969.

Adelson, J., The mystique of adolescence. *Psychiatry* 1964, *27,* 1–5.

Aldrich, C. K. Expectations of crime. *World Med. J.,* 1967, *14* (2).

Andersson, B. E. *Studies in Adolescent Behavior.* Stockholm: Almqvist & Wiksell, 1969.

Andersson, M.-L., Dahlryd, E., Domfors, L.-Å., Jonsson, L.-E., Leinonen, R. & Ljungquist, C., *Linjeval och yrkesvärderingar i årskurs 9 relaterade till den sociala klasstrukturen i årskurs 6. (Choice of line and evaluations of occupations in grade 9 as related to social composition of the class in grade 6.)* (Stencil.) Stockholm: Psyk. inst., 1969.

Andersson, B.-E., Ekholm, M & Hallborg, M. *Skolsegregation och vissa effekter därav. (School segregation and their effects.)* Report in Project UG, youth in Gothenburg. Göteborg: Ped. Inst., 1970.

Aronfreed, J. *Conduct and Conscience. The socialization of internalized control over behavior.* New York: Academic Press, 1968.

Bagge, L. *Effekter av social differentiering: Relationen mellan skolelevers trivsel och klassammansättning. (Effects of social differentiation: Relations between satisfaction and the social composition of the class.)* (Stencil.) Stockholm: Psyk. inst., 1971.

Baltes, P. B. & Nesselroade, J. R. Multivariate longitudinal and cross-sectional sequences for analyzing ontogenetic and generational change. A methodological note. *Development psychology,* 1970, *2* (2), 163–168.

Bandura, A. C. & Walters, R. H. *Social learning and personality development.* New York, London: Holt, Rinehart and Winston, 1965.

Baraff, A. S. & Cunningham, A. P. Interpersonal concepts of rapidly remitting and stereoid dependent asthmatics. *J. Psychosom. Res.,* 1966, *10.*

Baumrind, D. Child care practices anteceding three patterns of preschool behavior. *Genet. Psychol. Monogr.,* 1967, *75,* 43–88.

Bayley, N. Consistency and Variability in the Growth of Intelligence from Birth to Eighteen Years. *Journal of Genetic Psychology,* 1949, *75,* 165–196.

Bealer, R. C., Willits, F. K. & Maida, P. R. The rebellious Youth Culture—A Myth? In D. Rogers, (Ed.) *Issues in Adolescent Psychology.* New York: Appleton, 1969.

Becker, H. S. *Outsiders.* New York: Free Press of Glencoe, 1963.

Beckne, R. *Anpassning, beteende och prestation. En analys av data från elevenkäten. (Adjustment, behavior and achievement. An analysis of data from pupil questionnaires.)* Örebro project, special study 1. Stockholm: Psyk. inst., 1966.

Berglund, B. *Mental growth. A study of changes in test ability between the ages of nine and sixteen years.* Stockholm: Svenska bokförlaget, 1965.

Bergman, L. R. Some univariate models in studying change. *Report from the Psychological Laboratories, the University of Stockholm,* 1971.

Bergman, L. R. Change as the dependent variable. *Report from the Psychological Laboratories, the University of Stockholm,* 1972. Supplement 14.

Bergman, L. R. Parents' education and mean change in intelligence. *Scand. J. Psychol.,* 1973, *14,* 273–281.

Bernstein, B. Social class and linguistic development; A theory of social learning. In Halsey, Floud, Anderson (Eds.) *Education economy and society.* New York: Free Press of Glencoe, 1961.

Bernstein, B. *Social class and socialization.* London University: Institute of Education, 1970.

Bjerstedt, Å. *Interpretations of sociometric choice status.* Lund: Gleerups, 1956.

Blalock, H. M. *Causal inferences in nonexperimental research.* Chapel Hill: Univ. of North Carolina Press, 1964.

Blomberg, D. *Den svenska ungdomsbrottsligheten. (The Swedish juvenile delinquency.)* Stockholm: Natur & Kultur, 1963.

Bloom, B. S. *Stability and Change in Human Characteristics.* New York: Wiley, 1964.

Boalt, G. *Social mobility in Stockholm: A pilot investigation.* In *Transactions of the Second World Congress of Sociology,* vol. II. London: International Sociological Association, 1954.

Boersma, F. J. & O'Bryan, I. An investigation of the relationship between creativity and intelligence under two conditions of testing. *J. Pers.,* 1968, *36.*

Broadhurst, A. & Glass, A. Relationship of personality measures to the alpha rhythm of the electroencephalogram. *British J. of Psychiatry,* 1964, *115* (519).

Bronfenbrenner, U. *The measurement of sociometric status, structure and development.* New York: Beacon House, 1945.

Bronfenbrenner, U. Response to pressure from peers versus adults among Soviet and American schoolchildren. *Int. J. of Psychol.,* 1967, *2,* 199–207.

Bronfenbrenner, U. *Reaction to social pressure from adults versus peers among Soviet Day School and Boarding School pupils in the perspective of an American sample.* Symposium paper. Int. Congress of Psychol., London, 1969.

Bronson, W. C. Adult derivatives of emotional expressiveness and reactivity-control: Developmental continuities from childhood to adulthood. *Child Development,* 1967, *38,* 801–817.

Bruner, J. On perceptual readiness. *Psychological Review,* 1957, *64,* 123–152.

Carlsson, G. *Social mobility and class structure.* In *Lund studies in sociology.* Lund: Gleerups, 1958.

Cline, V. B., Richards, J. M., Jr. & Abe, C. The validity of a battery of creativity tests in a high school sample. *Educ. psychol. Measmt.,* 1962, *22.*

Cline, V. B., Richards, J. M., Jr. & Needham, W. E. Creativity tests and achievement in high school science. *J. Appl. Psychol.,* 1963, *47.*

Coleman, J. S. *The adolescent society.* New York: The Free Press of Glencoe, 1961.

Coleman, J. S. *Equality of educational opportunity. A publication of the Natio-*

nal Cent. of Educational Statistics. Washington D.C.: US Office of Education, 1966.

Comber, L. C. & Keeves, J. P. *International Studies in Evaluation.* I. *Science Education in Nineteen Countries.* Stockholm: Almqvist & Wiksell, 1973.

Cortés, J. B. & Gatti, F. M. *Delinquency and Crime. A biopsychological approach.* New York: Seminar Press, 1972.

Cox, S. H. *Family background effects on personality development and social acceptance.* Unpublished doctoral dissertation. Texas Christian University, 1966.

Crafoord, K. *Symtom eller ålderstypiskt beteende? En studie av 15-åriga flickor. (Symptom or phase? A study of 15 year old girls.)* Örebro project, special study 15. Stockholm: Psyk. inst., 1972.

Cronbach, L. J. Coefficient alfa and the internal structure of tests. *Psychometrica,* 1951, *16.*

Cronbach, L. J. Intelligence? Creativity? A parsimonious reinterpretation of the Wallach-Kogan data. *American Educational Research Journal,* 1968, *5,* 491–511.

Cronbach, L. J. & Furby, L. How we should measure "change"—or should we? *Psychological Bulletin,* 1970, *74,* no. 1, 68–80.

Cropley, A. J. A five year old study (longitudinal) of the validity of creativity tests. *Developmental Psychology,* 1972, *6* (1), 119–124.

Dahllöf, U. *Skoldifferentiering och undervisningsförlopp. Kognitiva mål- och processanalyser och processanalyser av skolsystem 1. (School differentiation and educational processes. Cognitive goal and process analyses and process analyses of school systems.)* Stockholm: Almqvist & Wiksell, 1967.

Davies, G. A. & Belcher, T. L. How Shall Creativity be Measured? *The Journal of Creative Behavior,* 1971, *5.*

Davis, K. The sociology of parent–youth conflict. *Am. Sociol. Rev.,* 1940, *5,* 523–535.

Davis, K. Social norms. In B. J. Biddle & E. J. Thomas (Eds.) *Role theory.* New York: Wiley, 1966.

De Lacey, P. R. A cross cultural study of classificatory ability in Australia. *Journal of cross cultural Psychology,* 1970, *1,* (4), 293–304.

Douglas, J. W. B. *The home and the school.* London: Mac Gibbon & Kee, 1964.

Douglas, J. W. B., Ross, J. M. & Simpson, H. R. *All our future. A longitudinal study of secondary education.* London: Peter Davies, 1968.

Douvan, E. & Adelson, J. *The adolescent experience.* New York: Wiley 1966.

Draper, N. R. & Smith, H. *Applied Regression Analysis.* New York: Wiley, 1966.

Duncan, O. D., Featherman, D. L. & Duncan, B. *Studies in Population, Socioeconomic Background, and Achievement.* New York: Seminar Press, 1972.

Dunér, A. *Bedömningsmetod och tillförlitlighet vid subjektiva bedömningar. (Rating method and dependability in person perception.)* (Stencil.) Stockholm: Psyk. inst., 1965.

Dunér, A. *Effekter av social differentiering. En förstudie. (Effects of social differentiation. A preliminary study.)* Stockholm: Psyk. inst., 1970.

Dunér, A. *Vad skall det bliva? Undersökningar om studie- och yrkesvalsprocessen. (Studies in the educational and vocational career process.)* Stockholm: Allmänna förlaget, 1972.

Ellingson, R. J. Relationship between EEG and test intelligence: A commentary. *Psychol. Bulletin,* 1966, *65* (2).

Elmhorn, K. Study in self-reported delinquency among school children in Stockholm. *Scandinavian Studies in Criminology,* 1965, *1,* 117–146.

Erikson, E. H. *Childhood and society.* New York: Norton, 1963.

Erikson, E. H. *Identity. Youth and crisis.* New York: Norton, 1968.

Euler, U. S. v. & Lishajko, F. Improved technique for the fluorimetric estimation of catecholamines. *Acta psychol. scand.* 1961, *51.*

Eysenck, H. J. *Crime and personality.* Boston: Houghton, 1964.

Fiedler, F., Osgood, C. E., Stolurow, L. M. & Triandis, II. C. *The behavioural differential: an instrument for the study of the behavioural component of social attitudes.* A. P. A. Meeting, 1964.

Fishbein, M. Attitude and the prediction of behavior. In M. Fishbein (Ed.) *Readings in attitude theory and measurement.* New York: Wiley, 1967.

Flanagan, J. L. et al. *The talents of American youth. 1. Design of a study of American youth.* Boston: Houghton Mifflin Comp., 1962.

Flescher, I. Anxiety and achievement of intellectually and creatively gifted children. *J. Psychol., 1963, 56.*

Frankenhaeuser, M. Behavior and circulating catecholamines. *Brain research,* 1971, *31,* 241–262.

Fraser, M. *Children in Conflict.* London: Secker & Warburg, 1973.

Freud, A. Adolescence. *Psychoanalytic Study of the Child,* 1958, *13,* 255–278.

Gagnerud, S. *Självvärdering och beteende. (Self evaluation and behaviour.)* Örebro project, special study 8. Stockholm: Psyk. inst., 1969.

Getzels, J. & Jackson, P. *Creativity and intelligence. Explorations with gifted students.* London & New York: Wiley, 1962.

Gibson, W. A. Three multivariate models: Factor analysis, latent structure analyses and latent profile analysis. *Psychometrica,* 1959, *24.*

Ginzberg, E. et al. *Occupational choice. An approach to a general theory.* New York: Columbia University Press, 1951.

Glavin, J. P. Persistence of behavior disorders in children. *Exceptional Children,* 1972, *38,* 367–376.

Glueck, S. & Glueck, E. *Unraveling juvenile delinquency.* Cambridge, Mass.: Harvard Univ. Press, 1950.

Goslin, D. A. *Handbook of Socialization Theory and Research.* Chicago: Rand McNally, 1969.

Gotkin, E. H. *Vocational behavior: Types and measurement.* Paper presented at the Convention of the American Personnel and Guidance Association, Washington, 1966.

Gottlieb, D. & Reeves, J. *Adolescent behavior in urban areas.* New York: The Free Press of Glencoe, 1963.

Gowan, J. C., Demos, G. D. & Torrance, E. P. (Eds.). *Creativity: Its educational implications.* New York: Wiley, 1967.

Gowan, J. C. *Development of the Creative Individual.* San Diego, California: R. R. Knopp, 1972.

Guilford, J. P. *The nature of human intelligence.* New York: McGraw-Hill Book Company, 1967.

Hall, G. S. *Adolescence: Its Pathology and Its Relations to Physiology. Antro-*

pology, Sociology, Sex, Crime, Religion and Education. Vols. I and II. New York: D. Appleton, 1904.

Hallgren, S. *Intelligens och miljö. En experimentell undersökning av barn i tredje skolåret vid Malmö folkskolor och privata skolor. (Intelligence and environment.)* Unpublished lic. thesis, Lund, 1939.

Hallgren, S. *Intelligens och social miljö. (Intelligence and social background.)* In *Studier tillägnade John Landqvist.* In *Studia Psychologica et Pedagogica.* Lund: Gleerups, 1946.

Harris, C. W. (Ed.) *Problems in Measuring Change.* Madison: Univ. of Wisconsin Press, 1963.

Healy, W. & Bronner, A. *New light on delinquency and its treatment.* New Haven: Yale Univ. Press, (1936), 1950.

Heaps, R. A. Use of the semantic differential technique in research: some precautions. *Journal of Psychology,* 1972, *80,* (1), 121–125.

Heise, D. R. Some methodological issues in semantic differential research. *Psychological Bulletin,* 1969, *72,* (6), 406–422.

Henricson, M. *Tonåringars normer och normklimat. (Adolescents' norms and norm climate.)* Örebro project, special study 14. Stockholm: Psyk. inst., 1971.

Henricson, M. *Tonåringar och normer. En undersökning av tonåringars normklimat. (Adolescents and norms. A study of adolescents' norm climate.)* Stockholm: Utbildningsförlaget, 1973. (With English summary.)

Herzberg, F., Mausner, B., Peterson, R. O. & Capwell, D. F. *Job attitudes; review of research and opinion.* Pittsburgh: Psychological Service of Pittsburgh, 1957.

Hirschi, T. *Causes of Delinquency.* Berkeley and Los Angeles: University of California Press, 1969.

Hollander, E. P. & Hunt, R. G. *Current Perspectives in Social Psychology.* London: University Press, 1967.

Husén, T. *Testresultatens prognosvärde. (The predictive value of test results.)* Stockholm: Gebers, 1950.

Husén, T. *Talent, opportunity and career.* Stockholm: Almqvist & Wiksell, 1969.

Husén, T. *Social Background and Educational Career. Research Perspectives on Equality of Educational Opportunity.* Paris: Org. for Economic Co-operation and Dev., 1972.

Husén, T. et al. *Svensk skola i internationell belysning. I. Naturorienterande ämnen.* Stockholm: Almqvist & Wiksell, 1973. (Swedish report from the IEA; see also Comber et al., 1973, Thorndike, 1973.)

Härnquist, K. *Manual till DBA-differentiell begåvningsanalys. (Manual to DIA—differential intelligence analysis.)* Stockholm: Skandinaviska Testförlaget, 1961.

Härnquist, K. Social factors and educational choice. *International Journal of the Educational Sciences,* 1966, *1,* 87–102.

Härnquist, K. Relative changes in intelligence from 13–18. *Scandinavian Journal of Psychology,* 1968, *9,* 50–82.

Jackson, P. & Messick, S. The person, the product and the response: Conceptual problems in the assessment of creativity. *J. Pers.* 1965, *33,* 309–329.

Jansson, C.-G. Project Metropolitan. *Acta Sociologica,* Vol. 9, fasc. 1–2, Copenhagen, 1965.

Jansson, S. & Ljung, B.-O. *Vägen genom högstadiet till gymnasiet. (The career through secondary school and gymnasium.*) (Stencil.) Stockholm: Ped. Inst., 1970.

Johannesson, I. *Sociala relationer mellan barn i folkskoleklasser. (Social relations between children in primary and secondary school classes.*) Lund: Gleerups, 1954.

Johannesson, I. & Magnusson, D. *Social- och personlighetspsykologiska faktorer i relation till skolans differentiering. (Social and personality factors in relation to school differentiation.*) 1957 års skolberedning. Official Report, SOU 1960: 42. Stockholm, 1960.

Johansson, G., Frankenhaeuser, M. & Magnusson, D. Catecholamine output in school children as related to performance and adjustment. *Scand. J. Psychol.*, 1973, *14*, 20–28.

Johnsson, A. U. & Szurek, S. A. Etiology of antisocial behaviour of delinquents and psychopaths. *J. Amer. Med. Assn.*, 1954.

Jonsson, G. *Undersökning angående vanartiga barn och asocial ungdom. (A study of depraved and asocial youth.*) Official Report, SOU 1944: 30, Bil. A.

Jonsson, G. Delinquent boys, their parents and grandparents. Uppsala: Almqvist & Wiksell, 1967.

Josephson, I. *Sociala relationer och skolprestation. (Social relations and achievement.*) Örebro project, special study 3. Stockholm: Psyk. inst., 1967.

Kagan, J. & Moss, H. A. *Birth to Maturity: A Study in Psychological Development.* New York: Wiley, 1962.

Kagan, J. American Longitudinal Research on Psychological Development. *Child Development*, 1964, *35*, 1–32.

Katz, D. & Kahn, R. L. *The social psychology of organisations.* New York, 1966.

Kendall, M. G. *Rank correlation methods.* London: Charles Griffin, 1948.

Kinberg, G. Kriminologiska grundproblem. (Fundamental criminological problems.) In Agge, I. (Ed.) *Kriminologi*, 1955.

Kockeis, E. The value clash between working class subcultures and the school. *Social Science Information*, 1970, *9*, (5), 165–183.

Kohlberg, L. Stage and sequence. The cognitive-developmental approach to socialization. In A. Goslin (Ed.) *Handbook of socialization theory and research.* Chicago: Rand McNally, 1969.

Kohlberg, L. & Turiel, E. *Research in moral development: The cognitive-developmental approach.* New York: Holt, 1971.

Kraus, P. E. *Yesterdays Children. A longitudinal Study of Children from Kindergarten into the Adult Years.* New York: Wiley, 1973.

La Belle, T. Differential perceptions of elementary school children representing distinct sociocultural backgrounds. *Journal of Cross cultural Psychology*, 1971, *2*, (2), 145–156.

Lambert, W. W., Johansson, G., Frankenhaeuser, M. & Klackenberg-Larsson, I. Catecholamine excretion in young children and their parents as related to behaviour. *Scand. J. Psychol.*, 1969, *10*.

Larsson, L. & Sandgren, B. *En studie av kreativitetsutvecklingen inom årskurserna 4–9 samt en undersökning av kreativitetens samvariation med intelligens. (A study of the development of creative ability in grades 4–9 and of the relation between creativity and intelligence.*) (Lic. thesis, stencil.) Göteborg: Ped. inst., 1968.

Lasowich, L. M. On the nature of identification. *J. Abnorm. Soc. Psychol.*, 1955, *51*.

Lazarsfeld, P. F. Latent structure analysis. In S. Koch (Ed.) *A study of a science.* Vol. 1. New York: McGraw Hill, 1959.

Lawshe, C. H. & Harris, D. H. *Manual of instructions to accompany Purdue creativity test. Forms G and H.* Purdue: Purdue Research Foundation, 1960.

Lieberman, J. Review of M. A. Wallach and N. Kogan's *Modes of thinking in young children.* In *J. Creat. Behav.*, 1968, *2*.

Locascio, R. (in collaboration with D. E. Super) *Long-term follow-up methods and results in the career pattern study.* Paper read to the American Personnel and Guidance Association Convention in Washington D.C., 1966.

Locke, J. *An Essay Concerning Human Understanding.* New York: Dover, 1959. Originally published 1690.

Lofquist, L. H. & Davis, R. V. *Adjustment to work.* Minnesota Univ.: Appleton Century Crafts, 1969.

Luria, Z. Semantic analysis of normal and neurotic groups. *J. Abnorm. Soc. Psychol.*, 1959, *58*.

Macfarlane, J. W., Allen, L. & Honzik, M. P. *A Developmental study of the behavior problems of normal children between 21 months and 14 years.* Univ. of California Press, 1954 (Reprinted 1962).

Macfarlane, J. W. From infancy to adulthood. *Childhood Education*, March issue, 1963.

Macpherson, J. S. *Eleven-year-olds grow up.* London: Scottish council of research in education Publications, 1958.

Magnusson, D. Självvärdering och skolmiljö. (Self-evaluation and school environment.) In I. Johannesson & D. Magnusson *Social- och personlighetspsykologiska faktorer i relation till skolans differentiering.* SOU, 1960: 42. Stockholm: Allmänna förlaget, 1960.

Magnusson, D. Self-evaluation as a function of age. *Rep. Psychol. Lab., Univ. Stockholm,* no. 124, 1962.

Magnusson, D. *Test theory.* Reading, Mass.: Addison & Wesley, 1967.

Magnusson, D. & Dunér, A. *Anpassning, beteende och prestation — Örebroprojektet.* (Adjustment, behaviour and achievement.) Rapport III. *Metoder och modeller.* (*Methods and Models.*) Stockholm: Psyk. inst., 1967.

Magnusson, D., Dunér, A., & Olofsson, B. *Anpassning, beteende och prestation — Örebroprojektet.* Rapport IX. *Kriminellt beteende: Modeller och undersökningsplanering.* (*Delinquent behaviour: Models and planning.*) Stockholm: Psyk. inst., 1968.

Marnell, M., Dunér, A. & Magnusson, D. *Tonåringar — relationer och reaktioner.* (*Teenagers—relations and reactions.*) Stockholm: Utbildningsförlaget, 1973. (With English summary.)

Masterson, J. F. The psychiatric significance of adolescence turmoil. *American Journal of Psychiatry*, 1968, *127*, 1549–1554.

Masterson, J. F. *Treatment of the borderline adolescent: a developmental approach.* New York: Wiley, 1972.

Maulsby, R. L. An illustration of emotionally evoked theta rhythm in infancy: Hedonic hypersynchrony. *Electroencephalography & Clinical Neurophysiology*, 1971, *31*, 151–165.

Maxwell, J. *Sixteen years on: A follow-up of the Scottish mental survey.* London: Univ. of London Press, 1969.

McCord, W. & McCord, J. *Origins of Crime.* New York: Columbia University Press, 1959.

McDonald, L. *Social Class and Delinquency.* London: Faber, 1969.

McNeil, K. A. A validity study of the semantic differential technique. *College Student Survey,* 1970, *4,* (2), p. 55–59.

Mead, M. *Coming of Age in Samoa.* New York: Morrow, 1928.

Mead, M. Social change and culture surrogates. *J. Educ. Sociol.,* 1940, *14,* 92–110.

Merton, R. K. *Social theory and social structure.* New York: Free Press of Glencoe (1957), 1968.

Mooney, R. L. & Razik, T. A. *Explorations in Creativity.* New York, London: Harper & Row, 1967.

Mosteller, F. & Moynihan, D. P. *On Equality of Educational Opportunity.* New York: Vintage Books, 1972.

Murphy, L. B. The Child's way of coping: a longitudinal study of normal children. *Bull. Menninger Clinic,* 1960, *24,* 97–103.

Musgrove, F. Role conflict in adolescence. *Brit. J. Educ. Psychol.,* 1964, *34.*

Musgrove, F. *Youth and the social order.* London: Routledge & Kegan Paul, 1964.

Mussen, P. H., Conger, J. J. & Kagan, J. *Child Development and Personality.* New York: Harper, 1970.

Mårdberg, B. A model for selection and classification in industrial psychology. *Rep. from the Psychological Laboratories, The University of Stockholm,* 1973, Supplement 19.

Nesselroade, J. R. & Reese, H. W. (Eds.) *Life-Span Developmental Psychology: Methodological Issues.* New York: Academic Press, 1973.

Nordenstam, K. *Attityder och värderingar hos skolbarn. En undersökning med semantisk differentialteknik.* (*Attitudes and values of school children. A study with semantic differential technique.*) Örebro project, special study 4. Stockholm: Psyk. inst., 1969.

Norman, W. T. Stability characteristics of the semantic differential. *Amer. J. Psychol.,* 1959, *72,* 581–584.

Nye, I. & Short, J., Jr. Scaling delinquent behavior. *Am. Soc. Rev.* 1957, *22.*

Nygren, A. *Social differentiering i skolan. En empirisk studie vid Örebro grundskolor.* (*Social differentiation at school. An empirical study of the Örebro schools.*) Örebro project, special study 10. Stockholm: Psyk. inst., 1970 *a.*

Nygren, A. *Effekter av klassens sociala sammansättning på elevgruppers prestationsnivå och motivation.* (*Effects of the social composition of the class on achievement and motivation.*) Örebro project, special study 11. Stockholm: Psyk. inst. 1970 *b.*

Ohlin, L. E. *Selection for parole: A manual for parole prediction.* New York, 1951.

Olofsson, B. *Brottslighet — konformitet. En utvecklingsstudie på grundval av självdeklarerad brottslighet.* (*Delinquency—conformity. A developmental study of self-reported delinquency.*) Örebro project, special study 13. Stockholm: Psyk. inst., 1971.

Olofsson, B. *Vad var det vi sa — om brottslighet och konformitet bland skol-*

pojkar. (Delinquency and conformity of school boys.) Stockholm: Utbildnings-förlaget, 1971.

Olsson, I. Empirisk kontroll av intressemätningsinstrument API 4 aktiviteter. (An empirical control of the interest inventory API 4 activities.) (Stencil.) Göteborg: Ped. inst., 1970.

Olvaeus, D. Hackkycklingar och översittare. (Mobbed and mobbing children.) Stockholm: Almqvist & Wiksell, 1973.

Osgood, C. E., Suci, G. & Tannenbaum, P. The measurement of meaning. Chicago: Univ. of Illinois Press, 1957.

O'Sullivan, M. Divergent, convergent, insurgent? Contemp. Psychol., 1967, 12.

Ottoson, D. Nervsystemets fysiologi. (The physiology of the nervous system.) Stockholm: Natur och Kultur, 1970.

Parson, T. An approach to psychological theory of action. In S. Koch (Ed.) Psychology. A study of science, vol. 3. New York, 1959.

Passow, A. H. Urban Education in the 1970's. Columbia University: Teachers College Press, 1971.

Pátkai, P. & Frankenhaeuser, M. Constancy of urinary catecholamine excretion. Percept. mot. Skills, 1964, 19.

Piliavin, A., Hardyck. B. & Vadum, A. C. Constraining effects of personal costs on the transgressions of juveniles. J. of Personality and Social Research, 1968, 10, 227–231.

Plowden Report. Teacher, 1967, 9 (2). Suppl.: The Plowden Report, 1967.

Porterfield, J. A. Youth in trouble. Fort Worth Texas, 1946.

Riesman, D. The lonely crowd. New Haven: Yale University Press, 1950.

Riley, M. W., Riley, J. W., Jr. & Moore, M. E. Adolescent values and the Riesman typology: An empirical analysis. In S. M. Lipset & L. Lowenthal (Eds.) Culture and social character. New York: The Free Press of Glencoe, 1961.

Robins, L. N. Deviant children grown up. A sociological and psychiatric study of sociopathic personality. Baltimore: The Williams & Wilkins company, 1966.

Roff, M. Childhood social interactions and young adult bad conduct. J. Abnorm. Psychol., 1961, 63, (2).

Roff, M. & Sells, S. B. Juvenile delinquency in relation to peer acceptance—rejection and sociometric status. Psychology in the schools, 1968, 5, 3–18.

Roff, M., Sells, S. B. & Golden, M. M. Social Adjustment and Personality Development in Children. Minneapolis: The University of Minnesota Press, 1972.

Rogers, D. (Ed.) Issues in Adolescent Psychology. New York: Appleton, 1969.

Rokeach, M. The open and the closed mind. In E. P. Hollander & R. G. Hunt, Current Perspectives in Social Psychology. London: University Press, 1967.

Rousseau, J. J. Emile. Translated to English by B. Foxley, London: J. M. Dent, 1911. Originally published 1762.

Rubin, R. & Balow, B. Learning and behavior disorders: A longitudinal study. Exceptional Children, 1971, 38, 4, 293–299.

Schur, E. Our Criminal Society. Englewood Cliffs, N.J.: Prentice Hall, 1969.

Sears, R. R., Maccoby, E. E. & Lewin, H. Patterns of child rearing. New York: Harper & Row, 1957.

Shapiro, R. L. Adolescence and the psychology of the age. *Psychiatry*, 1963, *26*, 77–87.

Sjöstrand, W. *Skolan och demokratin.* (*School and democracy.*) Malmö: Codex, 1966.

Smith, I. L. IQ, Creativity and Achievement: Interaction and Threshold. *Multivariate Behavioral Research*, 1971, *6*, (1), 51–62.

Stennett, R. G. Emotional handicap in the elementary years: Phase or disease? *American Journal of Orthopsychiatry*, 1966, *36*, 444–449.

Stewart, L. H. Social and emotional adjustment during adolescence as related to the development of psychosomatic illness in adulthood. *Genetic Psychol. Monograph*, 1962, *65*, 175–215.

Stievater, M. A comprehensive Bibliography of Books on Creativity and Problemsolving. *Journal of Creative Behavior*, 1971, *5*, (201–224, 291–296).

Super, D. E. A theory of vocational development. *Amer. Psychol.*, 1953, *8* (4).

Super, D. E. *The psychology of careers.* New York: Harper & Brothers, 1957.

Super, D. E. *Vocational development. A framework for research. Career Pattern Study I.* New York: Columbia Univ., 1957.

Super, D. E., Kowalski, R. & Gotkin, E. *Floundering and trial after high-school* (mimeo). New York: Columbia Univ., 1967.

Swedner, H. & Edstrand, G. Skolsegregation — visst finns den. (*School segregation.*) *Kommunal skoltidning*, 1969, *4*.

Swedner, H. & Edstrand, G. *Skolsegregation i Malmö.* (*Segregation at Malmö schools.*) (Stencil.) Lund: Soc. inst., 1969.

Svensson, A. *Relative achievement. School performance in relation to intelligence, sex, and home environment.* Stockholm: Almqvist & Wiksell, 1971.

Svensson, N. E. *Ability grouping and scholastic achievement.* Stockholm: Almqvist & Wiksell, 1962.

Sveri, K. *Persistenta brottslingar. Försök till socialpsykologisk analys.* (*Persistent delinquents. An attempt to a social psychological analysis.*) Stockholm: Inst. Allmän Kriminologi, 1964.

Takala, A. Socialistuminen ja yksilön henikenen kasvu. *Rep. Inst. of Educ.*, no. 12, University of Jyväskylä, 1965.

Tapp, J. & Kohlberg, L. Developing senses of law and legal justice. *Journal of Social Issues*, 1971, *27* (2), 65–91.

Taylor, C. W. (Ed.). *Climate for Creativity.* Report of the Seventh National Research Conference on Creativity. New York: Pergamon Press, 1972.

Taylor, I., Walton, P. & Young, J. *The new criminology.* London and Boston: Routledge & Kegan Paul, 1973.

Terman, L. M. et al. Mental and physical traits of a thousand gifted children. In L. M. Terman (Ed.) *Genetic studies of Genius.* Stanford: Stanford University Press, 1925.

Terman, L. M. & Oden, M. H. The gifted child grows up. In L. M. Terman (Ed.) *Genetics studies of genius.* IV. Stanford: Stanford Univ. Press, 1947.

Terman, L. M. & Oden, M. H. The gifted group at mid-life. In L. M. Terman (Ed.) *Genetic studies of genius.* V. Stanford & London, 1959.

Thorndike, E. L. The effect of the interval between test and retest on the constancy of the IQ. *J. Educ. Psychol.*, 1933, *24*.

Thorndike, R. *The concept of over- and underachievement.* New York, 1963.

Thorndike, R. L. *International Studies in Evaluation*. III. *Reading Comprehension Education in Fifteen Countries*. Stockholm: Almqvist & Wiksell, 1973.

Thorndike, R. L. & Hagen, E. *Ten thousand careers*. New York: Wiley, 1959.

Tiedeman, D. V. & O'Hara, R. P. *Career development. Choice and adjustment. Differentiation and integration in career development.* College entrance examinations board. Research monograph, no. 3, New York, 1963.

Torrance, E. P. Current research on the nature of creative talent. *J. Counsel. Psychol.*, 1959, *6*.

Triandis, H. C. Towards an analysis of the components of interpersonal attitudes. In M. Sherif & C. W. Sherif (Eds.) *Attitude, ego-involvement and change*. New York: Wiley, 1967.

Waern, Y. & Härnqvist, K. *Manual till intresseschema — sysselsättningar. (Manual to interest inventory—Activities.)* Stockholm: Skandinaviska Testförlaget, 1962.

Wallach, M. A. & Kogan, N. A new look at the creativity-intelligence distinction. *J. Personal.*, 1965, *33*.

Wallach, M. A. & Wing, C. W. *The talented student. A validation of the creativity—intelligence distinction.* New York: Holt, Rinehart & Winston, 1969.

Weiner, I. B. *Psychological disturbance in Adolescence.* New York: Wiley—Interscience, 1970.

Weinschenk, C. In prevention of juvenile delinquency. *World Med. J.*, 1967, *14* (2).

Werts, C. & Linn, R. A general linear model for studying growth. *Psychol. Bulletin,* 1970, *3*.

West, D. J. *Present conduct and future delinquency. First report of the Cambridge Study in Delinquent Development.* London: Heinemann, 1967.

Westrin, P. A. *Wit III Manual.* Stockholm: Skandinaviska testförlaget, 1967.

Wilson, A. B. Residential segregation of social classes and aspirations of high school boys. *American Sociological Review,* 1959, *24*, 836–845.

Wright, D. *The Psychology of Moral Behavior.* Harmondsworth: Penguin Books Ltd, 1971.

Vernon, P. E. *Secondary school selection.* London: Methuen, 1957.

Vernon, P. E. (Ed.) *Creativity.* Harmondsworth: Penguin Books, 1970.

Vogel W. & Broverman, M. Relationship between EEG and test intelligence: A critical review. *Psychol. Bulletin,* 1964, *62*.

Vogel, W. & Broverman, M. A reply to "Relationship between EEG and test intelligence: A commentary". *Psychol. Bulletin,* 1966, *65* (2).

Vroom, V. H. *Work and motivation.* New York: Wiley, 1964.

Yee, A. H. (Ed.) *Social interaction in educational settings.* Englewood Cliffs, N. J.: Prentice Hall, 1971.

Ziller, R. C. Vocational choice and utility for risk. *J. Counseling Psychol.*, 1957, *4*.

Subject index

Person index

264